A Land of
Two Halves

This book is dedicated to my drivers. I've changed the names of some of them but nothing else.

First published in Great Britain by Scribner, 2004
An imprint of Simon & Schuster UK Ltd
A Viacom Company

1 3 5 7 9 10 8 6 4 2

Simon & Schuster UK Ltd
Africa House
64–78 Kingsway
London WC2B 6AH

www.simonsays.co.uk

Simon & Schuster Australia
Sydney

A CIP catalogue record for this book
is available from the British Library

ISBN 0-7432-5713-8

Typeset by M Rules
Printed and bound in Finland
by WS Bookwell

Contents

The Introduction, mate

When I came to New Zealand I expected to stay for a year. I've stayed for sixteen. I like it here.

I arrived at the age of twenty-nine. Before then I'd lived in assorted safe countries but I didn't settle in any of them. The thought of other places excited me too much. New Zealand was not one of those places. But Australia was.

I had a romantic image of Australia. I got it from cricket. On winter nights in childhood, when Sussex was frozen like iron, I would lie in bed with a radio listening to John Arlott describing the seagulls fluttering into a sapphire sky above the SCG as Doug Walters cut another ball to the white picket fence. I saw Australia as bright-edged, happy and hot.

I did not have a romantic image of New Zealand. If I thought of it at all, I thought of it as a smaller, greener Australia. New Zealand was keen but bad at cricket. It did sheep and butter well, but these did not excite me. So when chance flung me a job in New Zealand I saw it as a stepping stone. After a year I would cross the Tasman Sea to Australia and then perhaps I'd settle down.

I was a teacher then. I came to a school in Christchurch in the South Island, where I was given a room in a boys' boarding house. The boys didn't seem typical of my image of New Zealand. They seemed archetypical. All were white and most were farmers' sons. They came from the huge high country stations where the muster of the merinos takes a week, or from the lowland farms that supplied my childhood on the other side of the world with lamb and butter, or from the orchards of Hawke Bay that sent me apples in spring.

Most of the boys were outgoing, honest, active and cheerful. Few starred in the classroom. When they wrote, they wrapped themselves around the pen and stuck their tongues out. The bell at the end of the day was a release into physical activity. These boys liked rugby and making things. On Sports Day they preferred to run barefoot. They could climb ropes. They could work dogs. They rarely complained. I liked them.

A couple of times a year their parents came to town in their dusty four-wheel-drives. I liked them too. The mothers wore moleskins and blue Guernseys, and their handshakes were firm. The fathers wore moleskins and Aertex shirts and brown check jackets and their handshakes broke bones. The housemaster would lay in vast quantities of whisky and throw a party. The laughter at the party would be rich and unrestrained, and the party never ended before the whisky did.

The first public holiday after I arrived was Waitangi Day. I knew nothing of the Treaty of Waitangi, the accord between the British Crown and Maori that is the official founding document of New Zealand. On television I watched displays of fat brown men in tribal costume somewhere in the North Island sticking out their tongues, paddling war canoes and waving spears at white dignitaries. It looked like a royal tour of Africa. And it seemed remote from anything I'd come up against in Christchurch.

Christchurch was a planned Anglican settlement, a transplant from England and still commonly described as the most English city outside England. It's about as English as Baltimore. But I found it easy to fit in here, so easy that I bought a house. It was ramshackle, it cost $40,000*, it was built on the flank of a dead volcano, and it was the first house of my life. A few years later I got a dog. I'd always wanted a dog. Then I got another dog. After a few more years I gave up teaching and became a

---

*At the time of writing there are roughly three dollars to the pound. What the exchange rate was sixteen years ago I've no idea.

newspaper columnist. Without ever meaning to, I'd become one of New Zealand's four million settlers.

This was the last country in the world to be settled. Maori came from Polynesia less than a thousand years ago. Europeans began to arrive in the eighteenth century.

From where I'm typing this I can see a six-pack of beer. 'Know who you are' says the slogan on the pack. It's an idea from deep in the nation's psyche. Though I've never met a New Zealander who frets about who he is, New Zealand as a country frets about it a lot. The question of national identity is raised so often and so tediously that there are times when New Zealand's most prominent characteristic seems to be wondering whether it has any prominent characteristics.

It does. It has an abundance of them, and the world is paying increasing attention to them. More and more visitors come every year for the bush, the birds, the high country sheep stations, the geysers, the mudpools, the Maori heritage, the mountains, the whales, the vineyards, the seafood, the filmsets, the trout, the rugby, the tramping, the vast spaces and the easygoing informal hospitality of most of the people.

It was a New Zealander who split the atom. It was a New Zealander who conquered Everest. New Zealanders sing at Covent Garden, make movies for Hollywood, write software for British dentists, farm more efficiently than anyone in the world, build boats for billionaires and do better at games than they have any right to. But still the country looks at itself and wonders, like a younger brother hovering on the edge of the big boys' game. And now I'm going to join in the wondering.

I've seen much of this country over the years, but I have never travelled merely to observe it. In the trip I am about to go on, I want to see the place as clearly as I can.

Superficially, New Zealand appears to be a land of contradictions. It has a masculine image but it was the first place in the world to give women the vote. It sits in the South Pacific but until recently it traded almost exclusively with Great

Britain. It sent soldiers to Vietnam but it has banned American warships. It promotes itself as a virgin paradise, but it has destroyed 90 per cent of its native bush. It's a rural country but most of its people live in cities. It has the land area of the UK under Elizabeth II, but the population of the UK under Elizabeth I. It has two main islands, and two main races. It seems, in short, a land of two halves.

But I distrust generalisations. I also distrust most travel writing. In an effort to avoid the dangers of both, and in order to meet as many people as possible, I have decided to make the trip by thumb. I used to casually hitchhike everywhere. Now, forty-six years old and bald, I'm a bit nervous.

I've got a rough idea of where I want to go. I want to see the southern tip of the South Island and the northern tip of the North. I want to cross the Southern Alps and tour the wild West Coast. I want to see the volcanic heart of the North Island. And I'll leave the rest to chance. It's best that way when you're hitching.

But my main purpose is selfish. I've lived a third of my life here now. One of my dogs is buried on the hill behind my house. Within a few years my other dog will die. And then there will be nothing to keep me here but habit. The question I want this trip to answer is whether, when that day comes, I should stay or go.

PART ONE

The South Island

1

On the dogless road

When I close the gate behind me, my dog looks utterly woe-begone. Laurie Lee said it was easier to kiss and leave than to stay and love. Laurie Lee can never have owned a dog.

I hump my bag onto my shoulder, resolve not to look back, and set off down the steep hill to the Lyttelton wharf. On the street I meet the mechanic who mends my car, and a fat man I sometimes drink with. I'm glad that neither of them asks me what I'm doing.

In brittle autumn sunshine, I lay my bag at my feet on Norwich Quay and stick my thumb out as I haven't done for twenty years. I feel that the whole of the township is looking at me. It's well positioned to do so. The town is built on steep volcanic hills that overlook me from three sides. The hills are still bleached from the recent summer.

Beside me is a tall mesh fence. Beyond that a pile of logs awaiting export, a railway line, and a vast yard of shipping containers stacked three high like monstrous shoeboxes. Forklifts and straddle cranes bleep and flash. Tied up at the wharf are two rusting Russian trawlers, a bulk carrier discharging fertiliser, and a container ship the length of a rugby pitch.

Sail a mile east from here and you're in the Pacific. Keep sailing east and the next land you see will be Chile.

An old woman passes me. I've seen her a thousand times on her way to the shops in London Street. She's bent forward at the hips like a shelf-bracket, her view restricted to the pavement a yard or two ahead of her, but she walks with determined speed. The sight of her always touches me. Today she makes me feel that what I'm doing is folly.

I've gone wilfully from local citizen to traveller, from pedestrian to beggar. And this beggar's incompetent. The place where you stand to hitch should allow the driver to pull over easily and should indicate the direction you want to go. The place where I'm standing does neither. But I've broken the rules because I want my first lift, assuming I get one, to determine my initial direction. From here I could go north, south or west.

There's a book to be written about the psychology of hitchhiking, and this may turn out to be it, but for now let me observe only that the business is a matter of demeanour and a large part of that demeanour is expressed in the thumb. It is possible to proffer a thumb demandingly, imploringly, jauntily, shyly, limply, apologetically or listlessly. My thumb is limp and embarrassed.

An elderly man shuffles past with an elderly dog. 'I'll shout you the bus fare, Joe,' he says. I feel increasingly keen to get away.

God gets me away. He takes flesh in the form of a sputtering diesel recreational vehicle driven by the local pastor. He and his wife are heading for a conference of pastors to the south of Christchurch, and thus, verily, it comes to pass that I go south.

As we drive the long tunnel that bores through the volcanic hill and emerges into the industrial suburbs of Christchurch, Mr and Mrs Pastor are all friendliness. They make such encouraging noises about my trip that I am encouraged. 'You're sloughing the skin of habit,' says the pastor.

There is one principal road in the South Island and they drop me on it. It runs from one tip of the Island to the other, and about half of the South Island's million citizens could stand in their living rooms and punt a rugby ball on to it.

Still in the suburbs of Christchurch, I position myself 100 yards beyond a set of traffic lights so that stationary drivers can study me and have their internal debate about whether or not to pick me up, without being able to discern that I am suspiciously middle-aged.

Away from Lyttelton I've got a better thumb already, three-quarters erect and jaunty. The driver of the first car past gestures that he's turning off to the right. He probably isn't, but that acknowledgment that I am there, that I exist and am doing what I am doing, brings a gust of what I want from this trip, a sense of being solitary, free and somehow small. It's a feeling I remember from youth. I like it.

And with it comes an abundance of random detail and the time to observe it. In the window of a wooden bungalow a very black woman is combing her hair with what looks like a leaf-rake. An old man with donkey-coloured trousers and a wart on his head is kneeling in his scrap of front garden with a trowel and a trug. Trucks pass within ten feet of him.

When an elderly cream-coloured Toyota van pulls up twenty yards beyond me, I pick up my bag and do the customary hitchhiker half-run up the road. The run expresses my status, acknowledges that the driver's time is more valuable than my physical comfort, even though the driver is not going to drive away. Unless, that is, he's a young male shit with a back seat full of giggling young female shits.

Richard isn't. He's gentle and endearing, thirty something perhaps, and like so many drivers who pick you up, he used to travel by thumb. 'But I do like to see a bag,' he says. The back of his van holds a rusted push-mower, a bicycle with one wheel, and a wooden bed head.

The flat suburbs give way to the flatter plains, vast, fertile and farmed in twenty different ways. We pass a vineyard with a rosebush at the end of each row of vines. Then the black-green wall of a pine plantation.

Though Richard has travelled a bit he likes it here. Everyone's got somewhere that's home, he says, and for him it's the province of Canterbury. But he hates the nor-wester, the hot summer wind that drops torrents on the west coast, then rips across the plains, sucking the soil dry, snapping tempers and distorting television reception. It's against the nor-wester that the shelter belts stand – thirty-foot-tall hedges of macrocarpa that divide the paddocks like straight green ribs. This is a landscape of horizontals, the sort of breadth that an amateur camera fails to capture.

'I once spent three months in London in winter,' says Richard. 'It got dark at half past three. But I quite liked being a tourist, seeing the sights. That's what you do when you're away, isn't it, see the sights? At home you don't bother.'

When I ask if he found the English friendly, he chuckles.

'I remember,' he says, 'asking directions to the Tower off a guy in a coat selling papers. He said he hadn't got time to waste giving people directions.'

Away to the west lie the purple foothills of the Southern

Alps, a range of mountains like a dog's back teeth that forms the spine of the island.

He drops me at Dunsandel, a place known only for a song about its dog-dosing strip. All the farm dogs from the district were brought there twice a year, tied up, dosed for hydatids, and then left until they'd shat themselves empty. But here on the main road I can see only a pub, a junk shop, a café-cum-store, a shop that sells crafts and a former church that also sells crafts. Not feeling in need of crafts, I buy a coffee.

A recent anthology of poems about Canterbury province is entitled *Big Sky*. It's apt. The plains stretch from the Pacific in the east to the mountains in the west, but the sky just stretches, as delicately blue as a thrush's egg. I light a cigarette and hitch again, feeling pleased by the freedom of ignorance. I know nothing of what's about to happen, who I'm going to meet, where I'm going to sleep. Travel stresses the present tense.

As each car approaches I crook my smoking hand behind my back, an action I haven't performed for a couple of decades but that comes as instinctively as walking.

Neil's a builder. The back of his ute rattles with tools. He wears a red check bush shirt and rolls his own cigarettes. Raised on the west coast, he crossed to this side of the mountains because there was more money and more building. I tell him that when I picture the west coast I see rank gardens and roofs of rusting iron. He turns slowly to me and gives a gap-toothed smile.

'Yeah,' he says, 'they don't get too carried away over there. You heading that way on this trip of yours?'

'I hope so.'

'Well,' he says, 'if you ever get to Ross, go see Thelma in the top pub and mention my name. She'll look after you.'

We're in sheep country now. There are fewer sheep than when I arrived here. Indeed over the last twenty years the national flock has roughly halved, but because of heavier carcases and higher lambing percentages the tonnage of sheep meat produced each year has fallen by only a quarter. It's the sort of thing you know in New Zealand, or at least in the South Island. Even if you live in a city, agriculture's in the air. For all its desire to become a dynamic, electronic economy, New Zealand still makes most of its money by growing food. When the weather's benign and commodity prices high, the shops boom and the All Blacks win.

Sheep are increasingly giving way to dairy herds, and dairy herds need water. Huge wheeled irrigation booms wander eerily across the paddocks like horizontal pylons, sucking the aquifers dry, draining the snow-fed rivers.

The bridge over the Rakaia River is half a mile long, but it passes mainly over shingle and clumps of scruffy willows. Such water as there is flows in shallow winding channels. But several times a year when the rain is torrential in the distant mountains, the waters come with such ferocity that the river bed fills from bank to bank, threatening the bridge supports and sweeping the carcases of cattle out to sea with their legs sticking up.

The township of Rakaia where Neil turns off is larger than Dunsandel in the way that a mouse is larger than a shrew. But both Rakaia and Dunsandel are towns. No one speaks of villages here. The word smacks of English twee.

Though it's lunchtime, Rakaia's asleep. I see only a petrol attendant standing impressively close to a petrol pump, smoking. By far the most vigorous thing on show is a fibreglass salmon, thirty foot tall and sculpted in the act of leaping, perhaps because of the telegraph pole up its arse. New Zealand abounds in such things. There's a giant kiwi fruit, a giant sheep, a giant kiwi. In Ohakune in the North Island there's apparently a giant carrot. It's a form of branding for the tourists, one that I would like to believe was tinged with irony, but I am not confident. To be fair, the Japanese do take photographs of these things, but then the Japanese take photographs of the Japanese taking photographs.

Tiny Rakaia has two giant pubs. The Railway Hotel, a

wooden building painted an unfetching blue, is situated, astonishingly, beside the railway. But there's no longer a station. In the 1980s New Zealand was under a Labour government, but it still felt keen to join the international trend for privatising state assets, and sold its railway network to an American outfit for three beans and a packet of smokes. The Americans then cheerfully set about stripping the passenger rail services back to nothing. At the time of writing only three passenger trains run in the South Island, and two of these are strictly for the tourists. The few trains that still pass through Rakaia carry nothing but freight.

I have the smoky-voiced landlady of the Railway Hotel and the waddling Labrador and the factory-sized public bar to myself. I order a pie and a pint. The pint is half a litre, but the pie is the real thing. In fifth-form physics I learned that if you filled a matchbox with nuclei and then dropped it, it would sink fifty feet into the ground. New Zealand pies are similar.

Defying instructions from the landlady I slip half the pie to the Labrador. The dog swallows it in a single gulp and collapses on the carpet, panting.

The door opens and an elderly man steps neatly over the dog, orders a pint of Speights without separating his jaws, turns and walks towards a wall. The landlady calls to him but he doesn't seem to hear. She comes out from behind the bar, lays her hands on his shoulders and steers him left through a flimsy partition above which stands the word 'Casino'.

'We've moved the pokie machines,' she confides on her return to the bar. 'Some of our regulars take a while to cotton on.' While I drink two beers and the landlady tells me about a local enterprise that grows tulips for the Dutch market, no other customers appear.

When I step outside and the sun performs its usual amusing tricks on the daytime drinker's retina, I'm confronted with a choice. I can carry on down the main road or cut inland on Thomson's Track, a country road that spears across the plains.

I take Thomson's Track, not just because it runs right past the front door of the pub, nor because it makes a change from the flat predictability of the main South Road, but because it has fine associations. It leads towards the Mackenzie Country, an inland plateau ringed by mountains, where the land is carpeted with tussock the colour of a lion's pelt, and threaded by a network of streams and rivers that abound in trout. Once or twice every year I go to the Mackenzie for a week of fishing with friends, and we spend our days thigh-deep in the Tekapo River and our nights telling lies in the pub.

The first car past stops. I drop my fresh-lit cigarette and get in.

'Got any smokes?' says Rick.

He's about thirty, darkish-skinned, stubbled, pony-tailed and his eyes open slightly wider than is either necessary or normal. They are eyes with the sort of intensity that low-budget aliens use to pierce holes in metal. Rick speaks with a rising intonation that turns every declarative sentence into a question.

'My missus told me to fuck off. So I'm fucking off.' He's fucking off very swiftly. What little traffic there is on Thomson's Track is doing 120 kph and Rick overtakes it. The road is ruler-straight, but it intersects more major roads at hilariously unheralded intervals. When I lay a hand like a brace against the dashboard, Rick turns his eyes on me full beam.

'I'm not fucking suicidal,' he says.

Rick's missus has a three-year-old child. The father, a no-good fucker, walked out on her soon after the child was born. But a couple of weeks ago the man came crawling back, and Rick's missus took pity on him and let him stay. She gave him a sofa bed in the bedroom that she shares with Rick.

'I lie in bed listening to the fucker snoring,' says Rick. 'The first thing I see when I wake up every morning is his crusty underpants on the floor beside the fucking bed.'

This morning things came to a head, there was some sort of altercation and Rick was told to leave.

'I'm not a bad fucker. I know right from wrong. I've never been to prison. I don't drink and drive. Sure, I've been done twice, but I was only just over. Last time I got six months' disqualification and fifty hours' community service.'

'What was that like?'

Rick's face softens and creases into a smile for the first time and his foot eases on the throttle. 'Cruisy, man. I fucking loved it. Had to paint the horses on this ride at Caroline Bay. The guy in charge didn't give a fuck. Said I could just sit on a horse all fucking day if I wanted. But I *liked* painting them.'

He's lived in both North and South Islands and reckons they are two different countries. Of his numerous jobs his favourite was driving the night shift on shuttle buses.

'I loved it, man. I love driving at night. You can see the lights coming a long way off and so you can, like, smooth out the corners so the passengers can sleep and you're all alone on the road. Then you get back to Christchurch at seven in the morning and clean the bus, and every other joker is just going off to work and you can get on the piss.'

He used to be a big drinker and fighter, but not any more.

'I got hep C, man. Don't know how I got it but I got it. Three jugs these days and I'm as pissed as a sheila on a glass of wine.'

He doesn't know what he's going to do for the next few days. He's just driving to get away, grateful that at least he's got a car. It's a battered saloon that's done 300,000k, 'but she's a goer, man. I love this fucking car,' and he pats it affectionately on the dashboard. He's planning to hit up on friends in Geraldine and Timaru, sleep on floors, maybe do the pubs.

All this as we drive through iron-flat plains, farmed from white weatherboard farmhouses. No people visible, only the slow silhouette of a distant tractor, mile upon mile of wheat, sheep and cattle, and a concrete water race running beside the road, carrying snow-melt from the distant ranges.

When Rick drops me in Geraldine I give him what's left of my packet of Rothmans. We shake hands and he treats me to a final brain-stabbing stare before gunning the car up the road.

Now that it's over, the lift from Rick gives me a tingle of retrospective pleasure. I've no desire to meet Rick again, but I liked him and I enjoyed his honesty and I felt sorry for him. He also provided the sort of thing that makes hitching what it is. It let me step briefly into the mess of his life. And it did us both good. I must have been the first person he'd spoken to since the bitterness of his row that morning. Before he picked me up he must have been stewing, grinding his teeth, clenching the wheel. My presence let him unburden himself of some of that. And I relished the details vicariously. They reminded me that the world is wide and full of differences. And then I was able to step back out of that life, unwounded, uninvolved, almost untouched.

The propaganda against hitchhiking has grown in recent times and you see fewer and fewer people doing it. But it's not as dangerous as the propagandists make out. Never once have I felt physically threatened by a driver. I've met nutters but they've been harmless nutters. And on the two occasions when I've been sexually propositioned, both the propositioners, though big men and spectacularly ugly ones, were oblique in their propositioning, and they accepted the rebuff without demur.

Indeed my experiences of hitching have affirmed human nature far more often than they have damned it. For one thing, every lift begins with an act of generosity. And once inside the vehicle I have met infinitely more vulnerability and honesty than I have met aggression, perhaps because the fleeting anonymous nature of a lift invites intimacy. Both parties are staring ahead through the windscreen, so that words can be spoken as if to the air. The best lifts are like confessionals on wheels, like psychiatric couches barrelling through the landscape. Hundreds of drivers have told me things that they have clearly never told their partners, their parents or their children.

I like all that. Indeed hitching is the only form of travel I know that makes the actual shifting of one's flesh from one place to another into something of interest, rather than a chore to be endured for the reward of arrival. Furthermore, the intimacy is temporary and carries none of the consequences of intimacy, and that suits me just fine. Never once, anywhere, have I met any of my drivers a second time. So when Rick drives off up the main street of Geraldine he is driving out of my life for good.

In comparison with the tumult of Rick's life, Geraldine seems as orderly as a vicarage linen cupboard. It's a town of a few thousand set in rich and gently undulating farmland that presages the hills to the west. Pairs of white-haired women parade the main street in cardigans and calf-length tartan skirts and shoes so sensible they'd go to church on their own. Behind them pad meek men in zippered jackets and ties. There's a sense of perpetual afternoon. Battered utes from the surrounding farms creep along the street with dogs chained to their decks. Even the dogs are subdued. At the far end of the main street beside a park and a camping ground stand the world's cleanest public toilets with a decorative paua-shell inlay in the wall tiles to gratify the tourists.

But there will never be many tourists to gratify, for Geraldine is just a toilet-and-coffee stop on the road to excitement. Beyond Geraldine lies the Mackenzie Country, 13,000 feet of Mount Cook, the Lindis Pass and then the dramatic mountainous playgrounds of Wanaka and Queenstown. Geraldine can't compete.

Nevertheless the place seems snug and prosperous, the archetype of the rural service town that has done well in recent years on the back of good commodity prices. In the police station a single constable sits at a desk yawning. And I decide that the place will do me for the night. I've done a couple of hundred kilometres and I'm in no rush and I've no intention on this trip of getting stuck in the heart of nowhere and having to sleep rough.

The landlord of the Crown Hotel flips open a huge guest register. It's blank as the Gobi.

'Might be able to squeeze you in,' he says, and asks me with undisguised curiosity what I'm doing in Geraldine. When I tell him he warns me that tomorrow could be a rough day for hitching. A southerly front is due to sweep up the island mid-morning. I say I'll be away early and he promises to see to it that a continental breakfast is delivered to my room.

The room comes with a smoking ban, frills on the bed-spread, chocolate toffees on the pillow and a system of ropes and pulleys on the bathroom window that would have baf-fled Hornblower. I dump my bag and, because of a piece of pie that has nagged me since Rakaia, I set out to buy tooth-picks.

In the main street there's a totara tree planted to commemo-rate the birth of the first European baby in Geraldine. The tree's not very tall. A shop called The Scottish Connection advertises gifts from Scotland. No doubt Scots settled here in the nine-teenth century but the place is now about as Scottish as the rest of New Zealand. So I manage to resist the tartan souvenirs, but not the shop next door. It contains the world's largest jersey. The thing is hanging from a wall. A printed notice tells me that it was knitted on a machine in 1993, took roughly a month to finish, is five foot something by seven foot something, and is authenticated by *The Guinness Book of Records*. It looks like, well, a remarkably large jersey.

'What do you think?' asks the woman behind the counter.

'What on earth,' I say, 'possessed anyone to make this thing?'

'Well,' she says, 'we went to Aussie and saw the giant pineapple and the giant koala and all that and we got the idea for a giant jersey. Why not?' Which seems to me to be the right observation but one word too long. I don't say so. Indeed, a minute later I am dropping a dollar coin into a box and being ushered into the back room of the shop. Two women stand lis-tening to one man. The women notice my entry, say, 'Thank you so much, that was wonderful but we really must be going,' and go. The man says, 'Hello.'

Did you know that the patterning discs of the 9RJ 36 double-jersey knitting machine made by Mellor Bromley of Leicester are edged with little steel teeth? Yes, so did I. But did you also know that one and a half million of these teeth can be broken off one by one with a pair of sharp-nosed pliers, attached to the sticky side of a double layer of masking tape to form a mosaic, and then individually painted to recreate the Bayeux Tapestry? Well it's true. The thing's framed and mounted on the wall in the back room of the giant jersey shop in Geraldine and, for only a dollar, the gentleman who spent twenty years of his life breaking off, attaching and painting those one and half million teeth will tell you quite a lot more about it than you want to know. He will tell you that he painted the teeth one colour at a time and that the gold teeth alone took two years to paint. He will tell you that he is an enthusiastic mathematician and that he has worked over fifty mathematical puzzles into the mosaic. And he will offer to sell you a cd rom explaining everything about the Bayeux Tapestry, the mathematical puzzles and the 9RJ 36. What he won't tell you is how to make your escape politely. I will. Just leave. I'm not convinced he noticed when I did.

In the supermarket 150 birch toothpicks made in China – 'best for quality and fun' – set me back 85 cents, then I head out past Paddons' Agricentre with its fetching display of harrows, into the back streets of Geraldine. I lever remnants of pie from a back molar as I go. It is enormous fun.

The Catholic church, a gaunt concrete relic of the nineteenth century, looks large enough to hold the entire population of Geraldine. It's locked. Two streets beyond, the town ends in a paddock of bullocks. They amble up to the fence, dreamily pissing. One bullock licks my hand with a tongue as rough as a cat's. Another reaches through the wires to suck at my shoelaces. They stare at me with long-lashed eyes and the deep docility of herbivorous dinosaurs.

To one side of me there's a scrap of native bush. When the Europeans arrived, the whole area was forested. I turn my back on this remnant. In a week or two I expect to be in country where this stuff stretches without relief for hundreds of miles.

The back streets of Geraldine would make the *Marie Celeste* seem busy. The bungalows stand amid neat gardens, a slight breeze nodding the few flowers of autumn. No two bungalows are the same, but they feel identical with their walls of timber or fibreboard or plaster-cement painted in pastel colours, roofs of corrugated steel, and a deep suburban silence. Around an old people's home it seems that not even the air is moving.

But the public bar of the Crown is busy. The walls are hung with pictures of trotting horses and rugby players. Pop music plays above a TV tuned to a sports channel. No one pays attention to either. The men are in work boots, work socks and shorts and are happy and say fuck a lot. The women are in track pants and just as happy and they say fuck even more. I am asked my opinion of a television programme shown the night before about men in Auckland who shave their arses. Everyone pretends to be appalled while being delighted. Arse-shaving confirms what the country wants to think of the city.

The Crown's dining room is crowded with what looks like a Rotary dinner. Roast meat and gravy, women with white hair and no waists; men with brown jackets and haircuts, none of which would have looked out of place in 1954. So I fetch fish and chips from a shop down the road and as dusk becomes darkness I eat on a footbridge, leaning over the rail and staring aimlessly into rippling silver-black water. It brings a surge of memories of former travels, some bright, some melancholic. And I feel pleased to be where I am, on my way, alone, and with the few ties in my life temporarily snapped. I've got a country to taste at my leisure. And out there somewhere is a band of drivers whose lives, though none of them knows it yet, are briefly going to intersect with mine.

'How's it going, mate?' The speaker is shaven-headed. He's being towed by a panting mastiff on a short thick lead.

'Good,' I say. 'It's going good.'

After a last beer in the rapidly emptying bar I climb the wide old stairs of the hotel, fail to find the light switch, and grope along the corridor. Outside the door to my room I stop to fumble with the key and step both firmly and centrally on my continental breakfast.

2

On the road with God

Half an hour after dawn and Geraldine is dank and silent, as if nerve gas had come in the night.

I dither at Geraldine's only junction. I can go further inland or turn back towards the east coast. Inland means the lush foothills to Burke's Pass and then the Mackenzie Country with its tussocky moonscape, its rivers, lakes and wild lupins. But it is empty country, and could bring long waits by the road in a southerly storm. Caution chooses the coast. The Mackenzie will keep.

Geraldine stretches further than I expected, one house deep on either side of the road. I pass fresh-painted bungalows with prim gardens, and peeling bungalows with children's tricycles lying where they fell, sparkling with dew and cobwebs. Cats stare, then slink under hedges. A shop-sign says 'Furniture, Joinery and Funeral Director.'

It feels good to be the only person about, but my shoulder aches. I didn't bring a backpack because backpacks are for the young, but my sports bag was a poor alternative. Its handles want to slide from my shoulder. I am travelling as light as I know how, but a mile of pavement turns six underpants, six T-shirts, a spare pair of trousers, a sweater, a couple of books, a wash-bag and a packet of fun-size Mars Bars into a bad companion. It's with relief that I pass the last building, drop the bag at my feet by a paddock of black cattle, and proffer my thumb to the cool air.

Peter's heading to Timaru for an auction. A trailer bounces behind his van. He buys sarking and old furniture, turns it into new furniture and sells it at fairs and markets. He makes a living. He wishes he'd done it before. He stayed in his last job for fifteen years even though he'd learned all there was to learn about it in six months. 'Why do we stay so long in our niches?' he asks, then answers the question himself. 'Because we're fools, and cowards.'

Peter loves wood so much that he calls it timber. He tells me that New Zealand white pine is the only timber in the world that has no smell so they used it to make butter boxes. I like learning stuff like that. It's precise, pleasing and quite without use.

Peter spent three years on the West Coast. 'Feral's the word for that place,' he says. 'I know a woman who taught secondary school over there. She called it missionary work.'

Timaru is Geraldine writ large. Well, reasonably large. It has an Edwardian air. It's one of several South Canterbury towns that never seem to grow or shrink. They battle on, younger sisters to Christchurch, lacking either the gravitational bulk or the single remarkable attraction needed to lure tourists. Timaru does have Caroline Bay, where Rick painted the horses, and it's a pretty enough beach and funfair, but it sings of the fifties. I once attended a panel discussion in Timaru on the subject of the town's future. The meeting was held in the Caroline Bay tearooms. There were five people on the panel and six in the audience.

But Timaru does have some famous sons. The most famous of these was a horse. Phar Lap was perhaps the greatest racehorse of all time. When he died at the age of five in 1932 as the result of an illness which was described at the time as a severe colic but which many suspected was severe poisoning, Australia and New Zealand squabbled over his corpse. In the end, Australia got his hide and heart, and New Zealand his bones. I've seen those bones in the national museum in Wellington. They look like horse bones.

Bob Fitzsimmons was not born in Timaru, but his family came here from Cornwall when Bob was small. He promptly got a lot bigger and in 1897 became the Heavyweight Boxing Champion of the World. One of his fights in the States was refereed by Wyatt Earp.

But the most remarkable man of these parts was Richard Pearse, a reclusive farmer. It seems reasonably certain that in 1903 he designed, built and flew a powered aircraft some months before the Wright brothers managed it. The plane landed in a hedge. In recognition of his being the first to gratify, however briefly, the oldest longing of humankind, and of his pioneering efforts in an industry that would put a man on the moon inside seventy years and would do more to change the face of the twentieth century than any other, the locals called him Mad Dick.

Timaru is sweet enough, its streets lined with the usual stores, its cafés now housing coffee-machines and paninis. But it doesn't tempt me to stay, mainly because I want to be inside a vehicle when the southerly strikes. After twenty minutes and a bizarre conversation with two fat women pushing prams, I reach the junction where Timaru stops being Timaru and becomes the road heading south again. I drop my bag, light a cigarette and a small brown car pulls up at my feet.

John shifts a guitar and a packet of sandwiches to the back seat, and we drive towards the storm. You can see it. It's sweeping up the island like a black stage curtain. Cars run ahead of it with their lights on.

This country's good for storms. Sometimes the hooked tails of cyclones swing down from the tropics. More often the great southern oceans brew up fierce beauties like this one and send them racing unstoppably north. When we reach it, it's like driving into a carwash. The little car is gripped by weather. It slows perceptibly. The air inside drops five degrees and rain smothers the windscreen, not in drops but in a seething wash. The landscape disappears. It's the sort of onslaught that turns a classroom dark, that momentarily silences kids and teacher, makes them stare as one at the suddenly noisy windows. But it doesn't silence us. John and I are discussing God.

He's a professional young man with a post-graduate degree in a scientific discipline. The Church slips into his fifth sentence. Jesus into his seventh. And if you believe, as he believes, that this life is a preparation for the next bash, and if you believe, as he believes, that the only way to heaven is through Jesus, and if you believe, as he believes, that if you don't know Jesus you will go directly to hell without passing go or collecting $200, then I suppose that's fair enough.

'Am I damned?' I ask.

'Yes,' he says cheerfully.

'And all Muslims, all Buddhists, all Hindus, Aztec sun-worshippers, Jews?'

'Yes.'

He's a member of the fifty-strong worship team at an Apostolic church in Dunedin and about to head into Central Otago for a weekend of guitar-playing and fellowship and prayer. His girlfriend, who's a member of the same church, has a degree in zoology. She wants to be a pastor.

Arguing about God is adolescent and futile and I like it. I like it because I think I've got all the arguments. I like John too, but here, in this rain-lashed little car, I feel, well, saddened. I tell him so. I tell him that to believe in God is not only demonstrably absurd, it is also to renounce your independence. He says that if I knew God, I wouldn't say that. And he tells me how to find Him. Apparently it's just a question of asking Him in. I say I wouldn't want to ask Him in even if He were capable of coming in. I want to be on my own.

John turns to look at me with the sort of expression one might give a loved grandmother on her deathbed.

'You're a scientist,' I say. 'Your belief defies scientific method.'

'Lots of scientists believe.'

'But that's not a scientific argument, either.'

I ask if God can do anything He wants. John says He can. I asked if God wants me to believe. John says He does.

'Then why doesn't He just make me believe?'

'God doesn't work like that.'

As evidence of God's bounty, John gestures at the sodden landscape. 'He made the world beautiful,' he says. 'Do you think it was just chance that put earth at the right distance from the sun to propagate life?'

'Yes, of course I do. And anyway, what about Pluto?'

You can go on like that for hours. We do.

When I happen to mention that I got my first lift on this trip from a pastor, John turns to me with a swiftly blossoming smile. 'I reckon God's got a little plan for you,' he says.

I ask if he's read *Decline and Fall* by Evelyn Waugh. He

hasn't. 'You should,' I say. 'There's a lapsed clergyman called Prendergast. He can understand the finer points of theology. What he can't understand is why God made the world at all.'

'Our purpose,' says John, 'is to praise and love God.'

'Well, that makes God into a selfish old wanker.'

John is so upset by that last comment that he offers me his flat in Dunedin for the weekend.

The rain abates and we stop for petrol in Oamaru, pronounced Omaroo by the locals but O-a-maroo by television newsreaders, in deference to Maori sensitivity. But there are very few Maori here to be sensitive. Though Maori travelled all over the South Island and some tribes lived permanently here, most have always lived in the North.

Oamaru has a rare main street. It's a mish-mash of architectural styles, but built in just the one material, a creamy local sandstone that's so soft you can saw it. Unlike most buildings in New Zealand these seem to belong to the landscape.

Otherwise, to the casual visitor, Oamaru is Timaru with penguins. The penguins nest close to the town and at dusk you can watch them waddle up the beach, like waiters with piles. But John and I move on.

In the aftermath of the southerly, the sheep, the hills, the houses and the occasional rivers are done in shades of grey, beneath a dishwater sky as low as a ceiling.

Having reached an impasse over God, I ask John about New Zealand. I tell him that I'm travelling partly to try to grasp the heart of the country I've found myself living in. Is there anything distinctive about New Zealanders? John thinks a bit, then says no.

'Come on,' I say. 'What about the vaunted practicality, the no-nonsense earthiness, the number-eight-wire ingenuity, the rugged independence, the compulsion to travel, the willingness to work hard?'

'Yes,' says John. 'There is all that.'

South of Oamaru the road runs closer to the coast. The

beaches are harsh, the wind harrowing. Sudsy waves fling smooth and monstrous hunks of driftwood onto the narrow strip of sand. The only tourist stop round here is Moeraki with its celebrated boulders. They are a metre or two in diameter, half-buried in the sand, and almost perfectly spherical. You can admire them from close quarters or you can admire them from a café built overlooking them. Oh look, you can say, some spherical boulders. Though what you say after that, I don't know.

'Somewhere round here,' says John, gesturing at the barely visible landscape, 'there's a monument, on top of a hill. To the bloke who invented marine refrigeration.'

If anyone in this country ever deserved a monument, it's this man. Until the 1880s New Zealand's industries were all extractive – sealing, whaling, gold-mining, logging, kauri gum. None could last indefinitely, and some were already exhausted. So when this man invented a device that enabled mutton to be shipped around the world, he gave the country the chance of a durable future. The country took it. It rode to prosperity on the sheep's frozen back. That sheep was born in New Zealand, raised on New Zealand grass, shorn in New Zealand, killed in New Zealand, frozen in New Zealand, but thawed and eaten in England. Abattoirs here are universally known as freezing works.

'What was the name of this bloke?'

John shrugs.

If you approach Dunedin from the north you first catch sight of it from a thousand feet above. It looks grand. There's a long and skinny inlet shaped like a sock and the city surrounds the toe. On the northern side of the sock is Aramoana, scene of New Zealand's largest mass murder. The southern side is the Otago Peninsula, popular with seals, penguins, albatrosses and tourists.

From closer to, Dunedin looks less lovely. On a day like this, it's gaunt. Driving into town, John points out his church. With

some pride he tells me it's a converted biscuit factory. It does-
n't look very converted.

Again John urges me to use his flat. I turn it down partly
because of my mulish reluctance to be indebted, but also
because of the posters. I can picture them – the shot of the
waterfall in the bush or the sun rising, and the uplifting spiritual apophthegm. God always gets the credit for the good bits.
I have yet to see a poster of a pox-raddled beggar's corpse in
Delhi, labelled 'I am the way the truth and the life'. God's gone
down the same route as nature. Just as nature has turned from
implacable enemy into colourful David Attenborough entertainment, and an ingredient in shampoo, health food and
happiness, so the fierce father of the Old Testament has turned
into a celestial Care-Bear. It's a form of cuddlification, like
making a musical about Jack the Ripper.

All of which I can no longer be bothered to say to John. He
drops me at the Octagon, which is the hub of Dunedin's city
centre and not noticeably octagonal. Traffic bisects it and circles
it and the buildings are a grey hodge-podge. When I thank
John he says that I'm welcome and he's enjoyed the chat and he
hopes I find Jesus.

I find Robbie Burns. His statue stands in the middle of the
Octagon with, as every guidebook amusingly regurgitates, 'his
back to the kirk and his face to the pub'. Dunedin is apparently
Gaelic for Edinburgh. Just as Christchurch was a planned
Anglican settlement, so Dunedin, the second largest city in the
South Island with a population similar to that of Cheltenham,
was a Scottish Presbyterian one. When the settlers arrived in
1848 the first thing that they did was to fall to their knees and
give thanks for having found a climate similar to the one they'd
left.

The wind knifes round corners and frisks me for skin. The
pavements are scattered with optimistic café tables, but
between them stand rather more realistic gas heaters, feebly
battling the latitude and warming the world. The people of

Dunedin are always keen to tell you that the climate isn't that bad, which suggests it's that bad. People in warm climates don't tell you about it. They just bask.

I ditch my bag in a hundred-year-old, three-storey Lubjanka of a hotel that's shaped like a wedge of cheese. The tip of the wedge splits the main flow of traffic coming into Dunedin from the south. The hotel is conveniently placed for the railway station that doesn't have trains any more.

The hotel lift clanks. I asked for the cheapest room and I've clearly got it. The door's a hollow thing of wood veneer that rings when you tap it. There's a plasterboard dado, the joins masked by square battens of customwood. The ceiling's stippled and, like the wall, painted a colour that hovers between nicotine and pus. An awkwardly angled contraption emerges from the wall to align the small modern television to the small but less modern bed. The place sings of commercial travellers of the fifties, with brilliantined hair, yellowing vests and Players Navy Cut cigarettes. In the corridor you can smell those cigarettes. You'll be able to until they flatten the building. At the end of the corridor in the triangular tip of the cheese wedge the residents' lounge is empty. Unmatching armchairs, a television identical to the one in my room, a rubber plant with chronic fatigue syndrome, and a shelf of paperback novels by authors of unremitting awfulness.

On my way out I ask the girl at reception what's on in Dunedin.

'Nothing much,' she says. 'The students are away.'

Students make up 15 per cent of Dunedin's population. With that army of youth off on holiday the town is quiet. The little houses the students occupy, weatherboard villas with bed-sheets for curtains, wasteland for gardens and wet, sagging sofas on the veranda, are normally cheerfully anarchic in counterpoint to the sober commercial strictness of the adult city. Today, under a sky like a morgue, they look derelict.

The height of Dunedin's prosperity came in the 1860s when

they discovered gold in the hills beyond. The gold paid for big buildings in grey stone; bank buildings, official buildings, buildings as bull-necked and four-square as that old trout Victoria. They're still there. They make Dunedin seem serious.

Though New Zealand is now awash with shopping malls, I find few in this city that seems well suited to them. The main shopping thoroughfare is thronged with sturdy white women in dateless coats. And though I've heard tell of Dunedin's growing cultural diversity I can see little evidence of it. Until, that is, I climb some stairs to an internet café and find fifty Asian students engrossed in computer war games, their dexterous fingers waltzing over the keys, destroying the world with little involuntary gasps.

The main university building is a pleasure in Victorian Gothic. The new university buildings are horrors in postwar concrete. Every sign tugs its forelock to biculturalism. 'Te Whare Wananga o Otago Te Tari Karuri' says one. It's pronounced Otago University School of Surveying.

The First Church of Otago was built in 1848 and looks it. To my ignorant eye it could be any largish Victorian parish church in Britain, with its vaulted roof, stone pillars, and a woman in gloves doing flowers at the altar. I sit in a pew for a while. It has nothing to do with the conversation with John. I often do it when travelling. A church is one of the few places where you can sit indoors without having to buy anything. And I like the sense of sanctuary. I like the held air.

New Zealand feels secular. For me it's one of the attractions of this country that the pronouncements of bishops seem even more of a footling irrelevance than they do elsewhere.

Few people in this country even bother to pretend that the great religious festivals are in any way religious. It helps that they're all six months misplaced, which throws the symbolism delightfully out of whack. Easter, with its eggs and baa-lambs and promise of new birth, happens in autumn. And Christmas is hot. In the annual Christmas parades through the city centres, Santa is a sweaty old man.

Nevertheless many Christmas cards still feature snow, shop windows are painted with holly leaves and, until recently, most families had a hot Christmas dinner of turkey and plum pudding. There have been efforts to replace the traditional iconography of a northern Christmas with local stuff – carols featuring pohutukawa trees and such, all of which are awful – but it can't be long before the inappropriate trappings of an imported festival just melt into the land like the snow we haven't got. Already the turkey is yielding to barbecues and beer and summer berries. In time, New Zealand may acknowledge Christmas for what it is – an annual spend-up, knees-up, booze-up and get-together, a Thanksgiving without a celestial thanksgivee, and none the worse for that.

But perhaps because much of colonial New Zealand was religiously founded, it's a slow progress. The first Europeans were explorers. The next wave were exploiters – the sealers and whalers and traders. But the next and by far the most influential arrivals were the missionaries.

But then again, the visions of religious Utopia never materialised. The association that founded Christchurch, for example, went bust within twenty years and with it went the ideal of a society of Anglicans, each in his allotted social rank. But no amount of cash could have stopped the ideal withering, because most of the people who came here did not come in order to recreate the old world, in however idealised a form. They came to escape. They came to better themselves. They came to make something new.

And something new has been made here and is still being made. But the stamp of the past is everywhere and is not lightly shaken off. Parliament still opens with a daily prayer. And even though church attendances continue to fall, little Geraldine, for example, where I spent last night, seemed to have a church for every Christian denomination.

The First Church of Otago has had plenty of visitors. A visitor from Minnesota has written 'So peaceful' in the visitors' book in the porch, a visitor from Taiwan has written 'very nice', several other visitors from Taiwan have also written 'very nice' underneath it, and Hamish Gibson of Brisbane Boys' College, for whom the church visit was obviously a highlight, has written that 'it was as good as a kangaroo'.

Dunedin railway station, according to a brochure, is 'perhaps the most photographed railway station in the world'. It's absurdly ornate. The waiting-room floor is tiled like a doge's lavatory. There's stained glass and an elaborate moulded ceiling and little Enid Blyton guichets with the word 'Tickets' embossed above them. There are no ticket-sellers in evidence. The building now houses a sports hall of fame, an art gallery and a function centre, but the principal tenants are ghosts. An endlessly looping video advertises the only remaining passenger train, a tourist trip up the Taeri Gorge to nowhere and back. In fruity tones the soundtrack tells and retells the story of the hardy labourers from Ireland and China who hewed their way through solid rock and built viaducts over the . . . I am the only person there. I leave the video to talk to the ghosts. I go to visit albatrosses.

They nest at the far end of the Otago Peninsula, which isn't very far. A road winds along the waterfront around quaint bays. Some have a fringe of small houses. Some have only wading birds. In forty-five minutes I'm at the headland with nothing between me and Chile but a visitors' centre, an ocean, and a few big birds.

'Look,' says the American woman behind me at the viewing hide, 'is that one?' It isn't one. It's a seagull. But the next one is one, an albatross, riding the fierce wind with consummate intuitive skill, a monarch of the skies, wheeling and swinging like, well, a big seagull.

The facts are more interesting than the birds. Here, just a few miles from the second largest city on the South Island is the only mainland colony of Royal Albatrosses in the world. They skim the winds of the great Southern Ocean where they eat squid. They sleep on the wing. They mate for life. Their chicks are huge balls of fluff that live in the nest for eight months. Their first hesitant flight takes them to Antarctica and can last for five years. Their only predator is man, who catches them by mistake when fishing for tuna.

You have to pay to see the albatrosses. You don't have to pay to see the shags. They nest on the cliffs by the car park. You can look down on them squabbling and plunging and gliding, and I do. Indeed I spend twice as long looking down at the shags as I do looking up at the albatrosses.

In the many little bays on the southern side of the peninsula it's possible to see yellow-eyed penguins in their black and white tuxedos, fur seals in their sleek dingy fur, and Hooker Sea-lions in their short skirts and fishnet stockings. I don't bother. I'm hungry, thirsty, cold and keen for profane urban pleasures. I want to go gambling. I like gambling, and Dunedin's got a casino.

I hitch back into town with a German couple who, unusually for Germans, speak lousy English. The distance from the albatrosses to the Dunedin Casino turns out to be exactly the distance required to ascertain that they come from Düsseldorf.

Until the late nineteen-eighties the punters of New Zealand had to make do with horses. Then that same Labour government with the social conscience that sold the railways, granted permits for the first casinos. The punters flocked to the green baize tables, the chandeliers, and the parody James Bond glamour. Everyone was happy, including the people who like to worry about other people. They acquired a whole slew of problem gamblers to fret for.

Dunedin Casino is full of the women I saw shopping. Each has ditched her coat, bouffed her hair and acquired a bucket of coins. She sits on a stool before a fruit machine which she feeds like a giant neon pet.

I always play blackjack, partly because it seems to be the game where the casino has least advantage, but mainly because I understand most of the rules. I also have a system. It's a sure-fire winner if you stick to it. All it requires is the self-restraint to stop when you're winning, and the courage to keep doubling your bets when you're losing. I have the self-restraint.

I take a seat next to a man called Olly. Certain stimuli produce certain responses in Olly. If an ace appears on the table, Olly says, 'Go the Ace.' If a promising hand turns sour, Olly says, 'Them's the breaks.' If there are no stimuli around to fire a little message across his synapses, Olly cracks his knuckles and tidies his chips into piles, like a planner's model of a city centre. And if the man sitting next to Olly chickens out of his system and walks away from the table having lost a substantial sum of money in a little under an hour, Olly says, 'Them's the breaks,' and 'Cheerio,' and goes back to tidying his chips.

Defeat is said to be good for the soul. It doesn't feel good. What I feel, as always, is not so much anger as embarrassment. Greed has given me a knee to the groin and a karate chop of self-knowledge.

With the money I've lost I could have rented the best suite in my hotel for a week, though that is not perhaps the most instantly appealing notion.

I drift around the casino a bit, watching other players, with greed still urging me to fetch yet more money from the cash-flow machine.

'Would you like a free beer?' A woman is holding out vouchers.

Management gave them to her and her husband for a reason which she explains, but that I don't take in because I'm still absorbed with self-loathing. But it's a relief to listen to someone other than Olly and the voice that whispers, 'Sucker.'

The husband and wife are very happy people. They're heading tomorrow for the Bluff Oyster Festival where they'll be selling kelp.

'Kelp?'

'Kelp.'

'Oh.'

They farm kelp. Then they dry it, grind it, bottle it and sell it. Kelp is the next big thing. It's going through the roof. They can barely satisfy the local demand, let alone think of exporting yet. Kelp contains 500 trace elements and you use it like salt. It's especially good on porridge.

I tell them that if I make it to the oyster festival I'll try their kelp and buy them a beer.

'You betcher,' says the husband, and they leave radiating delight. They are bursting with it, like suns. On my way back to the hotel I try to think about them and their kelp and their happiness. I fail. I think about the money I've lost. And returning to my cramped and dismal room does even more to cheer me up.

I set the radio alarm for 6 a.m., partly because I want to get away early again, but more because I want to punish my flesh.

3

Ecce homo with ditch on the Day Of the Dead

Bagpipes wake me. They're not on the radio. They're coming from the street. I recognise the tune as something that Kenneth McKellar used to sing, but I still quite like it. Immediately I realise what's happening, and my heart sinks a notch. This is Anzac Day, a public holiday in memory of the war-dead. It will make hitching difficult.

I pull on my jeans. Outside it's still dark and the air is cold as steel. A parade is coming raggedly down the hill, led by old people with medals, followed by young people who haven't been taught how to march. A crowd waits for them in Queen's Gardens, perhaps 2,000 people, wearing department-store Puffa jackets and woollen beanies and toting their children on their shoulders. They are quiet in the darkness.

Representatives of the armed forces stand on each side of the memorial. One is Maori. Against the bitterness of the weather, he's wearing a skirt and a thin cloak. His feet are bare. He's standing as still as the statue on the plinth.

'Let us join together in singing "God Save the Queen".' No one around me does more than murmur. The chaplain then begs us to join in the hymn 'Lead Kindly Light'. There's no light to read the hymn sheet by, but a choir has set up by now to rescue the chaplain.

'We groan inwardly,' says the chaplain, 'as we wait for our bodies to be let free.' I sense no groaning. This isn't a crowd of churchgoers. It's a crowd of the ordinary, drawn to this place by some sense of duty and nationhood. Today's the 88th anniversary of the day the first Anzac forces landed on Gallipoli.

Over the course of the Gallipoli campaign, 8,450 New Zealand soldiers disembarked. 7,473 of them were either killed or wounded.

It is generally accepted that Gallipoli marks the birth of New Zealand. This event more than any other caused New Zealand to cut its ties with the colonial mother ship and sail off as an independent nation.

It's a neat story, but it isn't true. A quarter of a century later, at the start of the next World War, the Prime Minister of New Zealand was still able to say this: 'With gratitude for the past and confidence in the future we range ourselves without fear by Britain. Where she goes, we go; where she stands, we stand.' And his people agreed with him.

Across the road from my first house in Lyttelton, an old

woman lived in a cottage. She was dying, and her doctor had forbidden her to smoke, but she loved to beckon me over and cadge a cigarette. She'd lived her whole life in Lyttelton. I asked her once if she had any unfulfilled ambition. 'Yes,' she said with no hesitation. 'I'd like to go home.' By home she meant England.

When the newly crowned Elizabeth came here in 1953, the whole country painted its front door, spruced up its garden, swept its vagrants under the carpet and curtseyed. It is estimated that three quarters of the population actually turned out to see the young Queen. The massive crowds were sparkle-eyed and they threw flowers at her feet.

In the late seventies the Queen came here again. A Maori protester threw a T-shirt at her.

But when the Queen came for a third time a couple of years ago, no one threw a thing, probably because the few people who turned out to greet her were all too old to be any good at throwing.

The process of dissociation from Britain has been a slow one and most of it has happened in the last fifty years. No one event caused it, though New Zealand felt betrayed when the UK joined the EEC in 1972. It was a betrayal that did the country good. It obliged New Zealand to see itself not as a distant farm for Britain, but as a trading nation in the South Pacific.

The old woman across the road from me has died. This year New Zealand established its own Supreme Court. Kiwis can no longer appeal to the Privy Council in London. Within twenty years New Zealand will be a republic. Though it wasn't Gallipoli that caused it, the separation of New Zealand from Great Britain is effectively complete.

And Anzac Day has come to symbolise that separation. In recent years the numbers attending the dawn services have risen. But as yet there is no new form of ceremonial. The service falls back on those old imperial stalwarts, God and the military. The Mayor of Dunedin, Sukhi Turner, reads unconvincingly from St John. The cold silent crowd endures it rather than listens. A bigwig from the Australian army manages to make two allusions to a rugby match to be played in Dunedin this evening between a Kiwi team and an Aussie one. One of these allusions may have been a joke.

As the service proceeds, the sky lightens from black to sunless grey. Wreaths are laid while the bagpipe band plays 'Speed Bonnie Boat' ten times in a row. During the 'Last Post', a massive Woolworth's truck rumbles past. A volley of rifle fire sends the seagulls sheering off across the clouds, mewing. The President of the Returned Services Association reads a list of other Anzac ceremonies to be held in the region. It seems that they've been co-ordinated at half-hour intervals throughout the morning so that an addict can attend them all. The President invites all former combatants to the RSA for refreshments. And that's that. It's taken an hour or so. People start to talk again.

'That Maori guy,' says an oldish man in a ski jacket, 'he must have been fucking freezing.'

In the thin cool morning the people drift back into lives with something affirmed. They seem cheerful, with a sense of duty done and identity bolstered. I follow a procession of them to breakfast in the dining room of my hotel, where amid the thick flock wallpaper and the moulded plaster ceiling and the chandeliers with obvious electric cables, breakfast is the real thing. A battalion of pigs have laid down their lives that we should eat. After a hand of sausages and a flank of bacon I am greased like a Channel swimmer and ready to try to hitch.

The road heading south out of town is wide as a paddock and all but empty. It's lined with tyre dealerships, carpet warehouses, and office furniture stores with not long to live. Among them stand enterprises already dead, their windows whited out and weeds at their feet. A car park of gravel is scattered with wet plastic bags. After perhaps a mile I set up at the base of the motorway that climbs past Carisbrook Stadium where the rugby will be played this evening.

There's predictably little traffic and what there is shows predictably little interest in me. The cars are all burdened with too many people and thoughts of the dead.

I take a perverse pleasure in mild misfortune. It's a form of self-pity. I envisage myself stuck here for the day, imagine my fingers slowly numbing as the hours pass and the first claws of hunger scratch at my gut. I consider resorting to a tactic I sometimes employed in the days of hair and energy. I would kneel as a car approached and join my hands in supplication and look up towards the driver with spaniel eyes. It always worked, and did so quickly. The irony and humour of the pose would pierce somebody's indifference. But I had to be desperate to find the nerve to do it, and I'm not desperate yet. Besides, I'm not sure that I can still do spaniel eyes.

I don't need to. After an hour or so, a bearded scoutmaster offers me a lift to Green Island in his bearded scoutmaster's car. I don't know where or what Green Island is, but it's a given of hitching that elsewhere is better than here.

Green Island isn't. It is neither an island nor especially green. It's effectively the last southern suburb of Dunedin. The scoutmaster drops me on the slip road off the motorway, so that I have to walk a mile or so through Green Island to find the slip road back on to the motorway. The place is preparing for its Anzac parade. Bagpipes are warming up like a groaning surgical ward. Four youths in naval uniform huddle behind a shed smoking. At the Memorial Gardens four more youths in army uniform stand guard under the supervision of a grizzled ex-army man. Their heads are penitently bowed, hands on rifle barrels, rifle butts on the ground. One of the youths looks up surreptitiously as I pass. His face is a mixture of boredom, cold, superciliousness and quite volcanic acne.

For understandable reasons I get few lifts from women. For less understandable reasons, the woman who picks me up outside Green Island insists that I get into the back seat. From there I am poorly positioned for fondling her knee or raiding the glove box. But I am ideally positioned for hooking an arm round her throat, putting a gun to her temple, and telling her to drive to Dead Woman Gulch.

Generously refraining from any of these activities, I make conversation and learn that she is a freelance inspector of rest homes. I've never met one before. We discuss the freelance inspection of rest homes for some time. In order to hear her I have to crane forward, and in order to see me, she has to look over her shoulder. This does little for her steering. Or rather it does too much for her steering. Had this been a motorway in any other country of the developed world we would have hit something. But on a motorway in the South Island of New Zealand there's little to hit. And on a public holiday there's nothing to hit.

When I use the word motorway you shouldn't think motorway. On the approach to a city it may become four lanes, and even perhaps with a median strip, but five miles out of the city the motorway reverts to something to which most countries would ascribe a less imposing title. Road, indeed, would cover it nicely.

Earlier this week *Statistics New Zealand* announced that the population of the country had reached four million. It is a statistical probability that the four millionth citizen was an immigrant from Asia, and even more of a statistical probability that he or she took up residence in Auckland. Auckland houses over a quarter of the country's people. The North Island, including Auckland, houses three quarters. The South Island, which is roughly the size of England, is home to just over one million people.

Take any back road in these parts, and if you see another driver you casually raise the right index finger from the steering wheel. It's an acknowledgment that you belong to the same rare species. It's like blackbirds tweeting.

The country gently rolls, gathering from time to time to a rural township comprising a few back streets of bungalows and a main street that is also State Highway 1. On each main street there's a vast wooden pub, and a sprinkling of shops all closed until 1 p.m. in deference to the war-dead. At Milton the road is blocked by yet another Anzac parade, a straggle of people raw-faced in the cold.

My driver, who is off to spend the long weekend camping by a high country lake, drops me in Balclutha. A concrete bridge with the aesthetic merit of a sixties tower block spans the forbidding Clutha River. This is water you don't want to fall into. In bitter wind, a lone man scoots downstream on a scarlet jet ski. What he's doing is not so much recreation as an act of defiance.

In the 1990s the South suffered. People moved North for money and sun. Although good commodity prices in the last few seasons have done something to reverse the exodus, in the real estate agent's window in Balclutha there's a house for sale down the road in Kaitangata for $28,000. You could pay more in London to kennel your dog.

The only place open on Anzac Day is the Café Italio. It's as Italian as you would expect in Balclutha. The proprietor's in jeans. His wife is less formally dressed. I lunch on a slice of cheesecake that takes the enamel off my teeth, and two cups of coffee that replace it.

In the South Island you barely need a map. You enter most towns at one end and emerge at the other. The road is the road. But Balclutha boasts a junction. You can go straight on towards Invercargill, or you can turn left towards Invercargill. But this road to the left is the long road, the designated scenic route, passing though the Catlins, a rugged land of rocks and sea and deep green emptiness down in the bottom right-hand corner of the inhabited world. The Catlins are one of the twenty-nine regions officially known as New Zealand's best-kept secret. The hitching so far has been easy. I go left.

On a bank of the Clutha, a pair of dogs is mustering a mob of sheep. A border collie darts and slinks round the front and sides of the mob, steering, eyeing, slinking. It seems to work almost independently of the shepherd who stands at the back and whistles. Beside the shepherd stands a huntaway, a tall black and tan beast unique to New Zealand. It looks like a generic dog, the archetype of the rugged mongrel found at the pound. Its job is to drive sheep from behind. It does this partly by barking but mainly by being a dog.

I can watch dogs working for hours, but I don't have to. The first car, which has taken an ominous fifteen minutes to appear, stops.

The driver owns two farms. One runs sheep, the other dairy cattle. When he says 'farm', he so crams the word with r's that he sounds like a hedge-trimmer. This is the Southland burr, the only distinctive regional accent in the country. It's a soft appealing noise, deriving, I presume, from the Scottish settlers, but resembling no known Scottish accent. It's simply Kiwi English with added r's.

Variations in accent here are based not on geography but on class. New Zealand likes to imagine itself to be classless but it is no such thing. And, by and large, the lower the class the broader the accent; the higher the class the closer to what used to be known as BBC English.

To generalise, the most distinctive kiwi characteristic is to move some vowels back one place on the palate. Thus pen becomes pin, tip becomes tup and bare becomes beer. But beer stays, more or less, as beer. Most Kiwis rhyme here with there, ear with air. Ferry and fairy are homophones.

But there's also a squattocracy with an accent of its own. The old-established farmers with huge sheep stations, particularly in North Canterbury or Hawke's Bay, sound like Lord Haw Haw with buggered vowels. They pronounce off 'orfe'. The only other people I have heard do that are British commentators on show-jumping.

There's also a distinctive Maori English, which is less an accent than a speech pattern. Its most distinctive characteristic is the rising intonation of each sentence terminating with eh. But there's little chance to study that around Balclutha. Instead I manipulate the conversation in the car to try to get the farmer to say words with lots of r's in them. After twenty minutes of hedge-trimming he drops me in Nowhere Central.

I watch him drive away down a gravel road that winds over the hills. He disappears into a valley and reappears on a crest, then does the same again only smaller and more distant, the sound of his engine fading. Then he's gone. It's like the opening scene of *Mississippi Burning* shown backwards. And it leaves me alone in the cinema.

The place is green as an ad. Nearby there's a white weatherboard farmhouse with a barking dog and a clothesline. White sheets flap audibly on the line, next to a pink thing that may or may not be a tablecloth, and three pairs of catering-size underpants.

Beyond and in every direction the deep green paddocks are dotted with grey sheep. The wooden fenceposts are weathered to grey, the barbed wire browning with rust. Hawks circle on the crisp air. And the silence is like a blanket.

A camper van passes. I don't remember seeing them in the UK but the Americans call them Winnebagoes. Big rented white beasts, they're the human equivalent of snail shells.

There's a long wait. I watch a hawk. I hear an engine a couple of hills away. A minute or two later it crests the rise. It's another camper van. It doesn't stop.

And so it goes on. Perhaps five vehicles an hour and all of them camper vans. The cab of each is occupied by a middle-aged couple whose children have understandably fled the nest. The husband drives. The wife wears glasses.

As each camper van comes into view I compose my face. I try to look like a bearer of humorous tales, a provider of local lore, a character, and a joy to be with. I don't believe it myself.

As the vehicle nears, I sense the woman in the passenger seat catch sight of me. I am a threat, a freeloader, a not-nice, and a blot on the pretty landscape. She won't look me in the eye but, and I am sure I'm not imagining this, my presence charges the cab of the camper van with a slight tension.

I'm confident that if the husband were on his own he might consider picking me up. But then again, if the husband were on his own, he wouldn't be driving a camper van through bloody scenery.

Twenty-five years ago I got a lift from Dieppe to Rouen with a middle-aged English couple in a big Rover. The husband asked me if I was married. I said no.

'Take my advice, son,' he said, 'and stay that way.'

I could think of nothing to say. I didn't have to. The man had tapped a pent seam of his own venom and discharged it in a stream of invective about traps and womanhood and money and handcuffs that took us half way to Rouen. His wife sat with a map on her lap and said nothing at all.

But here in the New Zealand wilderness it seems to me that Mrs Camper Van's distaste for me communicates itself to hubby and the steering wheel. Each vehicle moves fractionally but noticeably towards the centre line, not to avoid hitting me but to prevent me leaping onto the bonnet, a cutlass between my teeth, and clinging madly to the wipers as the hubby swerves and wrenches in an effort to throw me off. But I retain my grip, smash the windscreen and then force the couple to drive at cutlass point to some remote scenic beauty spot where I subject the pair of them to serial indecencies, before tossing them out bleeding, snivelling and naked to smell their way back to civilisation.

In other words, I'm there for a long time. And as the slow hours pass, with nothing much to think about, I allow my frustration to swell into loathing. Camper vans seem so primly self-contained and smug. They stop at designated camper-van sites where they can plug into electricity and fill their little water tanks and empty their little chemical toilets and draw their little curtains at 9 p.m. and change the film in their cameras and prepare for another day of safe, polite and point-less travel through prettiness, stopping to gawp at the things the guidebooks tell them to gawp at, and not daring to ask themselves whether there's any pleasure whatsoever to be had from what they're doing.

More to keep myself amused than for any other reason I try lowering my thumb as they approach, smiling an ironic smile and shrugging ironic shoulders as a sort of double-dare to them to recognise that I know that they won't stop and thus to induce them to defy their own stereotype and stop. It works every bit as well as trying to look nice. Furthermore, a little voice whispers to me that they may not be stopping because there's only room for two in the cab.

The signpost on the bend points back to Balclutha and onward to Owaka. Balclutha is fifteen kilometres, Owaka six-teen. Sixteen kilometres is ten miles. The Romans marched at four miles per hour. So a pasta-laden ancient Italian in a plumed helmet, carrying a sword and singing 'Roll Me Over in the Vineyard' could make it to Owaka in two and a half hours. I set off.

A stride is a yard. A mile is 1,760 yards. Ten miles are 17,600 yards. I am 17,600 strides from Owaka.

It's hilly. I concentrate on mental arithmetic to take my mind off the ache of my bag-carrying shoulder, and the throb of what threatens to become a blister on the knuckle of my left big toe, and the clouds ahead that threaten to become rain. Four miles per hour is a mile every fifteen minutes. That's 1,760 strides in fifteen minutes. That's a bit under a hundred and twenty strides a minute. That's two strides per second.

When I hear a vehicle behind me I try to discern from the rumble whether it's a camper van or something occupied by humans. If a camper van, I keep walking and just proffer a casual thumb which they are welcome to consider an insult. The first time that I hear something more promising approach

I turn to see a dirty green sedan with a single male driver. Here's a deadfire cert. For one thing I'm in the middle of nowhere. For another I am marching pluckily towards my destination rather than standing immobile and dependent by the road. Both my plight and my transparent virtue make me irresistible. I switch my bag onto the kerbside shoulder, smile like the sun, stick out a thumb so strong and jaunty it could have played for the All Blacks, and I even carry on walking backwards as if willing to race the car to Owaka for the sheer joy of exercise. My second step lands in a ditch. I go down with an abruptness that can only have looked comic. The driver doesn't appear to laugh. He doesn't appear to do anything. He just drives past. I stab a finger in the air at his disappearing exhaust, and then I lie back in the grass, let my bag slide from my shoulder and I laugh.

It's a surprisingly good moment. It evokes the sort of feeling that I can remember experiencing on the road a few times in the distant past, most memorably on the Canadian prairies, somewhere west of Winnipeg. It was winter. It was metal-snapping cold. I was standing in snow. Snow was banked up behind me. I wore boots and thermals and a borrowed jacket that was trimmed round the hood with wolverine fur. I loved that jacket. The land was as flat as a tray and the traffic thin. I had been there for half a day. I was numb.

I watched a dot approach from the horizon and swell from a dot to a shape, from a shape to a car, from a car to a car with a single occupant. And then, just as I was about to put my thumb out, I chose not to. The car slowed a little. It would have stopped. But I looked away and let it pass. Why? Why was simple. It was the sky and the land and the bubbling sense of little me as a speck upon it, tiny, trivial but utterly free. That's all. Big sky, little man, the essential human comedy. As if for a moment I was suspended above myself, looking down and seeing this vain and self-preoccupied insignificant figure all on his own in a big white land. That's all. Call it perspective, if you like, call it Zen, call it a pound of parsnips and eat it with butter for all I care. It felt exhilarating.

And lying on my back, half in and half out of a ditch between Balclutha and Owaka in the heart of agricultural nothing I get a great draught of the exact same ecce homo feeling. And five minutes later I get a lift from Rodney.

Rodney owns a mobile saw mill. He was born locally, became a shearer, shore the world from Cumbria to Nevada, and then came home and bought the saw mill from his father.

'Do you think you'll still be here in fifteen years?'

He thinks a bit, then says yes.

Much of his present work is coming from farm conversions. Because of the high price of milk fat, many farmers are switching from sheep to dairy. They hire Rodney to pull out the macrocarpa shelter belts, because macrocarpa is believed to cause cattle to abort. I file that little nugget away in the white pine butter box I use for such treasures.

When I tell Rodney I am heading for Owaka, I pronounce it oh-wocker in a more or less Maori manner. Rodney calls it a-whacker with the stress on the second syllable. And so, I soon discover, does everyone else.

Owaka's the biggest place in the Catlins. It's not big. It's got a motel, a pub, two ugly churches, a tearoom, a garage, a restaurant and, astonishingly, an internet café. The first person I meet is a boxer dog. He snuffles along beside me, nuzzling my hand as I trundle down to the information place. It's closed. There's a box on the wall labelled *Hunting Kill Returns*. The boxer and I cross to the motel.

Though it's late afternoon and cool, the doors to the motel rooms are all open, net curtains ballooning in the breeze, the rooms self-evidently empty.

'We're full,' says the girl in charge. 'Sorry.'

Where all the guests are, I've no idea. Crowding the internet café, perhaps, or polishing their camper vans, or filling in their kill returns. And so I do what I have never done or wanted to

do. I go to a Bed and Breakfast. The phrase makes me squirm.
It conjures images of chintz and frilled counterpanes and rubbery bacon, and of being welcomed into the bosom of a
matriarchal figure like a netball umpire.

I have always liked neutral territory. I like to drink in pubs,
not at people's homes. I prefer restaurants to dinner parties. I
may be driven by a fear of intimacy, I don't know. All I do
know is that a fear is a fear.

In my experience, growing older doesn't mean growing. It
means becoming more honest with yourself. And I honestly
don't like the idea of Bed and Breakfast. Nor does the boxer.
When I unlatch the neatly painted gate, the dog whimpers and
retreats.

Mrs Bed and Breakfast is warmly welcoming. It takes us half
a cup of coffee to discover mutual acquaintances in
Christchurch. And though Mrs B&B is not a local, she tells me
plenty about Owaka. The main employer is the freezing works
down the road. The church has split into factions. The social
centre is the pub. The big event of recent years was a murder
that made national headlines. It still causes rancour. And locals
are locals. However long he lives here, an outsider can never
become one. In essence it's the story of every small town.

My room has cushions on the bed that I can't see the point
of, and a chocolate on the pillow that I don't want, but do eat.
The curtains consist of yard upon yard of looped and draped
material that I couldn't imagine anyone wanting. Beside the
bed there's a copy of *Châteaux of the Loire*. A glass case in the
bathroom holds miniature specimens of honey and speargrass
soap, guava hair conditioner and root ginger shampoo as if
they were museum exhibits. On the cistern there's an aerosol of
forest fragrance so I won't have to smell my own shit.

But I can't fault the proprietor. She even offers to wash my
socks and underpants. No one has done that for me for over a
quarter of a century.

Owaka squats in a slight depression among undistinguished

rich green hills. The museum is closed. A peep over the fence
tells me that I'm missing out on a valuable learning opportunity with regard to rusting agricultural machinery and I shall
never know what else. But the internet café is open, and empty
save for the bearded owner.

'I didn't expect to find an internet café in Owaka.'

He looks at me with deep weariness. 'Yes,' he says.
'Everyone says that.'

Several hundred emails await my attention. Most want me
to enlarge my penis, though there are also several inviting me
to study other penises at work. All the rest are concerned with
money or drugs. Collectively they offer an inspiring view of the
human condition.

The pub in Owaka is called the Owaka Pub. It's a single-
storeyed building that could have been picked up by helicopter
and dropped into any small town in New Zealand without
anyone finding it odd. In the car park a man is lifting a set of
antlers from the back of his ute. In the bar, a swag of men and
women are warming up for the televised rugby from Dunedin.
The men are wearing track pants and check shirts. So are the
women.

Danny makes his living by cutting the heads off cattle. He's
off-his-head drunk. The booze triggers surreal semi-conscious
streams of comedy. I ask if he minds if I write some of them
down.

'You writing a book or something? What's it called?'

'*Danny's story*,' I say.

'Will it get me sheilas?'

I write that down.

'Fuck,' says Danny to the whole bar. 'He's writing without
looking. Fuuuuuuuuuck.' He launches into a bizarre fantasy of
riding bicycles at grandmothers in the forest and scattering a
thousand trays of pikelets. I give up on my notes. The story
could never work on paper. The words would die without his
tone, his manner, the daliesque grotesquerie of his delivery.

Danny tells me he can't read. I point at a bar mat and ask him what it says.

'Speights, pride of the south,' he says unhesitatingly. 'But that's easy. They all say that.'

I point at the smaller text beneath. It says 'Gold Medal Ale.'

Danny mouths at the letters like a fish. 'God something,' he says. 'Fuck, I don't know. It's new, that bit.'

He drops change into his pocket. It falls through a hole and lands in his gumboot. He raises his foot and shakes it. 'Good luck to it,' he says. 'It stinks down there.' Then he pulls off a boot and empties it onto the bar. 'Fuck,' he says. 'I'm a rich fucker.' He looks up at the giant screen where an ex-All Black is discussing the rugby match to come. 'Want some of this,' he says, offering coins to the screen. 'You big rich fucker?

'I played rugby once against this All Black guy. He just ran straight past me. And he patted my head as he went past. He patted my head like a little dog. Sit. Sit. I sat. The coach gave me arseholes.'

Before the rugby starts I eat in the restaurant attached to the pub. I have to press a buzzer to get in. The buzzer is next to and barely distinguishable from the fire alarm.

Inside the restaurant Ella Fitzgerald sings at a level just below conscious audibility. For $20 I get soup, battered cod and a dessert as rich as Getty. My waiter wears jeans and a sin-glet. He carries himself with the dignity of a maitre d', but without the condescension.

At the next table are three young couples. All three boys are in elastic-sided boots, moleskin trousers, Aertex shirts and homespun sweaters. All three order steak. All three have it medium-rare. All three drink beer with their meal.

All three girls have blonde hair, white wine and the cod.

When I return to the bar it's packed out for the rugby. It's a Super 12 match, the Otago franchise playing the Canberra fran-chise.

T.S. Eliot spoke of the divided sensibility. He never saw the

Owaka pub watch rugby. It pulses like a single organism. And as in an organism, every part of the creature functions. The head analyses tactics, the spirit hopes, the heart surges with passion, and the body lurches in sympathy with every tackle, every pass, every break. Here is thought, feeling, faith and movement, united in a single cause. And everyone's drunk.

When Otago score I'm in the loo. The urinal shakes. I feel the celebration through my feet. Ten minutes later, when Canberra are threatening a comeback, I am ordered to go for another piss. It works. Otago wins. It's a long night. I spend much of it laughing with a man who's spent the last twenty years working for the local branch of the Department of Conservation. He's responsible for preserving the place's scenic beauty. Late in the evening he tells me that his hobby is racing motor cars. The bigger, the louder, the thirstier the engine, he says, the better he likes it.

4

Popular mucus

The first thing I notice in the morning is that I didn't close the Belgian curtains before I went to bed. But an inspection of their tassels and straps reveals that I tried quite hard.

Mrs Bed and Breakfast takes the second half of her title seriously. No nonsense here about cooked or continental. It's both, and in substantial quantities. And beside my plate there's a little bag of fragrant socks and underpants. One could hardly ask for more.

For all I know the boxer may have slept the night outside my room, because the moment I step on to the street he's there beside me, insinuating his muzzle into my hand to demonstrate exactly how much saliva he can generate. It's an impressive quantity. Simultaneously he snuffles in the manner of a pig rooting for roots.

Dogs are a joy. Thanks to an abundance of neuroses I find them easier to love than people. I flirt with every dog I meet. Nevertheless if I am to hitch successfully I need to shake this one off. On my way up the street that is Owaka I try to interest him in the agricultural museum, the postman and some attractively bulging rubbish bags, all without success.

It's another nerve-gas morning. The postman is the sole representative of the human race in evidence, riding a little moped between the letterboxes and beeping his horn every time he delivers a letter. No one emerges to his beep. I lay my bag on the dewy grass at the eastern end of Owaka, and the dog and I turn to face the direction from which traffic would come if there were any. It's a grey Saturday morning in rural New Zealand and my companion is drooling. I've known better hitching prospects.

I instigate a game of fetch-that-stick. It will help to pass the time. And when a car does finally materialise, I'll be able to toss the stick a long way off and seem dogless.

I select a fine meaty stick and by waving it about and making stick-loving noises I rouse Rover to a point approaching orgasm. When he's leaping and yelping with joy I toss the stick a few yards. He watches it describe its brief parabola through the air, then looks up at me. I walk towards the stick. He follows me with curiosity. When I pick up the stick, the delight of recognition almost overwhelms him. I wave the stick around again. He leaps and yelps. I throw the stick and he looks puzzled again. I take another little walk. I'm playing fetch with myself.

The dog's still with me when the ute stops.

'That dog's a fucking pest,' says the driver and he drives me towards Papotaiwai and a mass of unappealing cloud.

By pretending to fiddle with my seatbelt I manage to see in the nearside mirror that the boxer stands and watches the car for the briefest of whiles and then ambles back into town. Here is a dog used to short romances. I am confident I haven't broken his heart.

'That dog's a fucking pest,' is a grammatically complete sentence of respectable length, and fucking is a word of two syllables. But my driver makes no further sallies into such linguistic complexity. I ask him if he farms. Then I ask him what he farms, then where he farms it, then whether he watched the rugby last night, then whether he thinks Otago played well, and then I give up. It is churlish to criticise one's Good Samaritan, but fuck it. He makes a stone seem blood-drenched.

He drops me at a parking area in Papatowai. It isn't quite raining. It also isn't quite Papatowai. Papatowai, such as it is, must be nearby, but nearer by is an estuary of sorts, some distressed grass and a pair of what turn out to be Swedes. They are packing bags into a dilapidated Subaru in anticipation of rain. And only just in anticipation.

During the lift with Mr Mute, I decided I would do a little coastal exploration on foot. Somewhere around here are the scenic works, a petrified forest a couple of hundred million years old, penguin colonies, blowholes, native bush. But as the first rain falls, the Swedes smile and offer me a lift. Reflecting that I may as well spend the duration of the shower heading further into the wilderness, I accept. The Swedes turn right instead of left out of the car park and drive me back to Owaka. I don't say a word. Or at least I don't say a word about the direction we're heading in. Instead I hold a conversation with the Swedes that you could spoon into a cup of tea.

New Zealand, they tell me, is very beautiful. New Zealanders are very nice. Everything is much nicer than

Sweden, although Sweden is very nice too. And every time either of them speaks, they politely turn to face me in the back seat, and they smile toothpaste-advertisement smiles, and they deliver their judgments of beauty and niceness with a lilting melodic intonation that reminds me for some reason of cow bells. And they are only twenty-two. Are they that nice to each other when they are alone? I rather fear that they may be. I feel the urge to say dissenting things, but overcome it without enormous difficulty.

I am back in Owaka about an hour after leaving it. It hasn't changed a lot, though the rain and the postman and the boxer have gone. Perhaps the boxer drowned in his own saliva. I scuttle through the place feeling faintly embarrassed, but also grateful. The suspicion has been growing that this detour through the Southern Scenic Route is not going to be a success, particularly at a holiday weekend. And now the generosity of Sweden has resolved the issue. I station myself opposite a sign saying 'Owaka Fire Brigade 50th Jubilee May 31', and rapidly get a lift back to Balclutha from a farmer who likes to kill magpies.

New Zealand magpies are not European magpies. New Zealand magpies are aggressive black and white crows. In spring they dive-bomb people in city parks, smacking hats with their beaks. And they make a noise like no other bird I know, a sort of gurgle, like panpipes under water, a sound famously rendered by the poet Denis Glover as 'quardle oodle ardle wardle doodle'. It doesn't sound anything like that.

According to this farmer, the magpie was officially declared a pest at the beginning of the year. He'd been waiting for that declaration. In just five months, he's killed 200 of them, using a decoy bird to lure them to a trap baited with tallow. Then he puts them away with 'a wee tap on the head with a hammer'. Already, he says, the native birds are returning to the bush on his farm.

Magpies were originally Australian. 'All Aussie birds are

squawkers or screechers,' says the farmer, and he lists a dozen of them including the spur-winged plover, a sort of lapwing, with jowls as yellow as lemon peel. Spur-winged plovers do indeed screech. Late at night my dog and I often disturb them roosting on the flat, and they take off into the night sky making a noise like train-brakes.

'Did you watch the rugby?'

'What a game, eh. An old mate came round to watch it at my place. He's got a crook ticker. If he gets excited he has to take this medication a drop at a time on his tongue. He must have got through about a pint of the stuff.'

And so back over the river and into Balclutha. For me at least, the Catlins will remain one of New Zealand's best-kept secrets. And though Balclutha is no metropolis, I am relieved to be back on the main road. I am urban man, softened by ease, unlike the pioneers.

Some of the first non-Maori to come this way were gold-miners who had been in California, the Klondike, South Australia. By definition their hope led them to places where no one else was. They lived lives effectively feral. But having dug and sluiced, and either prospered or missed out, some of them stayed. A proportion of the miners were Chinese; indeed, in 1874, Chinese made up 4 per cent of the population of Otago. Opposite me now there's a fish and chip shop called Wongy's Cod and Taties. It is likely that Wongy's roots in this country stretch back as far as any of his neighbours'.

And yet the Chinese have had a tough time here. In the late nineteenth century the government levied a poll tax specifically on Chinese immigrants. And in an even more bizarre measure they allowed ships to bring in only one Chinese passenger for every 200 tons of cargo. And those Chinese who did get in were subject to discrimination.

Despite its immigrant nature, New Zealand has never seen itself as a multi-racial society. It is officially bicultural, but for most of its short life it has been effectively monocultural.

Monocultural has meant white and proxy-British. It was only after the Second World War, when Maori began to shift to the towns from remote up-country settlements, that things began to change.

Last year the Prime Minister issued an official apology to Chinese New Zealanders for the injustices of the past. But suspicion remains. A recent television programme was called 'Asian Drivers – Are they really that bad?' And a prominent MP gets himself re-elected every three years by blowing rhetoric on the embers of racial fear in the coiffed skulls of ageing white women who remember a monocultural New Zealand, and the shaven skulls of white men who remember nothing but who like a bit of bigotry. His method is simple. He implies, but is careful never quite to state, that every social ill in this country, from the hospital waiting lists to the choked roads of Auckland, can be blamed on Asian immigrants. By doing so he taps a deep well of prejudice that gushes him a fat salary and no responsibility. He's part Maori.

A fresh wind has risen. It bends the trees but doesn't shift the louring grey. Across the road from where I'm hitching, an old woman sits in the window of her bungalow. The armchair is floral. It has a white antimacassar over its plump back. A television is on in the room but the woman chooses to watch me hitch. I wave to her. She gives a shy wave back, then turns to the telly. It's eleven in the morning.

I get a lift from Aaron and Peta. They're postgraduate students. Aaron's rowed for New Zealand and as the wind tries to toss their Fiat Uno about the road he clamps the wheel steady with huge clean hands. Aaron and Peta are heading, like the smiling kelp-sellers, for the Bluff Oyster festival.

When people want to refer to the whole of New Zealand, they say 'from Cape Reinga to the Bluff'. Bluff is Invercargill's port. It is on the same latitude as the Falkland Islands. It shares their bleakness.

We approach through brown salt marshes. A single withered

horse stands mute and disconsolate, failing to find shelter behind a skeletal bush. The bush is bent and flattened by the wind, its few branches streaming out to lee. The bush is the only thing between the horse and Antarctica.

I've been to Bluff once before, six years ago with a television crew. The landlord of the pub where we stayed sold me a beer on arrival, and then tried to sell me the pub. I thought he was joking. He wasn't. At the time you could buy a habitable house in Bluff for $2,000.

That evening we gathered the prominent citizens of Bluff in the pub. They said what a fine place Bluff was. They said that the weather wasn't bad. They said that there was more to Bluff than oysters. They acknowledged that Bluff had been through a period of decline, but they knew it would bounce back. One man in particular spoke up fervently for the place. He had a cravat and a moustache and he spoke with the accent of an ex-colonel in a Sussex pub. He couldn't imagine, he said, living anywhere else in New Zealand.

Late in the evening when the cameras had been packed away in their padded cases, he joined me at the bar. I offered him a drink. He shook his head, then paused heavily, as if debating whether or not to speak. He sighed and then he spoke. 'Bluff's fucked,' he said, and left.

Bluff still looks fucked. The wind screams up the street. It's wind you can lean on. Every third shop is empty. Every second shop sells secondhand goods. And there are only half a dozen shops. But for this one weekend, sad-looking Bluff is loaded to the gunwales with visitors. What has brought them here is oysters.

For several seasons the Bluff oyster beds have been closed because of the bonamia virus that stunts the mollusc's growth, but now the country is back on half-rations and the dredging of the year's first sacks has become once again an annual item on the television news. The rite requires a smug-looking reporter to scull an oyster straight from the shell and beam at the camera, at which point the studio anchor says, 'lucky man,' thereby establishing himself as a straight-up kiwi bloke.

For though the oyster is an expensive delicacy, it is nevertheless seen as a delicacy of the people. Like whitebait, in particular, and seafood in general, oysters are part of a national birthright, the right to go down to any stretch of the 18,000 kilometres of coast and 'get yourself a feed'.

This notion of living off the sea's bounty may owe something to tough pioneering days, and also to pre-European times when the Maori diet included so much seafood that the sand ground their teeth to stubs, but it is largely a reaction against the class-bound society of Great Britain and its dominant landowners. Because at heart this is an egalitarian country, where it is axiomatic that the sea and its contents belong equally to all. When Maori recently laid claim to ownership of the foreshore and seabed, they aroused an outcry of opposition so thunderous that the government defied all legal process in its rush to announce that everything belonged to everybody and would do so in perpetuity.

So it is partly a near-instinctive urge to celebrate a birthright that has drawn 10,000 people here today from all over the country. After all, it could hardly be the oysters themselves, in whose name the party is being held. They look like mucus and they taste like brine.

The wind is trying to ruin the party. It's thrown every sign out to sea, every piece of decoration. The west side of each marquee is concave. The eastern side balloons like a pregnancy. Any unsecured corner of canvas slaps like staccato applause. Guy ropes thrum like the strings of a double bass.

In the admissions tent, a brick pins a pile of banknotes to the trestle table and a woman with a purple face and blue hands ensures I have a firm grip on my change before she lets it go. We have a brief tug of war with $5.

In search of somewhere to piss I find the military-looking man who told me Bluff was fucked. He's grinning into the wind and greeting acquaintances with both question and answer. 'You well?' he booms. 'Good.' He doesn't recognise me.

I open the door of a Portaloo too far and the wind seizes it and wrenches it through 180 degrees, further than its hinges want. The little cabin tilts on its base and I hear the contents slosh.

Everywhere is crammed. In the huge refreshment marquee a boil of people in outdoor clothes besiege the stalls, then stand in knots in corners spooning chowder from plastic cups, sucking beer from bottles and generating a happy heat and noise that almost overrides the wind.

A local DJ hypes an oyster-eating competition. In the first heat there's a Western Australian, an Aucklander, a Southlander and an effervescent Korean girl with a camera crew in tow. Each stands poised with a toothpick above a paper plate of oysters. 'Go' says the DJ and they spear the oysters into their mouths, the DJ calling it like a horse race. The Korean girl falls behind, picks up the plate, tips down her oysters like soup, is instantly disqualified, raises both arms and parades before the delighted crowd in mock triumph, an oystery sludge slipping from the corner of her smile.

Meanwhile the Southlander's won at a canter.

'How was it?' asked the DJ.

'I'm hungry,' he says. 'When's the final?'

On a stage between tents a young woman in gloves sings 'Dixie', with the wind and an elderly jazz band behind her. Strands of hair whip round her face like snakes.

I meet half a dozen people that I half-know, two of whom have flown from the North Island just for this.

I eat a cup of chowder, grow tired of the wind and of battling through the crowd with a bag slung over my shoulder, can think of no reason to stay, so I head to the pub that the landlord tried to sell me. He told me then that the room I slept in was where one of New Zealand's early Prime Ministers was born. I've read since that he was born in Melbourne.

The pub hasn't changed. Unmatching Formica tables, unemptied ashtrays, a carpet like a disease, a drunk woman with three kids in need of a slap, and a lank youth with earrings, listlessly losing money to a pokie machine. In one corner a boat crew of Taiwanese midgets in identical jackets are playing bad pool in silence and drinking nothing. I had half thought of spending the night in Bluff but the pub changes my mind. I stay long enough to regain some feeling in my fingers then go out to hitch to Invercargill. It's mid-afternoon.

The wind now carries a freight of horizontal rain or sea-spray or both. Cars stream past with their lights on and I have to face into the wind to hitch. It's only now that I remember the kelp-sellers I met in Dunedin. As I do so the wind drives under the peak of my cap and cartwheels it high across the road and onto the rusted railway. Bugger the kelp-sellers, though I mean that in the nicest possible way. I fetch my cap.

I am pitied in the end by a shy rural couple in a double-cab ute. The driver glances nervously at me in the mirror throughout the short trip, as if he thinks he recognises me from a wanted poster. He answers my questions with evasive generalities. His wife says nothing.

Invercargill is the capital of the province of Southland. It has a population of 60,000 and a reputation for grimness. I take a room in the Bella Vista Motel. It has a bella vista of the Woolworth's car park and a Burger King. Too tired to go into town, I eat at Burger King. The soft, fat, smiling girl who serves me pronounces the word 'burger' as though it's infested with r's.

I spend the evening in bed reading Primo Levi and listening to the teenage boy racers rumbling past in their cherished cars. Their stereos thud with bass, like heartbeats heard through a stethoscope.

5

In the friendly arsehole

One of Noah's sons lived for 480 years. Noah managed 640. He spent 120 of them building his ark. It says all this in the Bible, and it's true. It's scientifically proven that people lived a lot longer back then because the earth's atmosphere was more heavily oxygenated. I don't know who the scientist was that said so, but I do know who it is that is telling me so. It is an

Invercargill carpenter and he is smiling and he is wearing an unignorable Hawaiian shirt.

I'm in church. I didn't mean to be. I set out to walk through Invercargill on a Sunday morning. The air was raw as a wound and cold as Calvinism. The very few people on the street were scurrying into churches. And partly because I was curious, and partly because I was cold, but mainly, I suspect, because of the lingering memory of John the driver and a desire to see the sort of thing he got up to, I went into one.

A dowdily dressed man greeted me as warmly as it is possible to greet someone without hugging them. I told him that this was the first church service I had ever attended voluntarily.

'Then you are very very welcome,' he said, and he smiled a very very wide smile and I felt very very uncomfortable.

It's more a lecture theatre than a church, with a stage, a lectern, a band, a projection screen and a scallop-shell arrangement of tiered seats. My seat's at the back as close as possible to the door. Half the seats are full. Most of the people are white. No one has dressed up. The conventional, social-standing notion of church seems to be missing. There are more women than men, and most are younger than I would expect. The pastor's away on some sort of sabbatical, so the worship is led by a woman with a microphone, a Polynesian-holiday blouse and an alarming grin. Every five minutes or so, the lyrics of a song appear on the screen. They're sub-pop hymns crammed with abstract nouns like love, duty, beauty and honour, some of which are spelled correctly. Backed by a happy three-piece band, she bashes out the songs with fervour. The congregation sings along with rather less. To say that it is like a tacky Cliff Richard concert would be unfair. It is like a Cliff Richard concert.

The prayers are apparently spontaneous and improvised. The effort to avoid the formality of traditional church ceremonies is obvious. Everyone on stage is relaxed and chatty. They smile full beam full time.

The congregation doesn't. A few raise a hand as they sing, in a sort of Baden Powell salute, but it seems half-hearted. Most merely mumble along with the songs, giving no sign of anything but the sort of clenched restraint that I expect I could find in the Presbyterian pews down the road.

But there's still a collection. 'God loves a cheerful giver,' says the worship leader. I sink my chin in my chest and choose to spend another day unloved by the Lord.

Then up gets the Hawaiian carpenter to tell the story of Noah and to ramble with deep irrationality for twenty minutes. When he loses his train of thought he just winds his smile up another notch. At the end of the service I'm at the door before any of the officials can get there to say warm things to me.

The moment I'm outside, I run. I run like a child. I run partly to dispel my guilt. I should not have intruded on this service. And I run partly so the adults can't catch me. I run to put as great a distance as possible between me and the grown-up stuff that was going on in that church. But above all I run because I can, because I've got a body and it works and I delight in its working and the very act of its working serves as antidote to the sad stuff. I run, in short, to be free, and I keep running till I feel good. Then I stop running to pant, hands on knees, sweat cooling almost instantly on my forehead, like prickles.

There's a café across the road. Its one patron is sitting in the window staring at me. I go in, say the most cheerful good morning, get a grunt in reply, and buy a vast bowl of excellent coffee and a muffin that tastes of suet. When ten minutes later the sun swings out from the clouds and spears low through the window, I set out to walk to the edge of Invercargill.

Invercargill has had a bad press. Its motto is The Friendly City, which implicitly acknowledges its lack of more tangible attractions. It's the southernmost city in the world, sitting only above Stewart Island which in turn sits above the most inhospitable ocean in the world. When Mick Jagger came here to perform he apparently, and charmingly, called Invercargill the arsehole of the universe. The image says little for Invercargill. But it says even less for Stewart Island. I am keen to find something to like about the place.

You couldn't call Invercargill intimate. Like Dunedin and Christchurch it is a planned settlement. The town planner gave little thought to the climate, building wide straight thoroughfares that funnel the fierce winds from the south and the west.

After the economic reforms of the eighties, Invercargill went into decline, its people lured north by sun and money. But now money has started to lure them back. The dairy boom has trebled the value of land, and an exuberant mayor has launched a scheme of free tertiary tuition that has pulled in the perpetually pauper young.

Three backpackers are struggling along the main street against the wind. Each is toting both a backpack and a frontpack. A sniper would despair of wounding them fatally. One even carries a third bag in her hand, from which protrudes the corner of a kitchen sink.

Time was when you could just push backpackers over and watch them writhe like flipped beetles. Today you have to trip them at the top of an incline so that they roll unstoppably down it in their casing of possessions. Or else you can do as I do now, and give an ironic middle-aged tut before passing by on the other side of the road.

Look up above the predictable plate-glass shopfronts, and Invercargill has a solid Edwardian feel – the colonnaded balconies of the Grand Hotel, the old NSW Bank building, and in particular the remnants of The Crescent. Old photographs suggest that a hundred years ago The Crescent would not have looked out of place in Bath. But stupidity and greed have torn most of it down and replaced it with buildings that resemble an aesthetic headbutt. And the stately bank building is now occupied by a New Life church.

The current city fathers, who include, I suspect, several mothers, have done their best to tart the place up. Sculptures dot the streets. These range from the agreeably witty – a steel umbrella that serves as a sundial – to the disagreeably witless. 'Sculpted in 2000 this artwork comprises two stone shapes representing our Maori and Celtic heritages turning and leaning towards each other in the hope that the future will hold unity without loss of cultural identity.' Another represents 'the hope that our future generations achieve the goals passed down by our ancestors.' A third represents 'the longed-for day when left-handed people are accepted as the equals of their right-handed brothers.' I made only one of these up.

The Invercargill prison was built in 1910. With thick cream walls and small barred windows it's like a cartoon prison in Mexico. A little beyond it lies the abrupt western edge of the city that is the Waihopai River. A lone woman strides the river-bank in threequarter-length leisurewear, power walking to the next cappuccino, and fiercely swinging her arms as if into the balls of an assailant. Ducks pootle, seagulls moan and just beyond the river there's a tract of native bush.

It's cool-climate jungle, dank and dark. At the heart of its few acres I sit on a decaying stump and feel the damp filter into the seat of my jeans. As the disturbance of my arrival fades, the bush around fills with native birds. They rattle, cluck, gurgle, pipe and squeal, granting an auditory snatch of what pre-European New Zealand sounded like. Darwin called it 'a chaos of delight.'

Fat native pigeons plunge from high branches, their wing-beats pulsing like tyres on wet asphalt. Tom tits, bellbirds, silvereyes, fantails. A pair of tuis chase each other through the small-leaved southern beech, their strange white pom poms bouncing on their chests. And huia, moa, piopio, saddleback, stitchbirds, kakapo, all of these are missing, being either extinct or confined to island sanctuaries.

When New Zealand broke off from the land mass now known as Gondwana however many millions of years ago, mammals and marsupials missed the boat. The only furry things that climbed aboard were a couple of vegetarian bats. So the place was an avian ark. Birds literally ruled the roost. They proliferated and evolved. And those that fed on the land became too lazy to fly because there was nothing they had to fly away from. Then men turned up.

The Maori ate all the moa. The white man dealt death to many of the other species. He felled the bush to make grazing. He imported British birds to make himself feel at home. He enjoyed himself with his shotgun. And he let loose the rat, the cat, the dog, the weasel and the stoat.

I sit a long while amid the birds. The bush makes a far better church than the church.

Then back across the river towards town, passing a muddy paddock marked out with strings. '31 exclusive sections', says a livid blue sign not two hundred yards from the gurgling tuis, 'for residential excellence'. Hundreds of acres of bush were felled to build Invercargill. I fear for the scrap that remains.

Back in the suburbs, imported birds predominate: chaffinches, starlings, blackbirds, sparrows. And the building materials are similarly alien: concrete, fibre cement, laminates, and the horror stuff known as summerhill stone. Just as few native birds have learned to fit into town, so town has yet to fit into the land. The towns of New Zealand are imposed upon the place, rather than being built out of it.

No one comes to this country to see what man has done. They come to see what he has not yet undone. They come to see the inhospitable land, the land that by and large the immigrants avoided as too harsh. They call it beautiful.

But such land lies ahead of me on my trip. Right now I couldn't be anywhere less harsh. Queen's Park is vast and immaculate. There's a gentle golf course, lawns mown to within half an inch of their lives, sycamores, oaks, a band rotunda, a rose garden and families on bicycles. The children are wrapped against the cold in puffy anoraks, like primary-coloured Michelin men. Mothers let loose their toddlers in a playground to kick the leaves. A child flings bread to the mobbing ducks and gulls then bursts into tears at the welter of wings. It could be a winter Sunday in the Tuileries Gardens.

There's even a children's zoo. I pluck blades of grass and feed them to a pair of ostriches with lunatic eyes, their heads lowering to their ankles or rising above mine on necks like vacuum cleaner hoses. Two wallabies lie splayed on a knoll as if they've been shot, and a little mob of alpacas stands bored beneath a sign saying 'red deer'.

At the city end of the park a futuristic pyramid turns out to be the Southland museum and art gallery. I've walked miles and eaten nothing. In the café I point at a substantial-looking sandwichy thing wrapped in clingfilm. 'Mince on panini,' says the girl. It is cheap and served with charm and it tastes, as one would expect, of vomit.

There's a tuatarium here and a gallery of contemporary art. I glance at the art, then hurry to the tuatarium.

Tuatara are lizards. As every guidebook will tell you, these lizards are living fossils. They haven't changed over 225 million years. With blank reptilian stares they witnessed New Zealand's slow drift into the ocean of isolation. They basked in the sun, survived changes of climate, caught innumerable insects with a rapid snatch of the jaws, and chewed each one with excruciating slowness. A tuatara can live for five hundred years. It is possible that one of the immobile beasts in front of me has lived through the reigns of both Elizabeths.

My route back to the Bella Vista takes me past the ornate nineteenth-century water tower that dominates northern Invercargill. You can buy postcards of it. On the main road outside the Bella Vista, a banner announces that Invercargill is proud to be hosting the National Conference on Fostercare.

A sign outside the Bella Vista announces 'It's Here!'. 'It' means Sky Television, the country's only pay TV station. The sports channel seems dedicated to highlights of the Manitoba water-skiing finals and endless footage of wastrel teenagers doing improbable but uninteresting things on skateboards in what appear to be dumps for disused concrete earthworking structures. To music. When I wake up they're still at it. It's dark and I have a craving for beer.

In Invercargill on a Sunday night a craving for beer is a hard thing to satisfy. On my way back into town I pass a grand total of no pubs. I eschew a fish restaurant whose menu is marked Fore Deck, Main Deck and Aft Deck – but no Poop Deck – on the grounds that (a) it's empty and (b) it's themed. And I eschew another restaurant-cum-bar that is playing music to the pavement outside and has a leopard on a bicycle hanging from the ceiling, on the grounds that (a) it's empty and (b) it has a leopard on a bicycle hanging from the ceiling.

A Scandinavian youth with the world's whitest teeth and skimpiest beard stops me in the street and tells me he's looking for a supermarket. I tell him I'm looking for a pub. It is only after we have both scratched our heads, shaken them, apologised, wished the other good luck and parted, that I remember the Woolworth's opposite the Bella Vista. I turn round. The youth has gone. But across from where he stood there's a pub. Well almost. It's called the Frog and Firkin. Themed it may be, and appallingly named, but it's indisputably a pub and I cross the road to it with gratitude and find it closed. I don't know if Invercargill is one of the numerous South Island towns that used to be dry but, if it was, it's beginning to seem that not a lot's changed. I thought the Scots were supposed to be drunks.

Back along the road a bit there's a convenience store that's conveniently open. Inside I find the Scandinavian youth. He is buying groceries that would be half the price in Woolworth's. I say nothing. The only other customer is a middle-aged dwarf openly studying a porn mag.

The girl behind the counter, who is as charming and helpful as every person who has served me so far in Invercargill, has to think for a while before directing me along a couple of empty streets to the city's main hotel, where the receptionist, who is as charming and helpful as the girl in the convenience store, directs me up a flight of stairs to Rosie O'Grady's Irish bar, where the barmaid, who is as charming and helpful as etc., has a clientèle of none.

The place is rendered Irish by serving Guinness, having a green rugby shirt pinned behind the bar, a series of cartoons illustrating Murphy's Law and a background tape of jigs and reels. Quite who is fooled by fake Irishness I don't know. Nor do I know who it was that arrived at the notion that pubs, those most civilised of places where the hair and the guard are let down and where the words flow with more honesty that is usual, need to be themed. Furthermore, the notion that pubs in Ireland are like 'Irish Pubs' is a fiction that one has only to spend five minutes in Ireland to dispel. Except, that is, in Dublin, which I am told has become so flush with Euro-dollars that it is replacing its Irish pubs with 'Irish Pubs'. Nevertheless my beer is fine. While my second is pouring I check Rosie O'Grady's menu. It's a crumbed-fish-bites-and-buffalo-wedges type menu. I order the all-day breakfast.

'I like it down here,' says Emma the barmaid when I ask her about Invercargill. 'I spent six months in Wellington. Wellington is the most unfriendliest city in the world. Not like here.'

Emma is joined by Melanie the barmaid. Melanie is my size and a bit. Early in the conversation she lets me know that she's knocked two men out. One was a stalker. The other was an accident. She found both funny.

'Everyone reckons,' says Melanie, 'that down here we sleep with our brothers and sisters. But it's just a friendly place. People say hello. Invercargill is the friendly city.'

And thus Melanie becomes the first person other than a city councillor ever to refer to a city motto with approval.

New Zealand is thick with city mottos. Most have been coined over the last twenty years, presumably with the intention of luring tourists, though whether one would want the sort of tourists who believe city mottos is another question. Christchurch, for example, was traditionally but unofficially known as 'The Garden City' for the undeniable reason that it had some gardens in it. Then a decade or so back the council invited suggestions for a more dynamic slogan. They whittled those suggestions down to three – The Garden City (old habits die hard), The City That Shines, and, thirdly, and altogether more impressively, The Most Beautiful City in the World, a notion that sent a chill through the heart of Venice.

After much discussion, and with a rare display of modesty, the civic leaders discarded the third option. They then chose both the others. Thus Christchurch is now officially and snappily 'The Garden City, The City That Shines'.

But at least Christchurch did better than Dunedin, where the motto until recently was 'Dunedin: It's all right here'. This no doubt seemed admirably punning to the consultants who cooked it up, but when it was spoken with a resigned shrug of the shoulders the slogan carried a freight of meaning that came uncomfortably close to the truth. And truth is not the job of slogans.

And now that Melanie has referred to Invercargill's motto I am half-expecting her to add that everyone gains from twinned towns. But instead she talks about young men. The few young men I have seen around the city have been scrawny types with loose clothes, slouches and beanies. But I have been unobservant. Melanie explains that there is a taxonomy of male youth. The boys divide into ruggers, who are slow and stupid, skaties, who take drugs and drink mild spirits, surfies, who smell and smoke dope, bogans who are rude and racist, wear tight black clothes and drive either Holdens or Fords and disparage either Fords or Holdens, boy racers, who drive laps round the city at night because they are too young to drink, homies, who derive their language and manner from Los Angeles street gangs, and then my all-day breakfast arrives.

Britain's sole contribution to gastronomy, the all-day

breakfast, is reliably bad. This one is up to scratch. Chair-stuffing sausages, a tangle of bacon with fat like blubber, two hothouse tomatoes halved and grilled to mush, rectilinear commercial hash-browns, and a brace of eggs with yolks the colour of the sun in Siberia in February. Salt, grease and no hint of green. Cardiac arrest on a plate. The nostalgic aura of the transport caff. There's no food I prefer. While listening to Melanie and Emma discussing boys and rolling their r's I eat even the gelatinous bit of the egg.

By the time I leave, it's late. Wide, cold and silent streets. Even the bogans and the boy racers have packed it in, garaged their cars, kissed them goodnight, drunk a cup of mild spirits to taste and gone to bed to dream of big women.

Heavy with Speights and breakfast I join the dreaming sixty thousand who are Invercargill, the southernmost city in the world, plain, ordinary, full of churches, and friendly.

6
The choc-box of indifference

L ast night's beer wakes me early. I deal with the bladder but
that leaves the dry throat. I struggle to tear open a sachet of
freeze-dried coffee with fingers that feel fat and remote from
my head. The coffee makes me want to smoke. I pull on jeans
without underpants – I like the rough feel of denim on buttock,
but am throat-grabbingly nervous of the zip – and go out on to

the balcony in the half-light. Suburban Invercargill is waking to a Monday morning. This town, this country, is young. It has seen only about 7,500 Mondays.

The streetlights weaken against the blanching grey of the sky. The sheen fades from the damp expanse of the Woolworth's car park and it becomes merely dull. In the giant neon windows of the store the shelf-stackers and cleaners are toiling midgets. The traffic on State Highway One is thin.

A cat slinks by the hedge. I mew and the cat freezes mid-stride. I mew again. The cat's head swings and fixes me with hunter's eyes, assesses me, then dismisses me. A taut and organised woman click-clacks out from the unit below mine, towing a suitcase on wheels and carrying two white blouses in dry-cleaning plastic. She stows the case in the boot and hangs the blouses in the back of her hyper-clean sales-rep saloon. I yawn and stretch. She catches the movement and glances up with momentary instinctive alarm, like the cat, like a gazelle sensing danger. I say good morning but she's looked away already, gone back inside. I stub my cigarette out, shiver and decide I'll make an early start myself. I've come as far south as I can on the mainland. Today I shall head north and west towards the uplands, towards the scenic wonderland that people from abroad imagine when they think of New Zealand, the place where the posters come from, the place which many visit but few inhabit. And where, if the many didn't visit, quite a few of the few would stop inhabiting.

Half an hour later as I head out to hitch, a man with a familiar face is loading bags into a sleek black ute, its chassis arching high above the wheels. I ask him if we've met. He says no. He lives in Dunedin now, but when he tells me that he comes from Western Australia I recognise him as the designated Aussie in the oyster-eating competition. He laughs when I say so. 'They wanted an international cast,' he says. 'I had to stress my Aussieness to get a go.'

He wouldn't go back to Australia. Perth has become too hot. Forty-degree days sap the will to do things. And New Zealand, he says, is empty and safe. His wife often forgets to lock the house at night. He does a bit of work here and there, mainly cooking. Three mornings a week he cooks breakfast at the Dunedin hotel where I stayed. I ask if he worked on Anzac morning and he says they did seventy-eight breakfasts that day, the most this year. When I tell him I was one of the seventy-eight, we agree that the coincidence is typical of this thinly peopled land.

'I like that,' he says. And I say that I like it too.

Just outside the northern edge of Invercargill, by the signs welcoming visitors to The Friendly City and the Fostercare Conference, there's a vast cemetery, as immaculate as everything municipal in Invercargill. Beneath the 20 kph sign at the entrance lie the fresh-tended graves of five young men who died in France in 1915. New Zealand has never had a foreign war of its own. But it has sent a lot of young men to die in other people's.

I cross the road and hitch. Beside me, a paddock with gorse, flax, scrubby grass and two knackered ponies in canvas coats. Beyond them, distantly purple in the west, the toe end of the Southern Alps. Behind me, the open road leading unmistakably to Gore. At my feet, a gravel layby inviting the driver to stop with ease and safety. There's no sun to inhibit his vision, no rain to make me sodden and unwelcome, no reason, in short, for him not to pick me up. I'm there for two hours. My lift, when it comes, is from a logging truck.

Twenty years ago about half my lifts were in trucks. I liked monkeying up into the cab, sitting magisterially above the puny domestic cars, seeming to be going slower than the speedometer said, feeding fags to the driver and, when in England, lowering my accent several classes without conscious intention. I liked the sense of being acknowledged by the working world.

And I liked it when a tyre blew out on a tanker carrying liquid sugar up the M26 somewhere north of Lancaster and the huge beast slewed across the road and came to a halt on the hard shoulder. The driver offered to flag a truck down for me but I was fat with time in those days and I said I'd stay with him until repairs arrived. On the dry warm bank above the motorway I shared drinking stories and a bottle of lemonade with the driver and we lay back in the coarse grass and watched a kestrel hover, and then I taught him how to catch grasshoppers. You get them from behind, sweeping your hand up the stem of the grass and closing over the kicking little beast. If you wait a while with your fist clenched hollow, the grasshopper becomes sedate and you can slowly open your palm and it will sit.

When at last the driver caught one he whooped with delight and rushed to me to show it as a child would do, but then, suddenly, a gust of self-consciousness checked him, and he stopped and threw the insect away, and sat down with his back to me, and for a long time after that he said nothing.

Trucks don't stop any more. The rules have got to them, debarred their generosity, and taken things one tiny step further down the road towards economic efficiency and human isolation. The tiny risk of picking up a hitchhiker is deemed too great a risk. The tiny loss of time is deemed too great a loss of time. The tiny act of generosity is deemed a waste.

I say as much, or more or less, to the driver of the logging truck. He tells me that by letting me into his cab he has invalidated his insurance. 'But fuck it,' he says. 'I've never made a claim yet.' Before he drops me in Edendale he tells me that Southland is New Zealand's best-kept secret.

Edendale is a cheese factory set in flat, green, unremarkable land. Some weatherboard houses cluster nearby, a few agricultural services and a 4-Square grocery with its green and yellow fascia and fifties-style logo, but if the cheese factory died these would die with it. The factory is vast and growing vaster.

Cranes swing slowly under a wide low sky. As I stand hitching at the gate a string of cement trucks like giant spinning eggs turn past me to disgorge. And every five minutes another milk tanker swings into the factory yard, its thousand gallons of sloshing load encased in a sleek steel cigar.

'Edendale,' says a sign. 'Home of New Zealand's Cheese Industry since 1881'. Throughout my childhood, cheddar from this monolith found its way into my mother's kitchen on the other side of the world.

Sixteen years ago when I came to this country there were only three types of cheese on the shelves – tasty, medium and colby. Colby was bland, Medium was bland, and Tasty, well, you could taste it. But now New Zealand makes brie wheels, fetta, goat's cheese in brine, huge waxed bowling balls of Gouda, and fresh Parmesan that crumbles like weather-worn sandstone.

And that transition is the country's transition in miniature. Post-war New Zealand was, by all reports, remarkably homogenous. Men married at twenty, worked and went to the pub. Women married at nineteen, had children and brought a plate to parties. Few people were poor, fewer still rich, and only the unemployable were unemployed. No doubt the place abounded in drunken husbands and suburban neuroses, but it seems in retrospect to have been a baby-boom la-la land. Though some people found it stifling, and Germaine Greer was arrested for publicly saying 'bullshit', it was, as everyone observed, a wonderful place to bring up children. And every burger had a slice of beetroot in it.

Now the beetroot burger's given way to the Big Mac, and most of the rest has gone too. The people have diversified, agriculture has diversified, markets have diversified. There are more skin colours, more languages spoken, more things on the shelves, more ways to earn a living, more television channels, more divorce, more vegetarians, more seriously rich people and more just as seriously poor ones. There is less certainty, less stability, less God, and fewer children.

But here, now, in the unremarkable rural heart of Southland, the date could still be 1950. A stock truck passes, leaving in its washing wake of air a distinctively New Zealand smell of woolshed and sheep piss. And utes go by with mud on the wheel arches and dogs on the flatbeds. The dogs lean clumsily into the bends, ears flapping, noses sucking in the smells of a hurtling world, a sort of olfactory speed-reading.

I get a lift from the gentlest man whose life runs parallel to the evolution of cheese and the country. He's Maori and he was brought up on ten acres in South Taranaki. Their house had no running water. His father swam rivers to stick wild pigs and he hung their jaws on the fence-line of the property. My driver, Terry, stuck his first pig at the age of ten.

At sixteen Terry came south to work in the meat industry. Now in his thirties, he has done every job in the business, from boner to inspector, but he's had enough. He tells me that he recently cured his father's prostate cancer with aloe vera and essential oils. In 1950 in New Zealand aloe vera was what you said to a woman at a party.

Terry now wants to become a naturopath, and to set up a shop in Southland selling Maori artefacts. He sees New Zealand as a small, good, battling place, infused by the spirit of the entrepreneur. It's a child of a country, he says, a long long way away from its big sisters, and just learning to stand up for itself.

He drops me in Gore which is a long long way away from most of New Zealand. Last time I came to Gore it was a Sunday and the place seemed aptly named. It was rain-lashed, gloomy, deserted and shut. But today, in late autumn sunshine, the shopfronts sparkle and women sit over coffee having intense mysterious conversations that seem barren of pauses. I eat a sandwich in the shadow of a fibreglass trout, twenty feet tall and sculpted in the act of leaping. The rendition is precise – the arch of the spine, the roseate spots, the white-yellow scales of the belly, even the lines of teeth in the palate, like a rank of tiny hacksaw blades.

Seagulls mob me. I toss them bits of sandwich, trying to favour a gull with one leg. It's a fierce bird, lowering its head, puffing its neck and cackling harsh atonal threats to ward the others off. Its handicap forces it to venture closer to me than it wants. I coax it forward. It doesn't trust me. It just wants my food. Its imperatives are emphatic and simple. Though I pity it, it doesn't pity itself. As often, I wonder where and how it will die. You see so many birds but so few corpses. Do they die at night, slowly shutting down in the cold and tumbling from the roost? Or, when they age and weaken, do the other birds attack them, driving them from feeding grounds so that they starve? Or do they suffer sudden seizures on the wing and plummet from the sky, their aerobatic sleekness converting on the instant to tumbling flesh-and-feather entropy?

The moment I finish my sandwich, the gulls lose interest and aggression. The one-legged basket case hops round the other side of the trout.

'Sol Campbell didn't even get a hearing.'

The speaker is a young woman emerging from an internet café. Going by her accent she's from somewhere in the Home Counties. Her boyfriend is waiting by a beaten-up camper van with a fishing rod and spin tackle.

'Did you get one?' she asks.

'It got off.'

'Trout?'

'Fink so. It was huge.'

'I bet. But Sol Campbell, it's just not fair.'

I head out of Gore, stepping briskly past the new-looking arts and heritage precinct on the grounds that it exists merely to draw tourists. And tourists, by definition, are other people. You're not a tourist, and nor am I. We travel, which is something altogether more worthy.

Every travel book I've read despises tourists and I was raised to do the same. On family caravan holidays in France, crowded places were dismissed as tourist traps where the shops sold tourist tat. But how vividly I recall pestering my mother in Paris to buy me a small bronze replica of the Eiffel Tower. How savagely I wanted it. I got it too. And it must be somewhere now, I suppose, mingling in some landfill with the corpses of gulls.

Barry, who picks me up ten minutes later, drives a dirty ute. Twenty years ago he came to Southland for a month's work as a cook. He's still here. Southland, he tells me, is New Zealand's best-kept secret. He cooks during the tourist season, but he also runs a business. He buys dags, the soiled bits of a sheep fleece, and runs them through a machine that crushes then washes them. 'The shit comes out one side, the wool out the other.' He smokes roll-ups, and plays as much golf as he can. A working man to the tips of his tattooed and yellowed fingers, he readily uses the word 'beautiful' to describe the land and the climate. New Zealand, he reckons, has a golden future.

The road stretches straight ahead across a high plain of unremarkable farmland towards the growing bulge of the foothills. A possum lies splayed in our lane, a hawk perching on it, plucking at its flesh. The bird takes off too late on cumbersome wings, momentarily blocks the windscreen, hits it with a thud that makes me raise an instinctive arm to ward it off. I turn and see the bundle of feathers cartwheeling in our wake.

'Hit one same place last month,' says Barry. 'Broke my grille.'

As we drive into Lumsden he gestures at a garage of rusting iron so almost-derelict you could push it over. 'My factory,' he says. His cell phone rings. He answers it with a grunt, looks up, points at a man in dirty overalls standing outside the garage and talking into a cell phone, honks his horn and stops the car. The man looks up, laughs, waves, closes his cell phone and I get out.

Lumsden is a single street, a garage-cum-store, a few weatherboard houses, a saw mill, poplars turning autumn lemon, a rust-red water-tank on stilts, and silence, the clamping midday silence of rural New Zealand. Most of the few inhabitants are two hours away, working in Queenstown where only the tourists can afford a bed. I expect to join them this evening, until Stuart pulls up beside me in his big clean station wagon. He tells me he's heading for Te Anau and asks me where I'm heading for. 'Te Anau,' I say.

Broad-shouldered, sharply dressed, twenty something, Stuart was raised on a farm. He's been a high-country shepherd with eleven dogs, has harvested cotton in Australia, wheat in Texas, peas in East Anglia, and is now about to return to Australia to work the mines. He likes hard work but has never really taken to reading and writing. Too many people, he reckons, stay at school too long in the hope of a desk job and a fat salary while there is always real work to be done. I find him engaging, cheerful, frank, gutsy, honest, modest and of a piece with many of the boys I used to teach here, boys from the farms, boys who found the city claustrophobic. Sturdy, bluff and likeable people.

We are driving towards the high lands, the grand lands, the lands you see in travel ads for New Zealand, the lands the tourism bureau calls, with their customary contempt for the language, 100% pure. As we climb, so the pasture yields to tussock, the native grass that grows in clumps like wind-tossed heads of hair. Normally tawny-brown, the tussock here is the colour of dried blood. Then through a pass of sorts and we have mountains.

The near ones are grassed, the mid-range ones wooded, the far ones rock and snow. The snow is like wedding-cake icing. This is the southern snub of the Southern Alps, the crinkle of land that the tectonic plates below have crimped to half the height of Everest. New Zealand looks small on the map, but here is a vastness as vast, it seems, as vastness goes. Away to the south and west lie a billion acres of Fiordland, all deep-hewn lakes and harsh ravines, glacier-carved and empty of people. It is bushed, impenetrable and wet. James Cook, dropped anchor in a Fiordland inlet 230 years ago. If he returned today he would recognise it. The trees would be the same height.

The road drops down towards the lake and the settlement of Te Anau. Te Anau is a Maori name. It translates as Place of Many Motels. They squat on the lake shore, diminished to Monopoly buildings by the expanse of dark water. On the far side of the lake the bush rises straight from the lake and climbs in receding vistas of black-green hills that meld and blur into sky. The scale of this landscape prompts the guidebook adjectives. Awesome, majestic, dramatic – every one of them drips with a tired, nineteenth-century romantic reverence. They falsify and chocolate-box this stark, raw and neutral land. But they lure the crowds that fill the beds and cram the tills.

The high season has passed but a few busloads of belated Japanese parade the shore in peaceable groups, tiny and tidy people, smothered with electronics, and not straying far from the shops.

It is late afternoon. I dump my bag at a motel and follow a track that hugs the long southern curve of the lake. Halfway round I find a small, almost-deserted aviary. Two cages of mountain parrots, a kaka chewing at a dangling chain, a kea roosting and eyeing me with venom. Then an enclosure stocked with takahe, a bird I've seen only in books. It was thought extinct until an Invercargill doctor found some in the bush near here in 1948. It's a flightless, blue-green beast the size of a chicken, with a beak like a gin-drinker's nose. Three of them plod to the mesh to study me. I cluck and croon to draw them even closer, touched by their lumpen trust and by thoughts of their rarity.

Water from Lake Te Anau drains down the Waiau River to Lake Manapouri. From Manapouri it once had nowhere to go. Now it passes through a tunnel drilled through a mountain on an extraordinary scale and drains into the fiord of Deep Cove and out to the sea, generating one tenth of the nation's electricity as it goes.

The power station is a tourist attraction. At the gates controlling the flow out of Te Anau a notice says 'No jumping off wall. Extreme danger below.' The drop is forty feet or more to where the water swirls in giant sucking vortexes. I doubt that the notice would be necessary in any other country.

With one hand firmly gripping the guard rail I piss over the edge. When I've done up my flies and taken a step back, the last drops are still falling.

The Keppler track starts here, one of the many famous walking tracks that thread across this region like tiny veins on the skin of a monstrous body. Some have huts dotted along them, and take a week to walk. If you want to tramp them at the height of the season, you have to book.

I'm standing in shadow but the sky holds tufts of clouds like fading vapour-trails lit pinky-orange from below. The sinking sun has turned the high lands to the north the colour of ginger biscuits, slashed by the deep black shadows of the gulleys. Waterfowl of all kinds are swinging across the sky to roost, like packs of slow arrows. The plaintive cawing of a pair of paradise ducks carries forever across the stillness. The lake's a mirror. Ducks tow rippled vee's across it. And on the far side of the water the lights come on in Te Anau and the town seems dwarfed, puny. Eye-candy comes no sweeter.

I go back the way I came. I would like to carry on round the lake, but for one thing I'm hungry, for another it would take six days, and for a third, I'd die. This land is vast, primeval and supremely indifferent. The only predators on human life in New Zealand are the sandfly and a single shy spider. The bite of each is little more than an irritant. But for all the lack of overt hostility, this raw and untamed land lies beyond our ecological niche. Half a day out here alone and they send out search-parties and choppers and you become a minor suburban thrill on the six o'clock news.

Back near Te Anau I can hear the trout at the lake edge,

sucking spent insects from the surface, sending steely concentric ripples widening over the black water. It would be sweet to borrow a rod, sneak down to the water's edge, study the patrolling route of a single fish and then, with trembling fingers, cast a fly with such delicacy that it lands like thistledown six inches in front of the feeding fish and scares it off.

Late-holidaying couples promenade along the front and a man with a tripod and several thousand dollars' worth of gear is taking a time-lapse study of the darkening lake. On a white timber jetty stands a docile queue of warmly dressed tourists awaiting the night ferry across the lake to the glow worm caves or, as the brochure puts it, the 'magical glow-worm grotto'. If the caves were across the road and empty I would visit them, but the notion of joining a guided tour makes my bowels squirm.

I tramp into Te Anau in search of a restaurant and a pub and find them both under the one roof. Neither is that good. The bar is tiny and the restaurant huge, an acreage of varnished pitch-pine tables empty but for one Australian family.

I order the suspiciously cheap roast of the day, drink a couple of beers alone at the horseshoe bar, am summoned to a table where a gravy-drenched plate of what may be lamb awaits me, and find I am positioned in the middle of a visual and aural smorgasbord. I can watch the huge screen which is displaying an interview between a rugby commentator as animated as a baboon and a brace of rugby players as animated as pastry. But in what I am now realising is official best practice in the hospitality industry, the television is muted. For my listening pleasure I get a medley of Abba, Simon and Garfunkel, the Beatles, Roxy Music, all of which I infuriatingly recognise and can name, and even in places sing along to with only slight inaccuracies in the lyrics. I've never owned copies of any of these tunes but they have slid into my head uninvited and have become as evocative as smells, summoning unbidden memories of places, people, loves and losses, fears and triumphs, hair. Is there a country in the world where these songs are unknown?

If I look away from the TV screen I get to watch the chef in tattoos and a black T-shirt preparing a stream of meals for what must be either invisible patrons or his own amusement. And if I blank out the music I get to tune into the Australian nuclear family which comprises fat mother, fat father with Hawaiian shirt, skinny teenage son with nose-stud, substantial teenage daughter, substantial teenage daughter's presumably illegitimate baby that has lungs like a ship lost in fog, and a conversation between father and son of which the following verbatim snippet is not a highlight but merely representative of the whole.

> Dad (stabbing a slice of roast pumpkin and raising it from
>   his plate): What the fuck's this?
> Son: Fuck knows, Dad, I ate it but—
> Dad: Yeah, well, who's the fuckwit? I'm fucking not.
> Son (with evident admiration for forthright paternal
>   honesty and gratitude for spiritual guidance through the
>   turbulent waters of life): Good on yer, Dad. Fuck.

I'm so engrossed that I find I've eaten several pieces of what may have been broccoli. I retreat to the bar and find Jeff.

Jeff's forty but looks thirty. He's American and a fisherman. Two pints later we find we agree on everything except Alan Greenspan and God. According to Jeff, the entire world economy is dependent on the money supply – whatever that may mean, though it doesn't seem to mean what it ought to mean – and Alan Greenspan controls it by being in cahoots with Wall Street and the World Bank and the IMF. I don't argue. On God, according to Jeff, 'the jury's out'. I feel on safer ground here and suggest that the jury's come back and unanimously agreed on a verdict of, 'Oh, come off it. Don't be so silly.' But mainly we talk about fishing.

This is Jeff's second trip to New Zealand. Back home he fishes for steelhead, which are, I believe, a variety of sea-run rainbow trout. In his many years of fishing for steelhead he has caught two. 'Count them,' says Jeff. 'Two.' But in New Zealand he catches trout in abundance. He wants to live here permanently. I tell him he should. He says he will and we drink to that. I tell him that the black gnat is the prince of dry flies. We drink to that. He tells me of the evening rise on the Upper Waiau. We drink to that. The Australians leave the restaurant. We drink to that twice.

When I leave, Te Anau is thick with mist. Mist is excellent for singing in, like a bathroom. I treat the place to a rendition of 'Que cuando vienen del campo', an Aragonese jota I learned when living in Spain in 1980. I learned it drunk and sing it that way. The lyrics are excellent. Here's the chorus in translation.

> And when they come from the fields
> They come singing
> Because they are so happy
> The agricultural labourers.

Dave, who taught me the song, knew only two others. One was the Hibernian FC supporters song and the other began, 'I love my mother-in-law.' One evening we sang 'Que cuando' in a little bar in the Tuvo in Zaragoza. The barman stood through it, smiling patiently. Then he led us into a back bar and introduced a man who looked like Humpty Dumpty with a single front tooth. The barman told us to buy him brandy. We bought him brandy. 'Canta,' said the barman to Humpty Dumpty and the man opened his mouth so wide I could see down the mottled horror of his throat, and out of that throat came a rendition of our song, so potent, so earthy, and so fiercely and sincerely felt, that it shook the bottles behind the bar. Dave and I felt such humiliation, such embarrassment at our feeble and insulting parody of local culture that we didn't sing that song again for, oh, at least an hour.

Still singing, I pass a camper van glowing an eerie blue like a recently-landed spaceship. The middle-aged couple inside are watching television. I raise the volume of my song a notch but they don't seem to notice.

Somewhere behind the mist stand the dwarfing mountains.

Greymouth

Hokitika

Franz-Josef

Christchurch
Lyttelton

Haast

Geraldine

Wanaka

Queenstown

Te Anau

Dunedin

Balclutha

Owaka

Invercargill

Bluff

7

Buddy Halftail

Mist is still muffling the town in the morning. But walking up the street hungover feels markedly different from waltzing down it singing.

Past the garage and the squash courts and a string of cheaper motels and over the brow of the hill and then my heart gives a little lurch and I stop. A hundred yards ahead of me stands another hitchhiker.

Immediately I am tempted to do the bad thing. It would be a simple matter to retreat a few yards back down the hill and set up shop out of sight of my rival, creaming the traffic. It would break the implicit code of hitchhiking, but it would be without risk. Even if the other were to come back down the road and discover me, I could credibly plead ignorance.

I have known numerous people who would unhesitatingly have done the bad thing. Rob was one such. I went to school with Rob. He was apparently without conscience. I haven't seen him for twenty years and I don't much mind. The last time we met was by chance at the southern end of the M1 at Cricklewood. A gaggle of hitchhikers were competing for lifts. Rob unfurled a giant cardboard arm bearing the felt-tip legend 'Entertaining Hitchhikers Ltd.' We had a lift inside ten minutes. I got into the front seat of the car while Rob slid into the back and went straight to sleep. He scared me.

I am not Rob. I keep on over the brow of the hill. Why? Goodness? Education? Conscience? I would be happy to lay claim to any of these but I instinctively know that the truth is less pretty. I do the right thing because I am afraid of the consequences of doing the wrong thing. I am afraid that I'll be caught. Where that fear comes from is one for the psychologists and the moral philosophers. It is of a piece with my fear of authority, my desire to be liked, my dread of confrontation. Selfishness vies with timidity. Both are strong, but timidity is the stronger. It does not sound right to call that goodness, though I suspect a lot of goodness is just that – submitting to Constable Fear.

My rival proves to be female, Japanese and the height of my lowest rib. She is surrounded by luggage amounting to roughly twice her body weight. How she got it there I couldn't say. Perhaps she hired a porter.

I say good morning.

She switches on a massively dental smile and says, 'Harrow.' Or rather she sings it in the manner of one who speaks a language dependent on tone. She is holding a sign against her chest like an orphan on a wartime railway station. It says Dunedin. Dunedin lies on the far side of the island and there is no direct route between here and there.

I ask if she's been here long. She smiles at me in charming incomprehension. I find myself admiring her. Monolingual, alone, tiny, vulnerable and defying the national trait of travelling in herds, she seems brave.

I wish her good ruck.

'Goo'bye,' she sings as I head into the mist. 'Goo'bye.'

I stand some hundred yards further on and feel oppressed by futility. Much of the trickle of traffic is clearly local, and the rest is camper vans. And if a driver spurns the smiling, pretty, youthful Miss Japan there's little chance that he will stop for me, middle-aged, male and bald as a billiard ball. The thumb I raise is a thing without stuffing. There is nothing I can do but wait in the mist, admire the water droplets that gather on my sweater and follow the progress of a worm.

I've ruined the worm's morning by turning over a stone with an idle toe and exposing the thing to air and light and predators. Alarmed to the degree that worms can register alarm, it sprints for safety with that odd, seemingly hydraulic process of movement, lengthening and shrinking as a hunch passes along its body like a wave along a skipping rope, but slowly. Its sleek snot-like flesh becomes encrusted with granules of soil and gravel. Driven by who knows what sense of navigation it executes a ninety-degree turn with excruciating slowness and burrows beneath a plantain leaf. This epic foot-long journey takes fifteen minutes.

Like a schoolboy torturer I lift the leaf. The worm has slumped there, exhausted. I tuck the leaf back down and let the worm be. This is the true stuff of hitching. I'm toying with a worm on my own by a road in some random unenchanted spot on the planet. I've been around for forty-six years and every moment of those forty-six years has been tending inevitably towards this moment. Ecce homo once more, and this homo sniggers.

The mist is thinning. Buildings have ghosted out of it and become solid. Over the course of an hour I watch the ironed sheet of the lake appear, shifting by imperceptible gradations from grey to black, from black to steel, from steel to pine green. Folded mountains emerge as hints of themselves, then gather bulk. Above the sharply defined treeline, some low vegetation, then what looks to be tussock, then bare rock and slides of scree and pockets of snow and then snow, all of it sharp in the sun. It is good to watch it happen. And there is no other form of travelling in which one would watch it happen. Hitching enforces immobility.

The sun strengthens. As I am taking my sweater off, a ute stops for the Japanese girl and she leans in the passenger window and presumably says Harrow and a man in a bush shirt gets out of the cab and loads all her bags on to the back beside an outboard motor, while she watches and smiles and does nothing. As the ute passes me the girl waves with frantic happiness from the passenger seat. I wave back, pick up my bag and walk a hundred yards to claim the space she's vacated, glad to be number one on the road again. Glad too to be alone.

'That the lion's share of happiness is found by couples', wrote Larkin, 'sheer inaccuracy as far as I'm concerned' – and as far as I'm concerned, too, at least when travelling. I have tried travelling in company and it has rarely worked. I once went down through France with a university friend. By the time we reached the Spanish border I thought I hated him. I didn't. What I hated was having to compromise, to discuss, to reach decisions together, to agree on the next move. But more significantly I hated showing my timidity on the road, exposing so much of my weakness.

In our little tent somewhere near St Jean de Luz I woke one morning about four o'clock and lay a while thinking and then slid cautiously from my sleeping bag and packed my things in awful, guilty silence and tiptoed away from the tent. When I reached the road I whooped and ran and I don't think I have ever felt freer. I got a lift from a lorry to San Sebastian and found a café there for breakfast and was drunk on carajillos by ten.

Beside me now a paddock holds four small sheep and six big boulders. The boulders lie roughly in a circle. In Europe they might be Neolithic. In New Zealand they are boulders.

An ancient black saloon climbs the hill out of Te Anau then slows and stops beside me. 'I been thinking,' says Jeff the fisherman, 'about what you said last night. 'About God and stuff. Do you believe there could be life on other planets?'

'Why not?'

'Right,' he says. 'Hey, good luck man. Be seeing you,' and he turns the car back round and heads towards the lake and the mountain rivers, a fly rod sticking from the rear window like an aerial.

Around me lies evidence that people have hitched here before Miss Japan and me: a cellophane pie wrapper gone yellow, a fading empty book of Zig Zag cigarette papers, a black and brittle banana skin.

A woman in lycra strides ferociously past, driven by an angry devotion to health. One of her swinging arms jerks a lead that tows an elderly limping retriever. They are heading away from the Te Anau towards nothing.

For three hours I stand, letting my mind drift, not minding much, until a battered Ford going the wrong way brakes and does a cornily squealing U-turn. The driver is young, shabbily dressed and wearing the sort of sunglasses favoured by bodyguards. 'I'll go anywhere for the gas money,' he says. I am wary. A Dalmatian pokes its head through the passenger window and tries to lick me. The dog acts as a character reference for the driver.

'How much to Queenstown?'

'Twenty bucks'll do it.'

He does another U-turn, we head into Te Anau, I buy twenty dollars' worth of petrol, and we go to Queenstown.

Reuben's twenty-three years old. He makes his living mostly by busking.

'I can play anything. Played with some great guys – Fat Boy Slim, Salmonella Dub. I've owned seventeen guitars, man. The Mongrel Mob smashed sixteen of them. Or just stole them. They fucking hate me, man.'

'Why?'

'I'm a short-arse. One metre seventy-three. One metre seventy-three's no use in a fight.'

The Dalmatian's got only half a tail. It lost the other half when the Mongrel Mob tried to run down the pair of them with a car in the streets of Invercargill. 'That dog's my best buddy, man. We go everywhere together, don't we, Buddy?'

As we drive through the near-empty landscape of tussock and hills and increasingly stark gulleys, every stretch of it brings out another little slice of autobiography. He did a bit of gardening here, collected pine cones there until the farmer took a shot at him, went to that farm to ask for work as a shepherd. The farmer laughed at his half-tailed Dalmatian and told him to fuck off.

'But I'll be back, man. I'll show them. I'm going to put Buddy in some sheepdog trials. He's the best, man. See that hill, that steep one? Been up it barefoot, mate. Up that gulley there, there's this brilliant natural spa-bath. No one knows about it.'

In the footwell in front of me there's a copy of *The Silmarillion*. He's read all of Tolkien several times. His mother's in Invercargill, his father's in Auckland and his brother's dead, killed in a car crash when hitchhiking north of Auckland.

'The bastards were pissed. Rolled the car at a hundred and eighty k. He was thrown out. Killed. The bastards only got a fine. And he knew it was going to happen, man. He told me that morning that something bad was going to happen to him.

And he told me his spirit would inhabit a hawk. I love hawks. I was in the paper as the hawk-man. I catch them.'

I ask him how. He is vague, but it seems that low cloud is essential. Having caught them he takes them into the mountains to release them again.

We are moving through more dramatic country. Athol, Garston – its name picked out in whitewashed stones – Five Rivers, hillsides steepening so I have to press my forehead against the cool window glass to see their stony outcrops, their jagged crests. Yellowing willows line a river bank, as picturesque as Switzerland.

The corpse of a possum on the road. Perched on top of it, as yesterday, a hawk, tawny and imperious, tearing at a strand of crimson innard with a beak curved like a pruning hook. Reuben brakes. The bird leaps and flaps with heavy laboured beats, bereft of the grace of thermal altitude, straining for impetus until it drops over the steep road bank towards the river below, turns on its side, catches a breeze and sweeps away with sudden aerobatic ease. We stop.

Reuben gets out and jogs back up the hill in his baggy track pants. Buddy the dog twists his neck to follow him with his eyes. Reuben takes the possum from the road and swings it by the tail like a hammer thrower. Its entrails and stomach detach at the point of release and fly off at a tangent. The furry carcase drops deep into the steep valley and Reuben trots back to the car.

'The hawks are too slow, aren't they, Buddy?' he says, getting back in. Buddy licks his face and whimpers. 'And some shits drive at them on purpose.'

Reuben promises to take me to the best place in Queenstown. 'You'll love it, man, you'll fucking love it.' And even Reuben, young, troubled, yearning, does not shy away from the adjective. 'It's fucking beautiful, Joe,' he says. 'Just fucking beautiful.'

Below us to the left the long eastern arm of Lake Wakatipu.

Beside it runs the Kingston Flier, a steam train for tourists, another attraction I fail to find attractive. I can understand the appeal of a steam train rattling beside the lake, its cottonwool plume flattening above the coaches like a squirrel's tail. I can admire the heavy engineering too, the gleaming beams of steel that link the wheels of the engine and circle like elbows. But to board that train, to be hauled by those beams beneath the squirrel's tail, I cannot see how the pleasure of that exceeds or differs from the pleasure of riding a diesel train. But I suppose it is something to do. We all need something to do.

We drop from the heights to the frayed end of the ribbon that is Queenstown. Hotels and houses cling to every buildable section. Through the crammed and cramped town centre and then up a side road, past dozers and concrete mixers, and the mud and marker posts of a new hillside subdivision, up a lane that flicks round a corner like a fishhook and then we stop. In front of us a boulder twice my height. Buddy bounds from the car, squats for an instantaneous and prodigious shit, then barrels down the hillside after a rabbit, his half-tail whipping with delight. Reuben and I climb the boulder and light cigarettes and look.

'What do you reckon?'

Below us in the last of the afternoon sun the lake is crinkled like kitchen foil. A paddle-steamer chugs across it like a toy in a bath. Away to the left the town itself huddles round the northern end of the lake. Mountains climb straight from the water, forested or sparsely grassed on the lower slopes but rising to rock, their jagged tops like the crest on a tuatara's spine. Behind them and away to the north, range after range, rising to snow and receding to a blur and then sky.

It's a view that appears in a million brochures. It's a view as startling as anything in Australasia, a view that puts tourists on the longest scheduled plane flights on the planet. And after five minutes I've had enough of it. So has Reuben. He calls Buddy who hasn't looked at the view but has found plenty to do, and we drive down into town where Reuben has to go to the bank. There is some problem with the payment of his benefit. The last I see of him and Buddy, they're bouncing down the pedestrian mall together and Buddy stops to sniff at a rail of kayaking gear. At the top of the mall a sign says 'No Skateboards, No Dogs'.

I liked the pair of them. I admired Reuben's insouciance, his tolerance of chaos, his seeming fearlessness. I suspect we all admire most readily the qualities we lack.

Queenstown squats beneath the mountains like a whore in a palace. But it's a pretty whore, and a rich one. The prices in the real-estate windows have strings of zeroes after them like the wheels on the Kingston Flier.

Now is the shoulder season, between the bungy-jumping, parapenting, jet-boating, scree-luging summer of fun, and the four-month winter carnival of snow. Queenstown's a playground. It bills itself as 'The Adventure Capital of New Zealand'. Home of the risk-free risk, of sanitised thrills and safety helmets, of a twenty-first-century parody of danger. What came free with the territory for the pioneers now comes very expensive for the tourist. The cash registers run on adrenalin.

Welshman William Rees from Haverford West was the first white man to settle here. 'No fires had cleared the country,' he wrote in 1860, going on to moan about the difficulty of battling through three-foot speargrass and matagouri scrub. The reward for his perseverance stands on the lakefront in the form of a bronze statue of himself and a merino ram. The ram looks quite convincing. But even Rees looks more convincing than the concrete statue of a kiwi a bit further along the wharf. And a lot more convincing than the concrete moa, which seems, at first glance, to have been surprised by a proctologist. At second glance, it still does.

Downtown Queenstown, such as it is, is compressed, the lanes pedestrianised, the buildings agreeably low, and despite the Gucci-style shops, the NZ Opal Centre, the racks of Ray-Bans, the countless vendors of outdoor experiences, the place achieves a sense of alpine village intimacy. Though the extremities of the town may be creeping round the lake-edge like a fungus, the heart of the place is pleasing. And more and more of the new buildings are echoing the earliest ones by being built of schist, the grey and flaky rock of the mountains.

Two haughty handsome Spanish youths are assaulting a minivan. They've locked their keys inside. The van's as old as they are and so rusted that it looks as though they could simply rip through the panelling, but though they kick it, shout at it, beat on it with fists, it resists them. One youth wrenches at the driver's door handle and it comes away. He flings it into the gutter where it bounces. Their distress is so intense that I take a seat at a café to watch, but they give up too soon and go away.

An absurdly young policeman in shirt-sleeves fingers a rack of thermal clothing marked 'Reduced'. Two older women in tramping boots slump onto a bench and bicker over the innards of a camera. Fifty tiny Japanese old people disgorge from a bus and so monopolise the pavement with their luggage and their sing-song swarm that shoppers cross the road. An executivish woman clicks past in heels, her skirt tight, her blouse black and expensive, her make-up too thick and too brown. A middle-aged American couple eat slices of cheesecake frilled with piped cream. He wears a plaid shirt, jeans and a cat hat, she a mandarin leisure-suit. She's got the arse of a shire horse, a mighty thing ballooning on either side of the chair like two taut bags of cement. It's more than an arse. It's a butt. An All-Star butt, a butt for America, a butt to block a supermarket aisle. I find it strangely compelling.

Queenstown is young but most of the young seem to be away now, mid-afternoon, expending themselves on river or mountain, doing the stuff for which Queenstown is famous. And in the afternoon sunshine, with my coffee-froth moustache,

I resolve to stay here a few days, take time off from the road, take time to see the fish. They're my favourite thing here, the attractive attraction. If you go to Queenstown, see them.

Go down to the wharf. Ignore the people trying to rent you a kayak, or take you parapenting, or strap you into a jet-boat, or chug you across the lake for an authentic New Zealand farm experience, involving authentic New Zealand shearing with a commentary in three languages, plus an authentic cream tea and/or barbecue alongside the authentic woolshed gift shoppe. Go instead to the jetty. Enter the hut, go down a flight of steps, turn right, pay five bucks and meet the fish. You can't miss them. There's only an inch of plate-glass between you and them.

The fish are wild. They are free to go anywhere in the lake. Most are rainbow trout the size of tuna, great slabs of fish-flesh, sleek, fat and untroubled, easing through the water like supple subs, slowly flicking a white-tipped fin, a tail, their faces set in lugubrious neutral. Each jackfish has the hooked lower jaw of a pantomime witch. Through and between them slide the long-fin eels, each thick as a thigh and long as a leg, up to ninety years old and all but blind. They wind up the glass with grey-black sinuous malice. Above them, buoyant and vulnerable, the bobbing undersides of ducks, New Zealand scaup, like little feathered dinghies. What draws the ducks and the fish to this place is your money.

Drop a dollar in a slot and a machine outside spews pellets. The frenzy is immediate. The trout change up through the gears and carve the water, their mouths like scoops. The eels writhe and stream, drawn by their noses, their mouths crammed with tiny and terrible teeth. And the scaup dive, their bodies gone silver with the feather-trapped air, their flat beaks weaving to either side, snapping like tiny plesiosaurs, until they lose the battle with their own buoyancy and erupt back to the surface like pneumatic missiles, their beaks tucked endearingly under their chins. The water clears. The eels sink out of sight to suck up the last crumbs. The trout slow. The ducks resume their bobbing. The wait restarts.

You can pull up a chair to the glass. I do. I fetch more dollar coins from the bored girl at the counter. I am not generally given to such things but here I sink into a sort of mesmeric communion. Several times I make up my mind to leave but my limbs don't move.

Robert Graves has catalogued the qualities of brute nature:

> Whose pleasures are excreting, poking,
> Havocking and sucking,
> Sleepy licking.
>
> Whose griefs are melancholy,
> Whose flowers are oafish,
> Whose waters, silly,
> Whose birds, raffish,
> Whose fish, fish.

Fish are fish. 'And saying so to some,' to quote another poet, 'means nothing. Others, it leaves nothing to be said.' I am among the others.

I stare at fish for their unrelenting fishiness. And these fish, by not being captive, by not being fishbowl fish, aquarium fish, are the best of all fish to watch, the fishmost fish.

A woman arrives with two children. The boy rushes to the glass and bangs on it. The girl sees an eel and recoils. I leave. Climbing the few steps onto the jetty is like changing elements. Queenstown wharf seems momentarily strange.

I am just in time to see the sun disappear behind the mountains with a click that drops the temperature an instantaneous handful of degrees. A single mallard paddles across the blackening water, towards the distant mountain that is still lit golden by the sun.

The shops are closing, rails and displays being wheeled

inside for the night. From outside a gift shop – pastel cardigans with rectangular sheep on them, sheepskin-covered coat-hangers, miniature All Blacks jerseys, possum-fur leg-warmers – a woman is bringing in a wicker basket of reasonably large pine cones. They are priced at $2 each. And I bump into Nico. I used to teach him. He's living here now. We go to the pub.

It's an Old English pub which, of course, is neither old nor English but it does employ a barmaid so cheerless, discourteous, inattentive, inefficient and unremittingly idle that there is almost no point in asking her where she's from. But I do.

'Barnstaple,' she says, and manages to turn its three syllables into 'fuck off'. It evokes a feeling in me that approaches nostalgia.

Lots of English people know exactly how to serve. Indeed they do so with both wit and a refreshing absence of unctuousness or corporate obedience. Nevertheless, if you encounter a bad shop assistant, or barman, or ticket-seller, a seriously bad one, anywhere in the world, the chances are that he or she, and it's probably she, will be English.

It approaches an art form, the talent to inject into someone else's day such a distillation of boredom, disaffection and even hostility, as will depress the spirits of all but the most stubbornly cheerful customers.

Nico is off to New York soon, something to do with design and fashion. Articulate, able, and generously broad of mind, he's representative of a species of young New Zealander who has to go away.

The business of going away has become so recognised a part of growing up here that it has shrunk to its initials. O.E. they call it – overseas experience. It's readily explicable. The population is so small that it is hard for the young to find somewhere on these islands where there isn't someone who knows someone who knows them. Or worse, someone who knows someone who knows their mum. For an adolescent trying to flee the nest, desperate for the intoxicating freedom of having no one to run to in distress, no one to fret for them, the whole country can seem like a nest. So they go. They used to go to England by steamer. Now they may fly to São Paulo, to Turkestan, to Los Angeles, but the UK remains the hub of most itineraries. When we were discussing titles for this book, the London publisher's first suggestion was *Where Backpackers Come From*.

The pubs of London are staffed by young kiwis better than the pubs of Queenstown are staffed by Barnstaplists. But it isn't only the pubs. The trading floors, the banks and business houses of London house several thousand willing and cheerful New Zealand young.

But there is more to O.E. than escape, or even than the perennial instinctive need of the young to walk over the horizon. On the New Zealand census form there's an ethnicity section. You can tick a box beside Maori or Tokelauan or Chinese or any of twenty others. But the box that the great majority of people tick, the box that you tick even if you're a fifth-generation New Zealander born on a high-country station in the bed that your great-grandfather was also born in, is NZ European.

The link remains. For all that this country is about as similar to Great Britain as Florida is, for all that this country will be a republic inside twenty years, the link remains. And the young have to go and see the other end of it. Some return to New Zealand within the year, others never. Typically they stay away perhaps three years. But it seems that they cannot be comfortable in these comfortable islands until they have seen their ancestral lands.

I ask Nico if he's pleased to be Kiwi. He says he is. 'But it's a small country,' he says, 'and it needs constant reassurance, a succession of pats on the head.'

And though that is less true than it was perhaps thirty years ago, a glance at any newspaper will tell you that it remains part of the psyche. If an American magazine says good things about New Zealand, it's news. If a survey of travellers reveals good things about New Zealand, it's news. I'm not sure that it's insecurity. I think it's just a consequence of being small and young and distant. And increasingly dependent on tourism.

I ring Louise's daughter. Whenever I visit Louise in England she takes me out to lunch and then discovers she's forgotten to bring money. She blushes. I pay. Her daughter's in Queenstown now and has received instructions from Louise to buy me dinner. Louise will forward the cash by international postal order, or Federal Express or carrier pigeon or whatever, which is fine by me.

When Louise's daughter arrives she looks like Louise. She buys me a fat pork steak. The evening dissolves into beer. I am garrulous, unserious, happy. I mention the reasonably large pine cones I saw earlier.

'Who buys them?'

'The Japs,' says Nico. 'They have to buy presents for all the people they know back home. That's a lot of presents.'

But a pine cone? 'And for you, Hiroshi, with my very best wishes, a reasonably large pine cone.'

'Arigato a thousand times, my little lotus flower.'

Late in the evening Nico bets me that I can't make Miss Barnstaple laugh. I devote twenty minutes to the task. And lose.

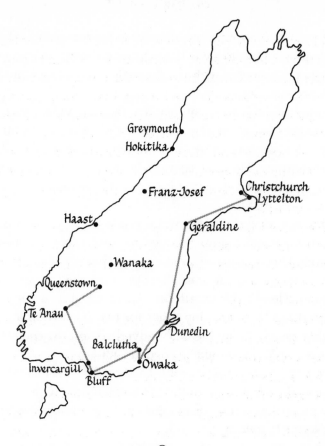

8

Trussed like a duck to shuffle the plank

Queenstown is part of Otago, a province that stretches from here in the mountains to Dunedin on the coast. Otago must be at least as large as Kent, Surrey, Sussex and Hampshire put together. Yet, the entire province is covered by a single phone book less than an inch thick. That includes the Yellow Pages.

Nine in the morning and already the tandem paragliders are circling over Queenstown, their chutes the shape of eyebrows, rising and lowering with the thermals. They hang beneath a dish-rag sky.

In light drizzle an Asian tourist is shooting video footage of a wooden bungalow. The bungalow isn't doing a lot, but it's labelled 'Queenstown's oldest building, built in 1864'. I say good morning. He turns in surprise and gives me a hundred-tooth smile and a nodding bow, but his camera hand stays statue-steady, as if independent of his body.

In a downtown café the waitress has a cough like a diesel engine on a cold morning. Between paroxysms she's cheerful enough. During paroxysms she's, well, paroxysmic, her body knifing forward at the waist, her apron clutched to her mouth like a murderer's chloroform pad. She uses a thirty-second bout of good health to take my order for two flat whites and the mighty mega all-day breakfast advertised on the chalkboard outside. At $19, it should be good. It isn't.

You can judge an all-day breakfast by the tomato. It should be grilled or fried to mouth-blistering sludge, with only the skin preserving it from disintegration. If the tomato's right, the rest seems to follow.

The tomato in front of me now is wrong. It's hot-house pale, and barely warm. And sure enough, cool on the heels of the tomato, the eggs are plasma, and the sausage small and solitary. The bacon is ringed with half an inch of whale blubber and has a rind from which you could make a serviceable catapult. The whole is bulked by a doorstop of foreign bread that may have dwelt under a grill for fifteen seconds but which has never so much as glimpsed the hot and fatty bottom of a frying pan. Worst of all are three fat potato wedges. Before noon potatoes are inedible and possibly poisonous.

When I'm done with pushing it round the plate, I tell the waitress it was delightful, accept her cough of gratitude, resist the urge to revisit the fish and succumb to the urge to visit the birds. They live on the site of a former rubbish dump.

Above the bird park, a gondola climbs through an avenue of dense fir trees, that may, for all I know, be pines. Either way, they're not indigenous. But the birds are.

In the first aviary an injured New Zealand falcon hops on a perch behind one of those irritating first-person notices. 'Hi, my name's Freddie. I was injured flying into some chicken wire and a kind farmer brought me in.' This bird is no Freddie. It is exquisite ferocity. Its beak is a weapon. Its eyes are black, unblinking and nameless.

In the nocturnal house, a kiwi scuttles through leaf mould among rotting logs, probing deep into the litter with a beak like a dipstick, then scuttling on, as monomaniac as all wild things. But this bird has none of the falcon's sleek efficiency. It's a fluffed football. Its wings are stumps. It lays an egg one-third of its body weight. Its eyes are weak as water. Its nostrils are on the end of its beak. It's a freak, a basket case. It could have evolved and survived nowhere in the world but on the avian ark that was New Zealand. And it's now unlikely to survive even here. Man has destroyed nine-tenths of the forests that the kiwi needs, and the remaining tenth is alive with stoats. Kiwi numbers have dwindled from the millions into the thousands. And despite the efforts of the conservationists it is likely that on the main islands those thousands will continue to dwindle towards zero. Eventually the bird will survive only in sanctuaries like this, and on offshore islands that have been cleared of predators.

I spend two gentle hours in the bird park. There are specimens of other less dramatic but equally threatened species: the dull-looking brown teal, the blue duck that is slate grey and lives only on the fierce tumbling streams of the high alps, and the black stilt, the world's rarest wading bird. They live on the braided riverbeds of the Mackenzie and I have seen them there.

One sweltering day last summer I gave up on fishing, and lay on my back on the river bank, tipping my fishing hat over my eyes to snooze under a sky as wide as the globe. A persistent insect woke me, and I sat up to see three immature black stilts, their plumage imperfectly black, high-stepping through the shallows, probing the silt with their beaks. I stayed still to watch them. They lacked the dainty elegance of their abundant pied cousins, but the thought of their rarity made the sight pleasing.

Half an hour later, brewing coffee at the car with friends who had caught a swag of fish, I could still see the birds as dots on the estuary mud.

Two men in shorts came down the gravel road carrying gear over their shoulders. As they neared, it became clear that the gear was a substantial telescope and tripod. The men were middle-aged, the flesh of their faces red from too much sun in too short a time. The armpits of their khaki shirts were black moons of sweat. They set up their telescope a little way away from us, swung it through an arc and fixed on the distant stilts. They looked through the scope in turns. One turned the pages of a book and passed it to the other. They returned to the scope. They turned to each other and beamed and then they shook hands.

On their way back up the track they were still beaming. I asked what they'd seen and they were extravagantly delighted to tell me that they had seen three black stilts. They had come to New Zealand for a fortnight and had designed an itinerary round rare birds. They came, they said, from Bolton.

It would be possible to say all manner of things about these men. But all I feel the urge to say was that it was good to see people so happy.

Back in town for more coffee I run into another former pupil. Queenstown is becoming my Piccadilly Circus.

Ed's a lawyer and a cheerful cynic. He tells me that his elder brother, whom I also used to teach, is now CEO of Croquet New Zealand. I'm not in the least surprised that Croquet New Zealand has a CEO. All sports matter here. There is, for example, a high performance academy for bowls. That's lawn bowls, the gentle recreation favoured by the elderly whom time has robbed of the ability to play more strenuous games. The high performance bowlers are young and keen and they wear track suits and they take bowls terribly seriously. Bowls New Zealand calls them athletes. But I prefer the bowls club near where I live. It's sponsored by Lamb and Hayward, a firm of undertakers.

I agree to meet Ed later for a beer, predictably in the local Irish bar called Pog Mahones. Somewhat less predictably, according to Ed, the name translates as 'Kiss my arse'.

Feeling the need for the sort of exercise that breeds a warm glow of virtue and an evening thirst, I climb to the top of the gondola hill with an Italian lesbian.

It takes a while for her to tell me she is lesbian. Indeed it takes a while for her to tell me her name. That name is Lucasta. I tell her I know of only one other Lucasta and she was the addressee of an Elizabethan poem: 'To Lucasta, on going to the wars', by Suckling.

'Not Suckling,' she says. 'Lovelace.'

'You know the poem?'

'I was named after it. My dad was English. He studied at Oxford or maybe Cambridge. I don't remember.'

'I suppose people are always mentioning that poem to you.'

'You're the first one.'

I feel absurdly smug.

Lucasta is quiet and cautious. She has the face of a young Virginia Woolf. If you're going to have a Virginia Woolf face, young is the one to have. Having glimpsed her on the footpath ahead of me I caught up with her when she stopped to drink from a metal water flask. I asked her where she was from and complimented her on her barely accented English and we walked on together following the line of an old water-pipe up through the steep bush.

Lucasta unfurls slowly, like a fern frond. She has come to

New Zealand because it is big, empty and beautiful. She is travelling alone by bus. She hopes to see penguins.

The track rises into a pine plantation, the trees all straight as poles and pruned of their lower branches. Beneath them a deep softness of dead needles and a perpetual sunlessness.

'New Zealand,' says Lucasta, 'is so clean. Not like Italy. Italians drop litter everywhere.'

I tell her that New Zealand has a romantic notion of Italy and Italians, or rather two romantic notions. According to one image, Italians are leaders of fashion and the civilised urban sophisticates of Europe. According to the other, they're all wise and wrinkled peasants, wedded to the soil and olive groves and families in hillside villages of white stone, cobbles and lou-vred shutters.

Lucasta is too gentle to say bullshit, but over the next few minutes she paints a picture of Italians as conventional, idle, repressive and grossly over-protective of their children. Kiwis, on the other hand, seem to her to be hospitable, easy-going and robust. In an unstartling conclusion she tells me she would like to come to live here.

'Are you married?'

'I have a partner,' she says.

'What does he do?'

She pauses a moment and looks at her feet and then she says, 'My partner is a woman,' and her eyes flash fearfully to mine.

When I smile, she laughs for the first time.

The path has widened into a track and brought us to the gondola's upper terminal, offering views of the town below, the lake, the receding ranges of mountains. But on this low grey day the gondola's bubbles of glass and steel wheel up and round and down on their endless looping hawser, with few people aboard. There's a luge-track up here, a sort of dry sledge run. The plastic luges wait to be rented like a static conga line of strange black insects.

'Do you want to have a go?'

Lucasta shakes her head, says she doesn't like all these adventure sports, can't understand why anyone would want to do a bungy jump.

'I've bungy jumped.'

'How was it?'

'It was OK,' I say.

And it was. I jumped last year, just up the road from here. They weighed me and wrote 86 on the back of my hand in red marker pen. They took me onto the bridge, put me into a sort of abseiling harness, like a jockstrap with buckles, then sat me down and trussed my ankles with a towel, an ordinary bath towel. Mine was red.

My knees were trembling. It was partly the cold – the air was laced with winter and the bridge exposed – but it was mainly nerves. 140 feet below, the Kawarau River was grey-brown and turbulent and I was going to fall to within a metre of it.

A young man, with a practised line in gallows humour, wrapped a strap round the towel, attached a clip here, a carabina there, helped me to my feet and led me onto the gantry. The gantry was a yard or so of planking. It ended in air.

To my left there was a viewing deck. It was early in the day and there were only half a dozen spectators. One was slapping himself for the cold. Music blared from a stereo behind me, techno-style music with a thunderous pulsing beat. Without it there would have been just the silence of wind and rock, a silence that would creep into the psyche and intensify the fear.

The worst of it was my feet. Bound at the ankles I could only shuffle to the edge like a trussed duck. I kept a grip on a metal loop for as long as I could. I looked ahead of me, striving to ignore the bubbles in my neck, the throat-catch of nausea. Above the music, instinct was shouting no. Every self-preserving synapse was on beeping red alert, screeching that to step off into nowhere was to step for the last time. But I knew that I would jump. I tried to concentrate on the scenery.

It was a stark place. Just thin soil, thinner vegetation, and bare rock ceding to sky.

'We'll count you down from five.'

They counted fast. On 'Go!' I flung myself outwards as I had been advised to do, diving onto the air, as if onto a mattress, throwing my arms out like a suppliant. At the exact moment when it was too late to go back, I wanted to go back. Then gravity grabbed me. I was conscious of its sudden seizure, wordlessly aware of my utter powerlessness.

And then I was bouncing. I had no sense of having come near the water. I bounced two, perhaps three times, each with a switchback lurch of weightlessness at the top. And then I was dangling. Dangling from a bridge by my ankles like a duck in a poulterer's window.

My shirt had untucked from the waistband of my trousers and was rouched around my chest, exposing my stomach. I felt the cold on my flesh. I didn't feel triumphant. I didn't feel exhilarated. I did feel some degree of relief, but mainly I felt impotent and strangely silly. To gain some dignity, some control, I pulled myself up into a half-pike, but couldn't hold the position for long.

A yellow dinghy pushed out into the current and the bungy rope lowered me towards it. The youth in the dinghy held out a pole for me to grab and I was laid on my back in the boat like a baby having its nappy changed. The youth asked me how it was. I said it was great. But I was lying. I found it ordinary. I found it exactly as you would expect to find it – frightening, then sudden, then over. It was, in short, OK.

What was missing in this adventure was adventure. What was missing from this perilous act was peril.

New Zealand is recognised as the capital of the synthetic adventure industry and Queenstown is the capital of that capital. But I don't think it's a particularly New Zealand thing. Most of the people who are tied onto rubber ropes, strapped into jet-boats, slung beneath hang-gliders or otherwise towed, suspended, rolled, dropped or flung are foreigners. Most come from the rich societies of Europe, North America and Asia. They lead urban lives, dedicated to the avoidance of risk. Their societies are moving towards the abolition of bad luck. Bad luck is somebody's fault. And somebody can be sued.

But swaddled lives are unsatisfactory. They lack the raw test of mettle that is danger. So the rich people come to New Zealand to get a fix of danger. It helps that the country is a long way away, set deep in the Southern ocean, a place, or so it seems, where you can peer over the edge of the map and catch a glimpse of the end of the world. Just to come here is to engage in a tame simulacrum of daring, a ghost of the urge that drove Tasman and Cook.

Even more conveniently New Zealand is a distant natural wilderness that hosts a safe white English-speaking civilisation with good coffee and modern hospitals. So even to make the journey here is a sort of bungy-jump. It has the tang of adventure, the salty-blood taste of risk, but it is safer than crossing the road. But you can't buy a T-shirt saying, 'I crossed the road, and survived'.

When the youth finally untrussed me I was relieved to sit up, to be autonomous again, and even more relieved to clamber out of the dinghy onto rocks, and to climb the steps back to the bridge. A pair of employees pumped my hand and gave me an certificate saying that I had received 'an instant injection of adrenalin and euphoria'.

I hadn't. I had been frightened but that was all. My job was to take a single step. I was 86 kg of paying luggage.

'How much did it cost?' asks Lucasta.

'Nothing,' I say. 'Someone else was paying.' Which is true. Otherwise I wouldn't have done it.

'Talk to me about something else,' I say, and over coffee in the gondola terminal Lucasta tells me about life as a lesbian in an Italian village.

Gradually I come to understand the fierce volley of

adjectives she fired at her compatriots a little earlier. The local priest condemns her. Some of the old folk ostracise her. She's a small and shy young woman with the wide and dark but nervous eyes of a gazelle. Yet she is brave and strong, braver and stronger than any bungy jumper, braver and stronger than I could ever be, and I tell her so. She disavows it, but she laughs.

We climb down the hill as friends and go for a late-afternoon Guinness in Kiss My Arse. We're still there at eight when Ed arrives with Bill. Bill's a ski-instructor who hails from the glittering winter playground of Wigan. He's boisterous, loud and funny. He tells me that when he takes a class of young Japanese women who have never skied before, most of them stay only long enough to get a photograph of themselves standing upright with both skis on. 'And then,' says Bill, 'that's it, they're off. They've done skiing.'

9

Noise in nowhere

I spend two more days in Queenstown, partly because it rains a bit and threatens to rain a lot, but mainly because of Wayne. Wayne runs the Caples Court Motel. He recognised me from the mug shot on my newspaper column and invited me to stay as long as I wished for free. I promised to take the first opportunity to plug his excellent motel with its film star clientele,

courtesy limousine service, hot and cold running chamber-
maids, stunning views of the lake from the Jacuzzi with the
floating minibar, and extraordinarily economical tariff, but
Wayne fell to his knees, clenched his hands in supplication and
begged me not to do so. So I'll refrain.

Queenstown's a pleasant place to mooch a while. It exists to
soak up the surplus of cash and leisure that the twenty-first
century has dumped on the Western world. And it's full of
the young, wearing the sort of trousers that have zips at the
knee and that can be turned into shorts by a flick of a velcro
tab, or into a rucksack, or a four-wheel drive amphibious vehicle with drinks cabinet and emergency whistle. A
disproportionate number of the young people are British. I
constantly eavesdrop on boastful discussions about parapenting and hangovers, conducted in accents that I can place to the
nearest soap opera.

I am drawn several times to the wharf and the lugubrious
trout. From the wharf the town looks like a football crowd on a
terrace, the buildings crammed into too small a space, all
jostling to glimpse the lake.

On the Friday morning the clouds dissolve . Wayne hates to
lose a guest. He kisses me on every available cheek, offers me a
Fortnum & Mason hamper and a complimentary flight to anywhere in the country in the motel's private jet, insisting all the
while that this is what he does for every guest. But I explain
that mine is the rugged road of manly independence, and I go.

I don't go far. I hitch outside the Bottle House. The Bottle
House is built of bottles. I don't know who built it but I bet he
was good company. The necks of the bottles are on the outside,
so the building resembles a porcupine, if, that is, you can imagine a rectangular glass porcupine with a front door.

There's plenty of traffic. Some of it slows as it passes, to stare
through me and at the Bottle House before accelerating away. I
don't mind. It feels right to be on the road again, bag at my feet,
my fun-size Mars Bars still untouched at the bottom of that

bag like charms against disaster, charms that are slowly flattening and widening in their black and red wrappers.

I offer my thumb to everything that passes, half-grateful for gaps in the traffic that allow the lactic acid to drain from my shoulder. The heart of hitching is its unpredictability, but I wordlessly assess each vehicle as it approaches. To dirty older-model cars driven by men without hats or passengers, I offer a tauter thumb and a brighter mien. For late model, well-washed cars, for women drivers, and inevitably for camper vans, the thumb and face droop.

But unpredictability wins another little victory because a sparkling scarlet BMW stops. As the side window lowers electronically it triggers a memory from many years ago in France, a memory I didn't know I retained. It was near the end of a trip. I had done perhaps 1,500 miles in trucks and Renault 4s and countless Citroën 2CVs. And then on a road so straight and poplar-lined that it was almost a parody of Frenchness, I got my first and only lift in an expensive Citroën, the sort they sometimes used as ambulances, with headlights that popped up like bulbous eyes to frame a raking bonnet narrowed like a nose. They had pneumatic suspension that emphasised the Frenchness of their engineering. Cut the engine and the car sat like a dog. For me those Citroëns had become a symbol of the world that was older than I was and that had more money than I did and that purred past and disdained my youth and poverty. I remember nothing of the Citroën's driver. But I retain, and am now assailed by, a tactile memory of the cool tautness of the leather seats, and a sense of unearned privilege.

I don't recall ever getting a lift in a BMW. This one's driven by a doctor heading a few miles up the road to his surgery in Arrowtown. He wears a tie, shades and leather driving gloves, and typically he has little of what you could call a New Zealand accent. He would not stand out on an edition of *The Antiques Roadshow* filmed in Tunbridge Wells.

As part of his O.E. he spent a few years working in a London hospital. 'The doctors were incompetent,' he says cheerfully, 'and the nurses idle.'

I ask him if some doctors are markedly better than others, and whether those in the profession instinctively judge and rank their colleagues, as they do in teaching. By way of reply he tells me of some graffiti on the wall of the junior doctors' common room in the London hospital. It listed the most common last words of patients. Top of the list was, 'I've got this pain in my chest.' Second was, 'My surgeon is Dr Andrews.'

He drops me at the foot of a long and shallow dip in a road as straight as a knife. Beside me a stand of poplars, their leaves autumnal lemon. Across the road a vineyard about the size of a football pitch. Behind me the weak morning sun, still low in the sky. My giant shadow stretches 30 metres down the road. My elongated bag looks like the giant's sleeping dog. Though there's no car in sight I put out my thumb and watch the stretched shadow do the same. I withdraw my thumb, then put it out again, make rabbit ears with my fingers and sense again the mild intoxication of utter and random freedom.

When a camper van approaches at dawdling tourist speed, instead of looking at the driver I watch the vehicle's wheels, waiting for them painlessly to run over the shadow of my arm. But instead, of course, at the last possible second, the shadow flicks up and over the bonnet and the body of the camper van, then clamps back down on the road. Because the driver sees me as a silhouette he cannot see that I am smiling with tiny surprise. Nor, if he did, would he be remotely interested.

I have plenty of time to practise shadow games. My shadow shrinks from thirty yards to ten to five. By eleven o'clock the fun has worn a little thin. I have sown a scatter of trodden cigarette butts.

A white saloon car, clean as a church, emerges from the Arrowtown turn-off. Because the car has three middle-aged people aboard, I drop my arm and merely smile as it passes. The noise of the car thins to nothing and I am left in silence once again, until a car comes down the hill behind me, heading towards Queenstown. I hear it braking and I turn to see the same white saloon do a U-turn and halt at my feet. The driver gets out. He's wearing shorts.

'You must be Joe,' he says. 'I read that column of yours about hitching near Owaka,' and he stows my bag in the boot.

The three of them, two men and a woman, are North Islanders here for a forestry conference. Being visitors they take the Crown Range road, the designated scenic route to Wanaka.

What you do affects what you see. I see wooded hillsides. They see trees. They tell me about trees. Apparently none of the autumn colours that surround us are indigenous. The postcard images of Queenstown and Arrowtown dappled with brown and fawn and gold are imposed and exotic, imported from the European North. I learn of wilding firs and larches, willows, sycamores and, well, even as I hear it and am interested by it, I know that it's also stuff that I will not retain in any detail.

I ask if there are any white pine around. 'Apparently,' I say, 'it's the only timber in the world with no smell.'

'Yes,' says the driver. 'That's why they used it to make butter boxes.'

'Oh really,' I say, and shut up.

We pass the Cardrona Pub, so archetypical with its verandah and its weatherboards and its stark high-country setting, that it's featured in a hundred ads for beer, then we wind down through golden tussock to Wanaka.

Ten years ago Wanaka was the poor man's Queenstown. And if the poor man bought land in Wanaka ten years ago, he is no longer poor. It's as if the flood of money had simply filled the crevice in the mountains that is Queenstown, and had overflowed the mountain lip and come to rest in a puddle on the shore of Lake Wanaka.

Wanaka lacks Queenstown's compressed alpine drama. To one side of Wanaka the land merely rolls pleasantly away. But the views on the other side, across the lake to the pleated mountains, are as choc-box paintable as anything in its more celebrated rival.

To get some idea of the place, take the English Lake District, heighten the mountains, file their edges, fold them more tightly, cover most of them with snow, iron that snow, enlarge the lakes, intensify the brightness of the light by a factor of ten, banish all drizzle and shoot fourteen out of every fifteen people.

The foresters drop me in sunshine that feels brittle, like elderly Sellotape. Grouted into the footpath that runs beside the lake are 2,000 tablets, one for each of the years since the birth of Christ, and significant events are scratched into the appropriate years. In 1539 Ambrose Parer invented the first commercial artificial limb. 103 years later, by which time the disabled had presumably mastered their prostheses and the English Civil War was making Mr Parer's descendants into millionaires, Abel Tasman became the first European to see these islands.

The café tables are sprinkled with people young enough to hope they might still be beautiful but old enough to own expensive low-slung cars and cashmere sweaters the colour of ducklings. Those sweaters are furled over their shoulders, and wraparound sunglasses are lodged in their hair, as they sit over coffee and look at the lake in silence, ageing. I fetch a coffee too and carrot cake. I like carrot cake. I like its moistness. I like its butter-textured icing. And I like the way it doesn't taste of carrots.

A sparrow makes raids on crumbs within inches of my plate, its tiny talons slipping on the painted metal. Its legs are jointed, fleshless filaments, reptilian, endearing.

Just out of Wanaka the road forks. Straight on leads to the Lindis Pass with its tussock like a sea of baby hair. And beyond the Lindis lies the Mackenzie Basin, the heart of the island with its moonlike landscape and its glacial lakes and rivers. I've looped round the bottom of this island and as the crow flies I am perhaps only 150 miles from sleepy Geraldine.

The left fork heads towards Lake Hawea, the Haast Pass and the West Coast of the island, and I take it. By doing so I cut off my last point of entry to the Mackenzie. But six months from now I shall be fishing there. The stones on the bank of the Tekapo River will feel hot through the soles of my boots, and as I stand thigh-deep in mountain water the sunlight will bounce from its surface and burn beneath my chin.

At the point of the junction there's a freshly decapitated rabbit, its white tail fluttering in the wake of passing cars, like a scene from a Beatrix Potter movie adapted by Hunter S. Thompson. A green and luxurious Land Rover stops beside me. It's towing a jet-boat. A tall young man climbs out of the driver's seat.

'Joe,' he says. 'What the hell are you doing here?' It takes a moment to recognise him. Last time I saw him he was in school uniform. He shakes my hand with a paw the size of a soup-plate, one of those distinctive rural New Zealand soup-plates that crush anything they grip. I knew him, everyone knew him, as Jojo. He knew me as sir. Now, instinctively, he calls me Joe, and I call him Jonathan.

His father is famous, knighted for his pioneering work and crippled by it. He and others founded deer farming in this country. They flew helicopters into the bush to capture feral deer, the descendants of animals released by earlier settlers. They caught the deer by throwing or firing nets over them, then leaping out of the chopper to wrestle the beasts to the ground, lash them to the runners and fly them out alive. It was perilous work. Jonathan's father crashed I don't know how many helicopters, walking away from some of his accidents, limping away from others and having to be carried from some on a stretcher, but always surviving. And his genes have survived too. His sons all like to fly and are big high-country men.

Jonathan's got an American film crew in the back of the Land Rover. He's taking them jet-boating. The Americans are from Virginia. One is called Drew, both of the others are Jim. In the mass, and I choose the word advisedly, they fill the large car. They are eating pies and dressed in camouflage jackets. The brand name on the jackets is Predator. They are making a documentary series about hunting around the world, to be called, if I remember rightly, *Shooting Things in Pretty Places*. Yesterday they shot chammy and thar. The cameraman shot them shooting them.

Wedged against the passenger door I sense that they resent my intrusion. But it is possible that what I take for a hostile silence is only the gaps between words. They talk slow in Virginia and as Jonathan and I catch up on the ten years since he left school we give them no chance to form and express a phrase.

We launch the jet-boat at the head of Lake Wanaka. Or rather they launch the jet-boat while I stand by admiring, as I always do, the practicality of practical men, and dreading that I may be asked to release the cotter pin spindle bracket.

The place is huge, silent and empty, a wind tousling the dark water. Beyond the far shore, tall mountains recede into taller mountains. Jonathan fires the engine and helps me into a life-jacket and the jet-boat, where I sit between two well-fed chunks of Virginia. The only way I could leave the boat is vertically, like a squeezed lemon pip.

The jet-boat is an archetypical New Zealand story, born in the Mackenzie Country. Bill Hamilton, a local farmer, wanted a vessel to navigate the shallow braided rivers of the region, so he made one. Now Hamilton jet-boats are common throughout the world.

A jet-boat sucks the water in from underneath the hull and fires it out the back. At full throttle it has a draught of nothing. It skims the water at monstrous speeds and it turns, as I'm sure one of the Jims would say if there were a quarter of an hour to spare, on a dime. But even if he did, no one would hear him. The engine drowns everything.

We roar to the neck of the lake and into the winding river

system. Jonathan shouts the names of the rivers but I don't catch them. He stands to steer the boat through ankle-deep rapids, wrenching at the sickening last moment round barely submerged rocks.

I am getting for nothing what the punters in Queenstown pay plentiful dollars for. I am intermittently frightened and unremittingly cold.

Herons take fright and labour into the air with crooked necks and long slow wing beats. We pass inches from over-hangs of rock and moss and ancient beech forest. Scree-slopes stretch from the sky to the water like grey scars on green flesh. At one spot of particularly scenic appeal we stop to let the cam-eraman off, wait for him to set up his gear, then scream past him three or four times, with Jonathan flinging out the tail of the boat to turn and turn again. The wash breaks over shingle that hasn't seen water since the last snow-melt.

For maybe three-quarters of an hour we writhe and thunder up ever-narrowing gorges, then suddenly Jonathan cuts the engine. My whole body relaxes. We drift into shore as the last reverberations fade into the air and silence seeps back in. We clamber out of the boat and stretch and rub cold limbs and say little. The place is primeval.

There's a tributary stream, its gorge so steep and narrow that sunlight would penetrate it for maybe half an hour a day. Fed further up the valley by waterfalls like straight white pen-cils, the stream gathers here in swirling pools of green translucency, deep distorting mindless vortexes of water, like thick stained glass slowly on the move.

There's a remoteness here, a gothic grandeur and a harshly beautiful indifference, a dwarfing mindlessness. And back in the mountains behind it there's a million hectares of the same stuff. I sit on a rock to make notes, to try to find some words that aren't entirely inadequate, inappropriate.

'Magical,' says Drew. 'The word you're looking for is "mag-ical".' I smile, but magical isn't the word I want. Get dropped in here alone without technology or food, and any magic would dissolve in minutes. The word I keep returning to is 'indifferent'.

Only the sandflies are not indifferent. They're delighted. Sandflies drink blood. They dig a snout into your flesh and they suck. If you tauten the skin to pin the snout in place, they suck until they explode. Otherwise they offer little entertainment and abundant annoyance. They are the bane of the West Coast. These are the first I've seen on the trip. (In the interests of entomological accuracy, I should add that it is only the adult females that are the bloodsuckers, a fact about which I propose to make no further comment.)

On the way back, the Americans and I have to disembark and clamber along the rocks of the bank so that Jonathan can steer a perilous rapid unencumbered. He does it standing up. It's a pure New Zealand image – the lone man in the wilderness in a homespun sweater and using homespun technology. Were he to hole the boat it would be a hard day's walking to get out of there. He doesn't hole the boat. Half an hour later we're hooking it back on to the Land Rover, or rather Jim, Jim, Drew and Jonathan are. In our wake the waters settle swiftly and the silence surges in to fill the hole we tore in it. There are only a couple of hours of daylight left and 150 kilometres of barren mountain pass between me and the West Coast, so I accept a lift back to Wanaka for the night.

An early evening stroll reveals a township that's booming in the wilderness. Wanaka's got an organic restaurant and a shop selling the sort of sleek retro furniture that appeared in Martini ads in the fifties.

A three-bedroom house is for sale near my motel. It has a lovely view of the lake for anyone prepared to stand on the roof. For the price they are asking, I calculate that I could rent my motel room for thirty years, with a weekly change of sheets and eleven thousand full cooked breakfasts.

In, oh dear, the Irish pub, an old man next to me at the bar in, oh dear, a green hat, asks after ten minutes of drinking side by side in silence, whether I'm a tourist.

'Yes, I am.'

'Well did you know there's an island in the middle of Lake Wanaka? On that island there's a lake with an island in it. So that island,' and here he gathers himself like a man preparing to dive and his forehead wrinkles with concentration, 'that island is in the middle of a lake, in the middle of an island in the middle of a lake in the middle of an island in the middle of a lake in the middle of an island in the middle of the Pacific Ocean.'

'Wasn't that,' I say, while careful to smile my appreciation of the conceit, 'one too many lakes and islands?'

'No,' he says and we resume our silent separation. I think of five contrite ways to restart conversation, but even as I turn towards him with the words prepared, I am deterred by the hat and by his worryingly wet lips.

This fake Irish pub is very much the real thing. It's authentically inauthentic, like an impersonator faultlessly impersonating an impersonator. There are sepia photos of bearded grandfathers in waistcoats operating breweries (and you just know the bearded ones pronounced waistcoat 'wisket'), a placard announcing that work is the curse of the drinking classes, several two-metre double-ended saws, something in copper that may be a still, and in a locked glass cabinet a 'My Goodness My Guinness' postcard is propped against a leatherbound *Poetical Works of Gray, Blair, Beattie, Collins, Thomson and Kirke White*. Neither Gray nor Collins nor Thomson were Irish, and Blair, Beattie and Kirke White belong to the land of literary oblivion, but none of that matters. The book is not a book. It's just a thing, an old thing in a young place. There must be someone making a living by importing containerloads of stuff like this, containerloads of age.

The barmaid's just back from her O.E., much of it spent in London where Turks and Greeks ogled her and called her their beautiful one.

'The English are lazy,' she says. 'They all want to be in the pub by two. And the service is dreadful.' But she says she had a good time. What drew her home eventually was a longing for space and wide skies and less hurry. One phrase, she says, sums up New Zealand: 'she'll be right, mate.'

And it's tempting to see truth in her remark. The ubiquitous 'mate' reflects a sense of equality among men. As is always likely to happen in a newly-occupied land, Jack learned to feel that he was as good as his master because both Jack and master were battling that land together. One cannot imagine any New Zealander addressing another as guv'nor. And 'she'll be right' catches a certain cheerful optimism, a refusal to be daunted by adversity, a make-do practicality and a trust in fate, qualities that characterise the best of rural New Zealand.

Those same qualities prevail in the barmaid's good-humoured manner, her lack of either servility or surliness. And they're there too in the huge-handed, generous Jonathan, standing up to steer his jet-boat through a wilderness.

I dine on a seafood pizza, knowing even as I choose it that it will taste only of cheese. It comes with sagging garlic bread and approximately 2 kilograms of chips, and it tastes of brine and virulent hollandaise sauce. And cheese.

10
Wanaka Wordsworth

There's a gumtree outside my motel room. It smells of throat lozenges. At six in the morning it seethes with sparrows, like a dormitory of squabbling schoolgirls. Somewhere behind them I can hear the impossibly pure fluting of a bellbird. There's a shred of mussel stuck in my teeth. When I explore it with my tongue it tangs faintly of hollandaise sauce.

A hole has worn in the corner of my packet of toothpicks, so that I have only to tap the packet and a single stick of quality Chinese birch slides into my palm and is ready for fun. I go outside to attack the mussel amid scenery. Wisps of mist swirl above the lake, and the lower slopes of the mountains are wearing fluffy underskirts of cloud. Above them, in the early sun, the snow looks impossibly smooth and dense, like the icing on a wedding cake. I shift the shred of mussel at the first flick of the birch. It's going to be a good day.

I'm away by eight, and for the first time on the trip I'm wearing only a T-shirt. Opposite the motel a mane-haired youth is hitching and smoking. As a car approaches he crooks his smoking hand behind his back and I feel a sort of inner chuckle at the slight deception, a band-of-brothers fellowship. I cross the road. He's German, taut with youth, buoyant as a cork, and hoping to get to Te Anau. I feel youngish by association. I wish him well and mean it.

On the half-hour walk out of town the turf of the verge feels springy underfoot, and my bag is packed with thistledown – the variety of thistledown that gains weight steadily over the course of a half-hour walk.

I pass Puzzling World, an attraction that toys with your senses like an Escher etching – houses built at angles, water flowing uphill, that sort of thing. In the pub last night I was told that its most popular exhibit is a mock Roman lavatory. Apparently, amid some of the world's most startling scenery, people like to be photographed on a communal bench pretending to shit.

I return to the junction where Jonathan picked me up yesterday. The freshly decapitated rabbit remains decapitated but its colours are less fresh, and the area it covers has trebled. But it's a superb place to hitch. Drivers can see me well ahead of reaching me and are obliged to slow to take the turn. The gravel layby I am standing in invites them just to add a touch more pressure to the brake and pull over at my feet. My position just beyond the junction shows emphatically the route

I wish to take and the fact I'm a mile or more from town asserts that I am no mere bludger, but rather a bona fide traveller. I can't go wrong. The hairs on my hitching arm gleam in the fresh-peeled sunlight like golden gossamer.

The driver of the first car past, a ute with a lawn-mower careening across the flatbed as he takes the corner, smiles at me and signals that he's turning off. I open my hitching palm to wave my recognition of his message and my thanks. The second car past does the same and again I acknowledge it. I feel like a vicar, this stretch of road my parish. I offer well-intentioned drivers the open palm of absolution.

And more than that. I fancy I am adding to the sum of happiness. To those who acknowledge me, my palm says, 'Go in peace, I shall be fine.' And any driver who stops to pick me up, well, he plunges into the waters of chance and raises his chances of being murdered or robbed. But I murder or rob very few of my drivers, and when he finds that he hasn't been murdered or robbed, he knows a three-fold happiness: he has taken a risk and been rewarded with gratitude; he has found time pass a little quicker on his journey; and he has the satisfaction of having performed an act of charity. When we part, both of us are happier than when we met.

A girl cycles past me in a wet weather top and those black cycle shorts that are nuder than nudity. The Gortex panniers of her long-distance carbon-fibre bike are bulging with essential stuff. It's an earnest way to do the country. She is travelling at little more than walking speed. I give her a cheery good morning. Her grimace of endeavour transmutes into the happiest of smiles and a Teutonic greeting, and then, before she is quite past me, reverts to grimace.

A ute stops. The driver has a beard and a deck full of delirious dogs. He is going to Lake Hawea, some fifteen minutes up the road. Because I doubt that he will drop me in a place as good as the one I'm in, I turn him down. He looks a little miffed. Half an hour later I accept a lift to Lake Hawea.

My driver is a young man who mends computers, making his monthly trip to fix a hard drive. The old man who owns the machine routinely clogs it with pornography.

'It takes about an hour to clean it up. He spends the hour telling me how the Maoris are ruining the country.'

We overtake the German cyclist. In comparison with our modest speed she seems stationary. In comparison with the landscape, she seems puny.

My driver lives and works in Wanaka.

'Been here a few years now. Renting. Should have bought, of course, I'd have trebled my money. But that's hindsight for you. Great place to live though. I mean,' and he gestures out the window at the mountains, 'look at it.'

'Yeah,' I say. The guy seems affable and smart, and I feel disinclined to engage in conversation that is merely polite. 'It's spectacular, but doesn't that wear off? I mean, in the end, what good are pretty mountains? Surely you can't go on playing the tourist where you live.'

He turns to me with a bunched and quizzical smile, as if both surprised and pleased that in our brief acquaintance we are going to go beyond pleasantries. 'But,' he says, 'it's not a question of playing the tourist, as you put it. Look,' and here he pauses to search for a way to say something that is clearly there in his head, but wordless. 'Look, sometimes I come home from work and I've had a shitty day and I've got a head buzzing with shitty little worries and I go outside and I look at the mountains. And I think, shit, those fuckers have been there one fuck of a long time. And then I feel better.'

It's pure Wordsworth. Wordsworth might have put it more decorously, but he could hardly have put it more honestly. For whatever ancestral reasons, it pleases us to see scenery. But more importantly the wilderness puts us in our place. It lends perspective. And it is that need for perspective, however vaguely felt, however unworded or unacknowledged, that draws jumboloads of human beings here each year from their boiling urban worlds.

I'm sorry when the Wordsworth of Wanaka drops me at the turn-off to Hawea and drives away with a beep of his horn to spend his Saturday morning with some wizened Prince of Porn.

Hawea is the last settlement deserving of the name on this side of the Haast Pass. Sir Johann Franz Julius von Haast was a geologist, sent here in 1858 to look into the possibilities of German immigration. He surveyed much of the South Island, assisted in the building of the Lyttelton rail tunnel, sought mineral deposits in the back country, became a British citizen, founded a philosophical society and the Canterbury Museum, and, in adherence to pioneering first principles, grew a beard that could have provided burrows for half a dozen kiwis.

Von Haast was not the first person to cross this pass. An anonymous prospector for gold preceded him by several weeks, and several thousand Maori preceded the prospector by several hundred years, but when it came to naming rights the prospector counted for little and the Maori for less.

When I first came this way in 1987 in an aircraft-carrier-size Holden Belmont with two giggling Swedish girls in the back seat, the highest section of the road was still a rough and unsealed track. You did not want to break down there. I broke down there.

The first three cars along all stopped and men got out and called me mate and fiddled with the engine and crawled underneath the chassis on their backs while I stood by in grateful impotence. Years later, a woman told me that the sexiest sight she knew was a man in overalls bending over a radiator grille to mend her engine. When she said that, I thought of the Haast Pass.

The men duly got the Holden going again. I had no way of thanking them except thanking them. The Swedish girls thought it was a hoot. I hated them.

There's a breeze blowing off Lake Hawea. I pull on a sweater. My hitching spot is less than ideal. There's no layby here, only a couple of feet of roadside gravel and then a steep tumble of scree surmounted by scraggly bushes that I couldn't name. A few camper vans trundle past, and sometimes, horribly, a plush white fifty-seater tourist bus, monstrous up close, its tyres as tall as my chest, and hauling a swirl of gritty wind that makes me avert my face and scrunch my eyes. But most of the time there's nothing, nothing but the lake, the crumpled mass of mountains, and half a mile of road with nothing moving along it but the breeze.

I eat a banana and toss the skin. It lodges in a bush. I pick up a sharp-edged stone, weigh it, take careful aim and miss. I throw again and again. Sometimes the stone rebounds from the bank and skitters across the road. It takes ten minutes to dislodge the banana skin. I scramble up the slope, replace the skin in the bush, slide back down and resume throwing. There is little else to do, or to keep me warm in the wind that is starting to whip the lake into cream-crested wavelets and make the grass stems flatten and bob.

As a child I used to spend hours on Brighton's shingle beach bombarding bottles in the grey water. Each hit was a ringing satisfaction, and I had a good arm. Today I have a bad shoulder. I damaged it with my final effort in a cricket-ball throwing competition when I was twenty-something. I tore the rotator cuff, whatever that may be. I can still biff stones at banana skins, but not over any distance or with any power. And each night for the last twenty years I have had to lie on my left shoulder to go to sleep.

We all collect damage over the years, the legacy of battles with the world, and I am fond of several of my scars, which I have only to glimpse in the mirror to be reminded of the goodness of the past, but I regret this damaged shoulder. I loved to throw. Not being able to feels like a loss, an unmanning, a literal disarming.

I'm scrambling up to reattach the skin for the second time when a car appears. I slide down and stick out my thumb. The car stops, the window winds down and a woman leans across a small boy in the front seat. 'My son told me to stop. Would you like a chip?'

The boy thrusts out a paper cone of chips. The sudden reality of meeting has rendered him mute. I extract a drooping pallid chip, hold it theatrically above my mouth, wiggle it like a worm then eat it and say thank you.

'You're welcome,' says the woman and drives away. Safely distant once more the boy leans out of the window and smiles extravagantly and waves and squeals. 'Bye bye,' he squeals. 'Bye bye, Mr Man.' The word 'man' always jolts me. I see myself as a child.

The German girl cycles past me again, her laden front wheel wobbling a little as she drives it into the wind. We smile at each other for the second time. I can think of nothing to say.

When the banana skin is shredded beyond use I pick out a red rock and aim at that. The forefinger on my throwing hand becomes raw from the sharp rims of the stones, but after an hour the rock is pocked with direct hits, each one a good white scar. I stop throwing only when cars approach, hoisting my thumb into the wind and composing myself into what I hope is the look of a roadside statue of the virgin Mary, an image of neglected benevolence. Nothing stops. Nothing looks like stopping.

When, after three hours, a ute swings out from Hawea township, with a boiler and sheets of plywood lashed to its deck, and spouting strapped over the cab, it is so clearly local traffic that I merely smile at it. The ute stops. It's going all the way to Haast.

I share the passenger seat with a brindled Staffordshire terrier. She leans her panting weight against my thigh and dribbles on my jeans. Her owner tells me stories.

He's a bluff and affable ex-butcher whose name I never learn. His stories are bloke stories. The local term is yarns. Backblocks New Zealand is a land of yarns. He tells of fishing and drinking, of barbecuing oysters, of dancing naked under a waterfall to be photographed by a Japanese tour party, of breaking an ankle, of being bitten on the testicles by a mosquito. He points out to me the island where his Staffie dropped four puppies. An hour later, he says, she dropped two more here in the cab of this ute.

And all the while we are climbing to the pass. We overtake the German cyclist. Lake Hawea gives way to beech forest and then to cold wet bush that climbs sheer to either side. White and skinny waterfalls launch themselves from invisible heights. Rock falls carve swathes through the vegetation and end in vertical deltas of raw stones.

I fail to notice the apex of the pass, but suddenly the streams are flowing towards a different ocean, and the bonnet of the car is tilted away from us, and the pressure of the dog against my thigh diminishes a fraction. The driver's stories continue unabated. Nothing is asked of me but to coo with wonder as the stories take their twists, and to laugh at the neat irony of their conclusions.

When he drops me at the Haast River bridge after perhaps two hours of journey the only thing he knows of me is that my name is Joe and that I listen. And that's just fine by me. Repeatedly laying out one's biographical stall to driver after driver is one of the more tedious parts of hitching. When younger I used to entertain myself by lying. Once I pretended to be in the army. My driver told me that he had been in the army himself and he asked me what regiment I belonged to. I knew only one army regiment. It turned out that he knew it too. He named and asked after several members of it. It was an uncomfortable lift.

It's late Saturday afternoon. I'm pleased to have crossed the pass, an absurd and unjustified ghost of the feeling that old Johann Franz Julius must have felt when he first hacked his way through. The settlement named after him remains a mere hamlet, a last-chance petrol stop. Though it's the official start of the notorious West Coast, Haast lies a mile or two inland. A lane leads down to the beach and Jackson's Bay where Lucasta could see her penguins, and where the Tasman Sea thuds against the island's flank. Here on the only main road, a road that heads north for hundreds of miles with the Alps to its right and the Tasman to its left, there's a visitor centre, a pub, a garage, damp pasture, scrub, a sprawling hotel and a squat disconsolate horse. I hitch half-heartedly for a while but there's next to no traffic, and when the first flicks of rain sow smudges on the canvas of my bag, I give in.

The hotel rents me a room for $30. I go looking for it down corridors empty but for disconcerting piles of bedsheets and a smell that's been long in the brewing. The $30 room would turn a monk's thoughts to suicide. The stain down the face of the radiator is the colour of desperation. The bed is as narrow as Calvinism. The veneer of the wardrobe door, never better than tacky when installed, is now . . . I return to reception where the girl doesn't seem in the least surprised to see me again and rents me a $60 room in which the double bed has a counterpane of brothel velvet and the orange Formica that surrounds the sink has a slot in it for the disposal of the sort of murderous double-edged razor blades that I remember my father using in the sixties. But the room is big and light and there's a door of glass that slides quite nicely if you put your shoulder to it and opens onto a patio, where sit two white and puddled plastic chairs and an ashtray.

Sudden full-blooded rain sweeps in from the Tasman Sea, hitting the roof like flung gravel. I lie on the bed and listen to it. Rain on a low roof is a primitive cocoon of comfort, an aural image that goes back to the cave. It is best listened to in a taut and leakproof tent. A taut and leak-proof tent, incidentally, is a textbook example of a double oxymoron.

When I wake it's dark and the rain has stopped. In the bathroom there's a spider the size of a fifty-cent piece. I capture it using a glass labelled 'Your Clean Glass' and a copy of *The*

Mirror. Your Free Community Newspaper. Not wanting to flush the spider down the loo, I open the door, look left and right and toss the thing onto a pile of used sheets. Quite who used the sheets I don't know, since I have yet to see another guest.

The other guests are in the bar, a party of middle-aged men from Auckland on their way home from an annual wife-free fishing trip in Fiordland. They tell me stories of blue cod the size of subs, and of giant crayfish that compete to be caught.

The walls of the bar are lined with dead heads of deer and thar and chammy, the bar itself with live men and women in thigh-length bush shirts. They lean like a picket fence, their backs to the bar, their elbows on it, their jugs beside them, watching a Super 12 rugby game between the Wellington Hurricanes and an Australian team.

'Get your fucking shit together, Hurricanes,' shouts a woman with widely spaced teeth. She knows every player's name.

An Aussie scores a try. 'Double movement,' she screams, her face twisted with rage. 'That was a double fucking movement.' It wasn't a double fucking movement. It was a try.

'Fuck off,' screams the woman at the TV, at everything, at fate.

She reserves her richest abuse for 'the fucking Aussie ref', who is South African.

11

Up Ship Creek

In the hotel dining room there are thirty tables for the Auckland fishermen and me and five varieties of breakfast: continental, cooked, whitebait, pancakes and West Coast. A bracket explains that 'West Coast' means both continental and cooked. The fishermen are all having the West Coast.

Whitebait is the signature food of the West Coast. The fry of a few varieties of secretive swamp-dwelling native fish, white-bait come up the rivers in wriggling swarms. Good whitebaiting spots are handed down through families like heir-looms. During a whitebait run the banks are lined with people wielding white nets the size and shape of windsocks. They look as though they are engaged in slowly choreographed sem-aphore.

Whitebait are cooked in omelettes known as patties. Like the oysters of Bluff, West Coast whitebait are not so much a foodstuff as a symbol of a relationship with the land. Mention whitebait and everyone smacks their lips. Free to catch and fiercely expensive to buy, they're eaten whole – eyes, guts, and anal passages. They taste mildly of fish.

While I wait for my pancakes to be cooked by the heavily tattooed chef, I can only admire the décor. It is a shrine to the seventies, like a period exhibit in a museum. Exposed ceiling beams, brass chains leading down to chandeliers of chunky yellow glass, dark wooden panelling of vertical louvres, and on my table a single plastic rose.

It's Sunday. I've had many a bad Sunday hitching. Business takes a rest and recreation takes over. Recreation isn't bored or looking for company. And recreation isn't going far. As I dump my bag on a patch of gravel just before the bridge, I feel a sense of foreboding like a little nauseous twist in the stomach.

Overnight the squat disconsolate horse has gained a blue tarpaulin coat, which makes it seem squatter but no less dis-consolate. The front has passed through but the tattered remnants of it linger up the valleys to the east as fat and dirty fluff. And the next front is visible on the western horizon, gath-ering low and brownish somewhere between here and Tasmania. The place is smothered in the silence of a rural Sunday, all deep and green and purposeless. There is no traffic except for occasional camper vans that are as productive as ever. I could not claim to be hitching. I am standing by a road, aged forty-six.

The birds accept my static presence as part of the scenery. A pipit fossicks through the verge a few feet from my bag. I have time in abundance to study its constant bobbing, its eye stripe, its whitish belly, its quivering alertness. A heron flaps slow and grey towards the river, its neck furled for flight, its legs trailing like primrose streamers.

The river is browned and fattened by last night's rain. Swallows flit and swerve and wheel under the bridge supports, as if dodging bullets. The bridge carries the road in a single lane for perhaps half a mile, narrowing with distance to a mere black path, then takes a turn to the left and disappears into the green wall of bush, as if swallowed.

After perhaps an hour of fruitless waiting I follow it, though not to any purpose. The nearest habitation of any size is several days' walk away. I move only in order to move, to do something, to break the grip of the inane. It is easy to think here, as the sole self-conscious being in the heart of an instinctive world. The trees stay where they are, mindlessly growing. The insects and birds move only to feed or to flee. All of them are held in a loose web of interdependency, just going on going on. And I, clothed, frail, unlikely to survive two nights lost in the bush, the sole visible representative of the dominant species, the species that burns and bulldozes the bush to suit its needs and frailties, am here just passing through to somewhere else. As mortal and transitory as the smallest insect, as undistinguished as a single stem of grass, and yet divorced from their unchanging battle to survive by the ease of civilisation.

With a head like a Hardy poem, I cross the bridge, ambling because there is no reason to do more. As I near the far bank I hear the distant drone of an engine and turn to see a saloon car take the bend, then slow for the bridge and swing onto it. The car's a battered Fiat, a young person's car or a poor one's. Two heads in the windscreen.

The footpath across the bridge is merely a kerb. To pass me the car will have to brush my thumb. The occupants are young.

They are smiling. They are smiling at me. They are waving with ludicrous good cheer. And they continue to wave and smile and mouth something merry through the glass as they pass me, accelerate off the bridge, and turn the corner to be eaten by the green. The car's noise takes perhaps a minute to dwindle to the level of the bush's constant murmur. Mindlessness settles back in.

When I step off the bridge and into the bush the temperature drops two degrees. Tree-ferns like feathery umbrellas, lancewood, pittosporums, beech, a tall and tasselly tree that may be a larch of sorts, the constant drip of water, and, underneath it all, impenetrable undergrowth, stuff with winding leafless stems as thick as a finger that bind and choke. How the pioneers carved through this stuff I don't know. Two strides from the road and you're drenched, torn, ensnared. I piss on the verge for something to do. It steams.

My progress is pointless. The black tongue of asphalt spears through the bush in straight undulations. Released from the hairpins of the Haast Pass, drivers now can plant the foot and race north. Cars going fast rarely stop. When a truck passes me going the wrong way I watch the ripple of its wake on the bush, making the branches whisper underneath the engine roar, fluttering the fringes of innumerable ferns.

A fresh possum carcase in the gutter. I turn it over with my toe. It's stiff with death but the dense fur is as soft and deep as cottonwool. Its snout looks made of pink rubber.

Three late-model cars approach in convoy. Each bears a cargo of old women dressed for church. They study me with undisguised disdain – a middle-aged man in the heart of nowhere with a dirty bag. I realise I look fishy, a convict on the lam, a murderer perhaps, and even as I offer them my thumb I feel my warm smile of beggary twisting into a leer and I slide my other hand into a jacket pocket to finger the honed and gleaming blade. To my surprise, the women don't stop.

Native pigeons lilt and gurgle through the treetops, their

wingbeats whirring like ill-adjusted brakes on a pushbike. A tomtit perches close, with its lemon-yellow breast and its black hangman's hood. In search of sunlight and to escape this dank and gothic world and this racetrack of a road, I return to the bridge where a car stops immediately and I'm offered a lift 'as far as Ship Creek'. I have never heard of Ship Creek. I get in without hesitation.

My driver's as jolly as Falstaff and as fat, so fat that his seat is pushed back as far as it can go to allow his gut to slide past the steering wheel. But wheel and gut are still so firmly wedged together that he can steer without hands. And he does, nudging us left or right with a twitch of the belly.

Born on the coast he's spent most of his life here. He's off now to meet a helicopter that will take him and some mates into the mountains for a week of deer-stalking. It seems unlikely that this man would succeed in stalking anything that wasn't deaf or crippled. But deer-stalking doesn't mean stalking deer. It means shooting them.

Falstaff works in an unspecified capacity in some hotel on the coast. I ask how tourism's going.

'Booming,' he says, 'but those Japs, they're dirty little bastards. Shit in the shower, they do. The girls hate cleaning up after them. I used to have this contract cleaning out the DOC toilets up the road there at the Point. I was up there one morning with the water blaster going and the earmuffs on and this Jap guy who's just got off a bus, he taps me on the shoulder and says, "We use?" "Hang on," I says, "just wait two minutes and they're yours." Well I keep going a bit, then I finish and go round the back and there's all these little Jap bastards lined up against the wall having a shit. Well, I'll tell you, I didn't hold back. I just pointed the water blaster and had a right fucking go at them. Shit, it was funny. Japs running everywhere there was, with their grundies round their ankles. I just couldn't stop laughing.' He's laughing again as he tells the story, a full Falstaffian belly laugh. The car nudges left or right with each gust of laughter. 'But those Japs, they're dirty little bastards.'

Ship Creek is a spot on the highway. It consists of a creek, which means a stream, and no ship. If there ever was a ship, it moored here a century or two ago, had a quick scout round, found lots of bush, nothing else, and left. But I don't look likely to leave any time soon.

I throw stones. I dance on the spot. I spend a while staring into the red-tinged water of the creek, I throw more stones, I dance on the spot, I try singing to the bush but it feels odd, I ransack my head for good memories of people, and then I devote an hour or more to the mental composition of the opening verses of what I am confident is the world's first epic poem on the subject of camper van drivers and extravagant sexual violation. None of it helps much.

Four hours later the bush is still there and so am I. The only mercy is that the sandflies aren't. The storyteller who drove me over the pass yesterday told me that sandflies can't fly if the wind exceeds 5 kph. I didn't believe him. But it seems that he may have been right. If he came round the bend now I would apologise for doubting him. He doesn't come round the bend. Nothing does.

It's two in the afternoon. I estimate that I am 20 kilometres north of Haast. On my crude brochure map that advertises a chain of motels, there is no settlement marked to the north for perhaps 100 kilometres. And that settlement is Harihari. I've seen Harihari. It's no metropolis. Indeed, it may be the only place in the world to be named after both its inhabitants. I pick up my bag and set off south towards Haast down the long green tunnel of bush, reciting my camper van epic in time with my footsteps. The rhythm of walking is good for metrical composition. I add several splendid verses. Then I get a lift from a camper van going north.

I don't hitch at it. It just pulls over. The driver's wearing a tie and a cardigan. As I climb in he hands me a small blackened banana and takes one for himself. I've eaten mine by the time he's unpeeled his. His every movement is laboured and deliberate. He chews as if making a series of unconnected conscious decisions to move his jaws. We remain stationary beside the road, him slowly chewing, me holding my banana skin on my lap. I don't mind. I am revelling in the soft cloth of the seat, the windlessness of the cabin, cherishing even the grey plastic mouldings of the dashboard, and in particular surprising myself with my delight simply to be back in human company.

The man is well over seventy, a Londoner from White City with an accent every bit as London as you would expect from one of eight offspring of a roadsweeper. The roadsweeper gambled and drank and beat his wife. 'I ain't been into a betting shop yet,' says my ancient driver as he starts the engine in this wilderness as far from White City as it is possible to be, 'and I ain't gonna start now.'

The van has five gears. They're marked on the head of the gear lever. He never finds fifth. Often he aims for fourth and hits second, thrusting us against seat belts, the engine squealing up the octaves. I find myself wincing and bracing at every bend, anticipating the next random thrash through the gearbox.

He spent his working life as a costermonger. He actually uses the word. He's got no kids and his wife's dead. So's his brother, who used to live in New Zealand and was the reason my driver first came here. He's now on his fifteenth trip. He rents a camper van and follows an unvarying route round the Returned Service Associations of the country.

'Every year I think I might go somewhere else, but they speak English here and they drive on the left. And most of the people are halfway decent at least, better than back home. England's changed for the worse. All them darkies. By the time I get back, Blair'll have invited another load of Iraqis over. But they won't be living next door to him, that's for sure. It's a bloody mess.'

The war was the event of his life. It provides him with 100 kilometres or more of stories. He fought in Italy.

'Served with a lot of Kiwis. They were all big blokes. I had a lot of trouble with my feet. Have done all my life.'

He is wearing black surgical shoes the size of loaves. When we stop to check the cause of untoward noises in the back of the van, he takes an age to lower himself from the cab and then walks with a laboured gait, as if wading upstream. He wrestles with the lock on the van, then struggles to haul himself up the step. A bag of apples has come loose. He hands me one through the door. 'These are all right. Not too tough. I bought a ten-kilo bag of apples in Gore but I couldn't get my teeth through the skin.' He pronounces teeth 'teef'. 'Had to give them away in the end, I did. Same as the sugar. Couldn't buy less than two kilos of sugar, but I've only got a five-hundred-gramme container. Gave the rest to some Dutchies.'

We pass through Harihari. He interrupts a story of the Pay Corps in Monte Cassino to say, 'Nice place, New Zealand, but some of the towns, well, you'd find more life in a cemetery. And some of the tourist places, they've got greedy. They didn't use to be. I don't mind paying, don't get me wrong, but I don't like being stitched up. Happened last night. I like a bit of steak, chips and a salad, nothing fancy, but I got stitched up thirty dollars for a steak in Wanaka. Thirty dollars. That's taking advantage, that is. But I know this place in Franz Josef, does a nice steak, reasonable like.'

It's late afternoon when he drops me opposite the Franz Josef motor camp. My thanks seem inadequate recompense for saving me from a 20-kilometre hike back to Haast, for an elderly banana and a soft apple, and for a startling confirmation of a truth that many have observed, that there is nothing so strange as the ordinary.

It's with surprising joy that I rent a motel room and dump my bag. The motelier is so affable and garrulous, so keen to ask and tell me things, that I fear I won't get away before dark, but eventually I am bounding out of town, over the ramshackle bridge of planking that carries both road and rail on the same single lane, then left up a gravel road into the foothills in order to stand face to face with the blunt end of the reason that Franz Josef exists. I'm going to see a glacier.

The light is dimming. I walk fast, delighted to have a purpose and no bag. Near the top of the road into the hills, an empty bus draws alongside me and the doors whoosh open.

'Joe.'

The face of a kid I used to teach beams from the driver's seat. A kid no longer, he is hugely tall, his hands on the roundabout-sized steering wheel are twice the size of mine. But he retains the open, guileless grin that made him an endearing pupil. Nevertheless I can't remember his name.

'Hamish,' he says and he gives me a lift. By the time he's driven me the last quarter of a mile to the glacier car park, we've arranged to eat and drink in a few hours time at a place called the Blue Something.

That I keep bumping into former pupils is beginning to test my belief that the world is a random place. But a bit of arithmetic resolves the matter. I taught here for ten years. The school took a hundred new pupils each year. So I know over a thousand kids. In the South Island there are a million people, therefore I taught one in every thousand. Since I've been on the road, at least fifty thousand people must have driven past me, and I must have walked past I don't know how many thousand in the streets. Which means then that I'm not the victim of spooky coincidence, but rather that at least forty former pupils must have ducked below dashboards or scuttled up alleyways to avoid me. They know who they are and will report to my study.

All of which helps to explain why young New Zealanders like to go abroad.

'The well-prepared visitor has alert eyes to see hazard signs and rope barriers; and is well-informed with the knowledge to

stay out of closed, roped-off areas.' The text of this sign is decorated with illustrations showing what an alert-eyed and
well-informed visitor looks like. The people who are now dribbling down the paths away from the glacier don't look
alert-eyed or well-informed. They look tired and morose. The
back markers in a straggling gaggle of schoolchildren look
dangerously fractious.

A path winds through scrub then is blocked by a rope.
Before me a valley of scree, the rocks the size of suitcases. A
grubby grey stream of snow-melt chunters down it. Half a mile
up, compressed in a gorge between gaunt mountains, stands
the snout of the glacier. It's a dirty wall of crumbling ice, perhaps 100 feet tall. Safely positioned with my well-informed
hands resting on the rope barrier I stare at it, then I read the
explanatory notices, then I stare at it again.

We did glaciers at school. I found them more memorable
than the exports of the Yangtse Basin. I got good marks for
labelling cwms and corries, arrets and mounds of terminal
moraine. I can't see any of these.

The valley of scree is sprinkled with the figures of unalert,
uninformed tourists, every one of whom has ducked under the
rope barrier for a closer view. I join them. A guided group
trudges past me in neon safety vests. Each carries an ice-pick.
The guide wears a skein of rope and is alone in looking mod-
erately cheerful.

A family of Indians picks its way over the rocks in inadequate urban footwear. Though I read recently that India has
more millionaires than New Zealand has people, I am always
surprised to see Indian tourists. I picture Indians as cricketers,
shopkeepers, bicycle riders, beggars in dhotis, or scrawny mys-
tics with foot-long fingernails, but not as air travellers or seers
of sights. This lot look as though they would rather be growing
their fingernails.

But I am not yet laden with the full glacier experience. I
boulder-hop up the valley floor until I am standing within fifty

feet or so of the face. The ice radiates cold. Streams gush from its crevices. Those molecules of water fell as mountain snow any number of years back, got compressed and absorbed, have spent all my lifetime and more making the grinding journey down the valley at the heart of this monstrosity, and now and now and now are being released by the billion to return to the sea. Apparently the glacier used to stretch to the township, but has receded more than a mile in the last fifty years. Whether that is cyclical or the effect of climate change, no one seems to know.

It draws people from all parts of the globe. It's a must-see of the South Island. 'Today we saw the glacier' runs the line on a thousand postcards a day in a hundred languages, and like so many things it is more dramatic as words than it is as a deed. When the postcard lands on the mat in London, Tokyo or Delhi, it bespeaks geographical wonder, the lure of elsewhere, like the elaborate traveller's tales with which Othello softened Desdemona's homely heart. Othello spoke of Anthropothagi and 'the men whose heads do grow beneath their shoulders'. I've never quite managed to picture the men whose heads do grow beneath their shoulders, but I expect they were just as dirty as the wall of ice in front of me.

The glacier looks, well, rather as one would expect a wall of dirty ice to look. But to be there, to stare at it, to feel it radiating coldness, to watch an ancient chunk crash from its face and shatter on the rocks, validates a day of holiday. Today I saw the glacier and now I can go eat and drink with a sense of duty done.

It's dusk and the lights and warmth and company of the hotels and the bars and the restaurants of little Franz Josef are hauling me and all the other tourists off the mountains and out of the bush, sucking us back like a vast flock of starlings, wheeling in from everywhere to roost with massive chattering in town.

In dimming light I run leaping down the scree, accelerating,

deciding only in mid-air where I will plant a foot, confident of
my dexterity, and keen for a beer. I am better at beer than at
sightseeing.

It's eight or more years since I taught Hamish. In the Blue
Something over pizza and lager he recounts those years.
They're crammed with unique, but typical, detail.

After school Hamish became a ski-bum in Queenstown, then
worked on a gold mine in remotest West Australia, did a
Management and Marketing degree in Dunedin, didn't want to
manage or market, taught English in Korea for a year or two,
spent time meandering through Thailand, Cambodia, Laos,
Vietnam, then felt the tug of home, the lure of the rich green
hills and the comfortable distance between people, flew back,
pulled on his leggings and became a glacier guide.

'Want a free guided tour tomorrow? I can slip you into one
of the parties.'

'Thanks,' I say, 'but no thanks.'

'Why not?'

'Sorry, but I hate guided tours. I've never been on one, of
course, but I know exactly what they're like, the safety lecture,
the ill-fitting gear I'll be obliged to wear, the fat guy who lags at
the back, the ex-schoolteacher type who's scrawny fit and who
stays close to the guide to ask earnest questions, the guide's
repertoire of stock jokes, the packed lunch with the ham, lettuce
and boiled-egg roll wrapped in clingfilm, and as for the glacier
itself, well there'll be informative stuff about Alpine faultlines
that the schoolmaster-type will listen to critically with his head
cocked, and there'll be crevasses and ice caves and ice tunnels,
all of which will look exactly as you would expect them to
look, and frankly when you've seen one you've seen them all,
and by halfway through the tour everyone will be wanting it to
end, indeed would pay money to get out of it right now, but it's
a bit like a church service in that it simply has to run its allotted
course however dull it may be, because that's the deal, that's
how it's done. And when it does finally stop, everyone scatters

instantly to the comfort of bars and shops, except for the schoolteacher type who hangs around to say he found it really interesting but he'd just like to clarify a couple of points, even though his quiet and plain-looking wife is clearly both embarrassed and very keen to establish as wide as possible a gap between herself and her present situation.'

'I see,' says Hamish, grinning in the beguiling guileless way of his that made him good to teach, 'so we'll have another beer, shall we?'

12

Vinously underelevated

Franz Josef was named by von Haast. Having got the pass for himself, he gave the glacier to the Emperor of his native Austria.

It's dawn, and the roofs of Franz Josef are frosted white, the mountains to the east silhouetted against a bleaching sky. A single bellbird pipes. There should be a CD of bellbirds –

although, now that I think about it, I bet there already is, which puts me off the idea. But the assorted songs of the bellbird, none of which sounds remotely like a bell, are all of such ineffable purity and unlike any bird song I have heard anywhere else in the world, as if the little beast were trilling an achingly exquisite lament for a lost Eden, that some travel writers have been known to go just a little over the top.

The air is cold enough to cloud my breath. A scrappy weatherboard bungalow squats behind the township, half smothered by the bush. White woodsmoke rises thin from its chimney – the authentic pioneer image, unchanged in a century and a half.

On the brief main street the businesses are stirring: the Okarito White Heron Experience, the Ultimate Amphibious Off-Road Experience, the Most Incredible Glacier Experience. Few words in the language are as misused as 'experience'. One of these words is 'ultimate'. Another is 'incredible'. Incredible means ultimate. And both mean readily credible. Experience, meanwhile, means almost nothing.

Down the road in tiny Okarito, where the rare white herons roost and serve up an experience to anyone who pays, there also roosts New Zealand's only winner of the Booker Prize. Keri Hulme describes herself as writer and whitebaiter. I've met her. She's chubby and cheerful and I liked her. I've even read a third of her novel, *The Bone People*, which for me and a Booker Prize-winner is an unusually protracted relationship. In the best traditions, the novel was turned down by several New Zealand publishers, apparently because the author refused to allow it to be edited, before being accepted by a women's collective and rising to international prominence.

New Zealand's literature reflects its history. For the first 100 years or so it lived in the literary shadow of Great Britain. Its poets warbled about crystal morns and sylvan scenes. And it was almost automatic for anyone with the urge to write, or, for that matter, to paint, to go to the far side of the globe and stay there. Katherine Mansfield is the best known of these, but there were many others.

It was only when the brave and queer short-story writer Frank Sargeson resolved to stay in Takapuna and to write New Zealand literature for New Zealand in New Zealand – and, incidentally, gave Janet Frame a bed in his garden shed – that local literature began to flourish locally. But even though there are more bookshops per capita in New Zealand than in most European countries, publishing here remains a precarious business, largely because there are so few actual capita. The only sure way to make money is to publish biographies of All Blacks or books like *Your Guide to Ultimate Incredible Outdoor Experiences*.

At the back of Franz Josef's Cheeky Kea restaurant a scruffy chef is frying bacon for a clientele that has yet to arrive. A girl lodges a freestanding sign on the pavement. 'Crampons', it says. I buy a paper and cigarettes from the garage. The proprietor asks me where I'm from. I ask him to guess.

'Well,' he says, 'I knew when you walked in you couldn't be German. The Germans are uptight. Not like Kiwis. We're laid back, easy-going. Me, I've changed career three times – lineman, kayak instructor, now this. You go with the flow. We don't get uptight like the Germans do if a bus is fifteen minutes late.'

'But,' says his wife, 'you never travel by bus.'

She laughs. He looks at her with momentary resentment, then laughs himself. 'Fair point,' he says.

As I leave the forecourt, three tour-bus engines simultaneously kick into life, and the first helicopter of the morning rises like a giant wasp against a Ming-blue sky, its rotors pulsing a drumbeat. The daily migration to the glacier has begun.

Outside the motel room next to mine sit three Australian sisters. They drove up yesterday from Queenstown. 'Very beautiful here. Lovely scenery. In Queenstown it snowed.'

Two of the sisters are smoking. Two of them are fat. One of

them is both. And she turns out to be both good fun, and the wife of the man who is driving the three of them around New Zealand. He's built like a tentpole and less good fun.

'Haven't I seen you somewhere before?' asks the wife.

'You may have seen me hitching by the road.'

'Jeez,' she exclaims, throwing more e's than I have into the exclamation. 'That's right. We drove past you all right. See him, Beth? He's the crim on the run, remember.' Her peal of rapturous laughter degenerates into such a deep and gurgling cough that Beth has to beat her on the back.

I feel rather flattered. We sit a while and smoke and talk about Australia, and as the sun comes over the mountains we watch the frost recede from the roofs like a slowly withdrawn tablecloth. And I realise with a little jolt of anticipatory happiness that it is Monday, and that there will be traffic. People will be going about their business, doing what they need to do to live, and I will be swanning, going where I wish at the pace that I wish, and exploiting their goodwill to travel for free. I feel no guilt whatsoever. Back in my room as I'm getting ready to leave, not even the marble-finish Formica in the bathroom can diminish my good mood, nor yet the shower with the pressure of a pensioner's bladder.

And hitching proves a breeze. Within minutes I'm in the back of a car fronted by a Canadian couple who are a blueprint for goodness. They are father and son, aged perhaps sixty and thirty. Both are intelligent professional men, prosperous but modest. They have maturely crossed the gap between the generations, stamped out the psychological fires of family, and occupied the common ground of friendship.

Having promised themselves this trip for years, they have not been disappointed. They've found the people warm, the scenery a constant source of admiration. They ask me questions about me and take a sincere interest in my answers. If the world were composed entirely of their kind it would be clean, peaceable, stable, fair and boring. I'm sorry.

The only vigorous moment in our conversation arrives when I say that I have had enough of bush.

'But it's beautiful,' says the father, and he gestures at the postcard framed in the windscreen.

'For a short while, yes,' I say, wondering whether I should follow this line or not. I am after all a guest in their car and I have sensed a hint of hackles rising. But these are mature intelligent professional men. I go on. 'But bush is eye-candy, and only from a distance. Close up it's cold, wet, impenetrable and inimical. That's why men have burned it down.'

But we don't argue. The subject changes. Any hint of conflict is ironed over by the tacit agreement of both sides. We are civilised people.

When we reach Hokitika I civilly offer to buy them coffee and to my surprise they civilly accept. Fifteen civil minutes later I am pleased to thank them, wave goodbye and be alone again.

In 1864 the town of Hokitika was made of canvas. By 1866 it had 6000 residents, a street of hotels, and a Casino de Venice. In that year 43 per cent of all the immigrants to New Zealand landed here. One third of those immigrants were Irish, the rest Chinese, Scots, Australians and Americans. What drew them was gold. In 1866, 15 tonnes of the stuff was hacked and sifted from the hills and rivers behind the town.

When the gold ran out, so did most of the immigrants. Those that stayed became Coasters. The baker in Hokitika, from whom I buy an apple turnover in a brown paper bag, is a Coaster of several generations' standing. The Coast, he says, is just one skinny village. He knows people in Haast and he knows people in Westport, the distance between Haast and Westport being greater, as he points out, than between Auckland and Wellington.

I bite into the turnover. Pastry and icing sugar fly. Without breaking his sociological analysis he passes me a bigger bag to hold beneath my chin.

'We're a bunch of mongrels, really,' he says, and his word reminds me of the things I was told about the coast by drivers on the other side of the mountains. I remember 'feral'. I remember talk of missionary work. 'Me,' says the baker, 'I've got Irish in me, and Scots and Jew and I don't know what else.'

The turnover is too generously filled. I drop sweet gobs of apple on my sleeve, on the floor. Still without pausing the baker reaches behind him and hands me a damp cloth and a plastic tray to use like a bib.

'It's always been a working place. The Labour Party started here on the Coast. But industry's pretty well dried up these days. The place is changing. Tourism's big, of course, but we get a long wet winter and the tourists go south to the snow.'

I hand back the tray, buy a steak and cheese pie and take it down an alleyway to the beach. The beach runs parallel to the main street. Though it's masked by the squat commercial buildings the sea is constantly audible in Hokitika, a muted beat of crashing water.

The beach is stark. Waves the colour of dishwater pound the sand, receding to leave a scum of soiled froth that gasps and subsides like a spent fish. The sea has thrown whole trees up onto the sand, trees from which it's stripped every shred of bark and then polished the timber to a silver-grey smoothness.

Dogs abound, seemingly ownerless. I play throw-and-chase with a terrier of sorts, good-natured as the baker and ugly as the water. A black-and-white beast, a lab/spaniel/pointer cross perhaps, hangs around as I eat my pie, catches a scrap of pastry in mid-air, misses another one, goes foraging for it among spear grass, and surprises a cat. The cat becomes a hissing arch of porcupine. The dog yelps, whips its tail between its legs, runs to me for succour and we become friends.

Together we wander down to the Hokitika River, where the estuary is half-closed by a spit so that the sailing ships of old had to come in broadside to the breakers. Between 1865 and

1867 there was a grounding or a collision or a wreck every ten days. Men died here.

In commemoration, the Hokitika heritage people have built a crude concrete schooner on the point, with picnic tables on the deck. It's a parody boat, but the only one now at the wharf. It lies beached beside well-mown lawns and a little road with dirty puddles for the dog to drink from.

I turn back into the township and the dog just stands and watches me go, as if the beach were his territory, the streets mine.

It's hard to imagine what the place was like in the gold rush. The general stores and chandler's shops and assay offices have long since gone. Revell Street held fifty-five hotels. The lot burned down. Now there are shops selling pretty things, a café with 'one of New Zealand's largest teapot collections', and a dentist called Charles Dickens.

In the aquarium the fish are mainly unspectacularly local. I like them that way. Tropical gaudiness does nothing for me. I press my face to the glass to meet wrasse and groper eye to eye, and I spend a while gawping at what may be the world's biggest whitebait, a short-jawed kokupu aged twenty or so. It hangs immobile in its tank, so plain and unremarkable that it's remarkable, like a generic illustration of a fish in a child's encyclopaedia.

Most of the eels are sleeping, which I didn't know they did. They lie draped over rocks and ledges and each other, their faces as expressionless as ever, their bodies swaying slightly with the water, like malicious seaweed. Apparently they go all the way to Tonga to mate, but then so do quite a lot of tourists.

Few Maori lived on the coast but for centuries they travelled here from as far as the far north to collect greenstone. Greenstone was their metal. Hard, dense and heavy, it could be fashioned into axes, weapons, items of ceremony. Then, in a typically cracking deal, a local tribe sold the entire coast to the white man for three hundred pounds.

Greenstone is a form of jade. It's big business here now. 'Touch these beautiful pieces of nephrite jade,' says a sign in a carvery window, 'and consider the intense forces that created them . . . This modest circular disc symbolises the universe on its outer rim. While the whole in the middle is representative of you, encompassed by the universe.'

Nearby is 'Literacy Westland'. A shame it's not next door.

A plumber's van is parked outside, the driver unloading plastic piping and explaining to his boss the state of a job he's just come from.

'She's fucked, mate.'

'How do you mean fucked?'

'Fucked as in fucked, mate, rooted.'

'These stones,' continues the notice, 'are one of the great products of nature... which has given jade qualities denied to other rocks. Jade is said to strengthen heart, kidneys, and the immune system. It helps to clean blood, increase longevity and dispel negativity . . . We must learn to love and respect our great oneness.'

A bumper sticker on a four-wheel-drive across the road reads, 'Don't like my driving? Email me @gofuckyourself.com.' I wonder whether our great oneness isn't still a year or two off.

In the visitors' book at the museum, Simona and Jan from Germany have written 'New Zealand are beautiful.'

The museum's a pleasure, small enough to absorb as a whole, and drenched with a rich yesterday of wiskets, beards, sailing ships and Wild West recklessness. On 31 August 1865, E. Mallard, Charles Brookes and Charles Cuiped were charged with being 'in a state of vinous elevation, totally inconsistent with their own wellbeing and the public peace'. Good to know that the law was as pompous then as now.

Before I go in search of a little vinous elevation myself, I've got glow-worms to visit. There's a cave apparently full of them just across the road from my motel. I while away the hours until darkness with dogs on the beach, though as the sun lowers into the froth of clouds on the horizon and the light thickens, they disappear as one, padding off home as if summoned by a single whistle.

At the entrance to the glow-worm cave, a sign suggests you grasp the handrail and let it guide you. With typical smugness I stride up the path, take a turn to the right and plunge into utter lightlessness. I grope for the handrail and inch my way along it. Being blind heightens my other senses. I can hear breathing. I follow the curve of the rail and I make out the shape of a woman silhouetted against a bank of glow-worms. I don't know if she knows I am there. I don't want to frighten her. 'Hello,' I say.

When she stops screaming we study the glow-worms together. Or at least we look at them. There's not much else to do with glow-worms.

'They're pretty,' she says, and they are. They dangle from a dank and mossy overhang of rock. Thick bush blocks out all light from the nocturnal sky and the worms form dainty chains of little sparkling gleams. To the human eye they're fairy lights.

But whether fairy, dainty, pretty, or, in Te Anau, magical are the adjectives one should apply to larvae whose excretory organs extrude a sticky phosphorescent substance with the purpose of attracting other insects to a slow death, I shall leave to you.

Emerging from the grotto with pupils widened by lightlessness, I note that Hokitika's good for stars. Actually, New Zealand's good for stars. The sparse human population means a lack of interfering light. Lie on your back at midnight in the Mackenzie and as your eyes relax you can see stars forming behind other stars, and more behind them. It's like looking through a microscope at the self-replication of bacteria, not that I've ever done much of that. It was Sylvia Plath, I think, who compared stars to full stops in a carbon paper. Here above Hokitika there's more punctuation than carbon.

There's no lack of pubs either, unsurprisingly perhaps, given the place's Irish and masculine heritage.

John welcomes me as I walk into the bar. He was raised on the coast, went away for a while but now is back for good. 'Coasters are friendly,' he says, 'and if you can't make friends what can you do?' As a young man he culled deer in the mountains for the government. He was paid by the tail. 'Six weeks at a stretch under canvas, then four days on the piss in town. A young man couldn't wish for a better life.' Or a more typically West Coast one. Or a more feral one.

Recently, at the age of sixty something, he visited Milford Sound for the first time. Kipling called Milford Sound the eighth wonder of the world. I ask John how he found it.

'All right, I suppose,' he says. 'But mate, if I want to see mountains I can look out my back window. And if I want to see the sea I can look out the front.'

And if Kipling were to roll into the pub now and start an argument, I'd side with John.

John worked at the butter factory down the road for a while, 'Just general labouring, you know, shifting stuff. Then I had a heart attack.' He interrupts himself to order a jug of Monteith's, the indigenous West Coast beer. By being brewed on the coast it is the marketer's dream. Its origin confers on it by association a rugged masculinity and pioneering strength, the connotations that sell beer to men in cities. Indeed in recent years Monteith's has become so popular that they now brew it in Auckland.

'The old days of industry on the coast have gone,' says John. 'There's just a bit of mining left, moss and tourism.'

Moss is the sphagnum moss that grows wild in the swamps. Antiseptic and absorbent, it was used during the Boer War to make bandages. Today, apparently, it goes into sanitary pads.

John is a product of his time and of this place. But the times are changing and so is the place. Nowhere in the country is the transition from old to new more marked than here. Separated by the Alps from the rest of the country, the coast has retained the tang of an older New Zealand. It has always been a man's place, a place of hunting and drinking and of hard physical work. But the industries that kept it going are all extractive industries, the industries that scar and exploit the land. Yesterday's industries.

Because of its big terrain and small population, the coast is home to more unspoilt native bush than anywhere else in New Zealand. And that bush has been an ideological battlefield. The coasters wanted to continue to log bits of it. The government, and much of the rest of New Zealand, wanted to conserve every inch of it.

The current government is a Labour government, but it is not a Labour government as the coast thinks of Labour governments. It is not a working man's government. It is a more urban, eco-friendly, overtly multicultural and female government. The Prime Minister herself is a woman, and one whose idea of a good relaxing holiday is to pull on unflattering thermal underwear and tramp into the bush for a bit of self-flagellating communion with the wet and the wild.

The government won the battle. The new New Zealand won. The logging of native bush is now banned and the primeval forests have become part of the conservation estate. The coast's future now lies in tourism, and it seems a bright future. The tourists come in greater numbers every year. Tomorrow belongs to the Canadian father and son, and the jade carvers. But it is a tomorrow that differs radically from yesterday and I suspect that it is too late for people like John to adjust. I can't see him learning to love and respect our great oneness. At the same time, I can't imagine a friendlier bloke.

In the days when the pubs shut at six o'clock, the Coast was famous for flouting the rule. When the pubs were allowed to stay open till ten it became harder work, but they stuck at it. They had an image to maintain. But now, when the pubs can effectively choose their own hours, they seem to have given up the battle. I buy pints for John and myself at 9.30 p.m. and am told that they're the last of the evening. Having spent time with the glow-worms, in terms of vinous elevation I'm barely taxiing for take-off.

I try three other pubs. Two are closing. The third allows me in for a single quick beer. I am alone. The ashtrays have been washed. The stools are upside down on the leaners. The bar-maid silently watches me drink.

Back to my motel along the wide and empty streets of Hokitika, silent but for the distant thud of the waves. A tangerine moon has risen from the Tasman Sea. Ten more paces and the moon turns out to be a street-lamp.

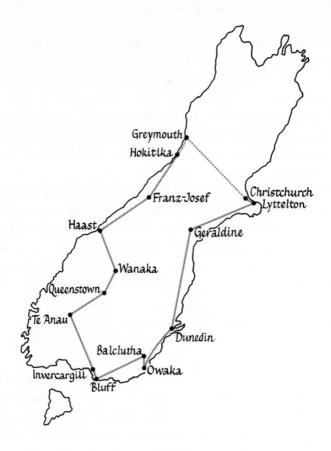

13
See George; go home

The South Island has had some wonderfully named lunatic asylums. My favourites were Sunnyside and Cherry Farm. In recent years both places have been renamed, and lunatic asylums have quite rightly become psychiatric hospitals, but it was fun while it lasted. The psychiatric hospital opposite which I am hitching now is disappointingly known only as Sea View. Even more disappointingly it's got one.

The first vehicle to pass me is a wailing ambulance. The third is a newish saloon driven by the garrulous motelier from Franz Josef.

'It's a small world, the coast,' I say as I get in.

'It's smaller than that,' he says. 'I know who's in that ambulance. And what's wrong with her.' What's wrong with her is apparently serious.

'Today we're roosters,' says the motelier, 'tomorrow, feather-dusters,' and he drives me cheerfully the short distance to Greymouth. On the way we pass the beach where the Coast to Coast race starts at 6 a.m. on the first Saturday of every February. Hundreds of people enter the race, some of them top-flight athletes, most of them ordinary Kiwis. Cow farmers, plumbers, nurses and quantity surveyors cycle into the mountains, then run over the pass, then kayak down the Waimakariri River, then cycle again to Christchurch. The winner breaks the tape on Sumner beach about six in the evening, having crossed a country in a day. The last ones roll in about midnight.

The hills behind Greymouth lack the snowy drama of the high alps. They are tame foothills, dressed in bush that is less forest than scrub. From a distance, that scrub looks like green fungus, lurking at the limits of the town, waiting to reinfest. The main approach road lies above most of the town so the pedestrian overlooks an expanse of corrugated iron. And because the rainfall is prodigious, the signature colour of Greymouth roofs is rust.

Few places are as aptly named as Greymouth. It tries hard not to seem depressing but I find it depressing. It shouldn't be. It's the capital of the West Coast and it's got the lot. On the long walk in from where the motelier drops me I note a musculoskeletal centre, a Mormon church, a Honda dealership, several chiropractors and a spanking new Warehouse, but somehow Greymouth has the smalltown blues.

Perhaps it is precisely because it's got the lot that Greymouth lacks the sense of pioneering outback, of being dwarfed by the land, that gives savour to the rest of the coast. Walking its streets feels like touring a cemetery that's not quite historic enough to be interesting. Old women battle against the stabbing wind in clothes that would not look out of place in a photo from the fifties.

Greymouth stands by the sea but turns its back on it, probably because the sea has so often invaded it. In order to see water, I have to climb the new flood barrier, and then I wish I hadn't. The Grey River is grey. The sea beyond is greyer. The wind punches and buffets me, balloons my jacket.

The wharf is bleak and shipless. Out beyond the end of it lies the invisible bar that has caught countless ships, drowned hundreds of men.

The little museum does nothing to lighten my mood. Its walls are hung with a chaos of black and white photographs, hundreds of which show Greymouth under two feet of water. And then there are the shots of the wharf between 1850 and 1950. Every one of them shows a fleet tied up to it, sailing ships, steam ships, seagoing barges, and the railway sidings heaped high with wealth-making timber. All gone now.

I've three days left before I need to be home for work, and here in the museum, in front of a photograph of George Fairweather Moonlight, I decide to go now. It's partly because three days is insufficient to do justice to the trek round the top of the island, and it's partly because there's a tourist train that runs from Greymouth to Christchurch, the TranzAlpine route. It is billed as one of the great rail journeys of the world and I have always wanted to take it.

But it's mainly because of George Fairweather Moonlight. In 1865 he found gold in the hills and named the spot after himself. The photograph shows him looking like a smug bandit, but what matters, what affects me, is that he's got a dog. It's leaning an adoring head on his knee. I can sense the warm weight of that head. I pick up my bag and head for the railway station.

It's smack downtown. And it retains, delightfully, some

Victorian vestiges, such as the peaked roof with a dentate wooden fringe above the single platform. But they're mending the track. The first half of the journey, from Greymouth to Otira, will be done by coach. I hate coaches. The old ones smell of schoolboy sick. The new ones smell of moulded plastic. And the moulded plastic somehow smells of schoolboy sick.

And coaches restrict you. Your seat is your seat and you stay there. On trains you can rise and wander, can sometimes find a buffet car and drink expensive bottled beer to the rhythm of wheels over welds, or you can enjoy the lavatory with its metal flap that opens on a glimpse of blurred sleepers. I can completely understand Paul Theroux choosing trains to tour the world in. Trains are for journeys. Coaches are for children and pensioners, people whose choices are limited by age or the lack of it. But I buy a ticket and a coffee and I wait.

It is not like waiting beside the road for a lift. In this waiting there is no doubt, no freedom. This wait won't end in a sudden blast of chance. There's no danger of danger, no fear of being marooned, no hope of happiness. This wait will end when the clock says it will. The bus will come and we will go.

'We' means the crowd that is gradually gathering, a polyglot mob, all of us tourists. Here's a pair of twenty-something Germans squatting among their possessions rolling cigarettes. Their monstrous backpacks have littler backpacks attached to them like suckling young. Near them, two sturdy Englishwomen, widows at a guess, with small neutrally-coloured suitcases that you just know have been efficiently packed, every item of clothing justified and folded. A middle-aged husband and wife occupy a bench, their nationality undisclosed because they sit in silence. The husband looks south-west, the wife north-west. I seem to be the only solo traveller, but no group or couple mixes with any other. Fifty or more existences all about to share a journey, but with tall fences between us. I hate being a part of it. I feel like a penned sheep. I am impatient to be away.

Two huge, clean and loathsome buses swallow us then lug us round the back of the town, through little semi-derelict settlements among swamps, and past graveyards holding the dead from ancient mine explosions. Grey sheep, brown cattle, green tree ferns. The couple in the seat behind me turn out to be New Zealanders. They are obsessed with ragwort, the tough and vivid yellow weed that can choke a farm. They tut at every passing clump of it, berate the unknown farmer.

Beyond Lake Brunner we join the only road that runs east, the road to Arthur's Pass. It climbs through bush and paddock, follows riverbeds, passes hotels where they changed the nineteenth-century horse-teams, and then enters second-gear terrain, winding and remote. I catch glimpses of the railway diving through tunnels, crossing old bridges of skeletal timber, and new ones of neat concrete.

Beyond the pass the landscape changes with sudden emphasis. Behind us now the dense wet vegetation of the west. Here on the dry east there's just a skin of wiry tussock over rock, speared by great rivers of scree. And the peaks soar either side to startling snow and sky.

The bus draws up at a station as alpine as Switzerland. Our train is waiting. We disgorge into mountain air as cold and sharp as a chisel. The train takes us on to the east, following a route like a cross-section carved through a papier-mâché model in a museum. From diminishing mountains to the foothills, and then down into the long alluvial plains of Canterbury, the paddocks slide-rule square, the sheep fat and numerous.

I buy beer from the buffet car and chat with two Cornishwomen with accents like butter. They tell me of their adventures in New Zealand. They love the place. But I have only half a mind for them. I am hoping that friends will have brought my dog to the station, and they have.

PART TWO

The North Island

14
Palmy bloody Palmy

It's more than a month before I can get away again north. The
North Island is different from the South Island. It has a dif-
ferent history, a different geography and a different climate.
Seventy per cent of all New Zealanders live there, and ninety
per cent of Maori. Crudely put, the North Island thinks of the
South Island as scenery dotted with yokels. The South Island

thinks of the North Island as Auckland. And it thinks of Auckland as hell.

The day before leaving I buy a new bag. It's the colour of fresh asparagus and it's got too many pockets and zips. But it's also got a pair of unobtrusive wheels at one end. I was tempted by another wheeled bag with hard corners and a retractable towing handle, but decided in the end that it was too natty, too embarrassingly flash for hitching. And also too old-person.

I fly to Palmerston North, partly because I've never been there, but mainly because I can get a ticket for $68. To my surprise the plane is not a twenty-seater where the co-pilot doubles as the steward and the cabin has the diameter of a sewer, but a rather substantial beast. It's still hauled by propellers but it comes with coffee and a stewardess from Lyttelton. I've met her dog-walking on the hills.

We talk about our dogs and my trip. She tells me she's hitch-hiked only once, fifteen years ago, straight out of high school, when she and three girlfriends went to Queenstown. Their parents had given them the bus money, 'but that went on booze and smokes, of course.'

She was amazed by the lifts they got. For her, as for so many, hitching sits in the memory as an emblem of an all-too brief period of youth and freedom, a time of impoverished adventure. And I feel a twinge of unease at the thought of sticking out the thumb again with more hair on my forearm than on my head. It smacks of fraud.

International flying is a trip into limbo-land. Only take-off and landing feel like real events. For the rest of the time your watch tells you lies and you live in suspension, like a foetus in a pickling jar. But flying over New Zealand on a clear day is how the ancient dreamers must have imagined flying. To the east now, the morning sun hangs low over the Pacific. The blue-black sea is crimped and sparkle-ridged, and trimmed with white like piping on a high-ranking naval uniform.

I can see the township of Kaikoura, but not the deep offshore trench that renders its waters so fertile. Whales grow fat there. The early settlers came to hunt them. The modern tourists come to watch them.

A few years ago, my mother was a tourist. She didn't fancy whale-watching by boat so we went up in a little plane that circled the sea, waiting. When a whale rose, it rose like an island, a grey-brown hugeness. Immediately three planes swung down towards it, circling and banking to give their paying passengers the view. And three boats skimmed across to it, and stopped to give their paying passengers the view. A hundred or so people, watching a whale being a whale. The whale did nothing. It breathed. Perhaps a fifth of its bulk lay inert above the waterline for ten minutes or so. Then the tail rose high, each fluke the size of a double bed, and it dived and was gone. The boats and planes dispersed. The whale had been watched.

From this plane window now the emptiness of the land is striking, the insignificance of man's footprint. There's none of the chessboard intimacy of English counties. Beyond Kaikoura the folded hills stretch interminably west, brownish-purple, sharply divided between sun and shade, with rivers and tracks winding like filaments along the routes of least resistance. The only buildings are farms in green valleys, utterly remote and the size of Monopoly hotels. I lean my forehead against the scratched and shuddering Perspex skin of the window and gaze. As always I feel half an urge to go live in the hills as a hermit, but at the same time I know I lack almost all the qualities such a life would require. A plane offers a view we probably shouldn't have, a view we can't live in. It presents the land like a brochure.

My first sight of the North Island is the Wairarapa cliffs where the fields just stop and fall to the sea. As the plane descends, dots become sheep, boxes houses, and a scatter of puzzling dice turns out to be silage bales wrapped in green plastic The land looks gentle and prosperously rural.

The sudden transformation from air speed to land speed,

from flying to friction, presses us against our seatbelts, then lets us back and we are creatures of the earth again, where we belong. Everyone stands too soon, takes stuff down, gathers stuff up, queues in the aisle, is eager to go.

The tarmac is painted with bright hieroglyphs, like a children's playground. On the 50-yard walk across it to the terminal doors, the passengers look around, absorbing the air, the temperature, the wind, the smell of the new place to which they've been hermetically transported. Flying is not so much travel as displacement. That's what gives the arrivals hall of any international airport its exotic feel. The clothes now being worn in Helsinki were donned in Delhi.

Palmerston North Airport resembles a provincial bus station. I sit outside on a bench of perforated steel and feel unsure what to do. The fifty people from the flight have all dispersed in cars. Sparrows twitter under an arch of soiled perspex. The town lies to the west beneath a ridge of unspectacular hills. It's too close to hitch so I walk.

As I tow my new bag across the car park the wheels roll fine, but the fat cloth handle is too low. It twists my spine, makes it ache. I tow it for 100 yards and then, with a sighing familiar motion, I hoist the thing onto my shoulder. And somehow I feel relieved. Wheeled bags are for suntanned, striding pilots and holidaymakers with pumpkin paunches and regrettable shirts.

I doubt that anyone has walked this airport road in months. It's nowhere country, with no footpath, a rank verge, and a ditch dotted with stuff tossed from cars: Burger King wrappers, waxed milk-shake cartons, a crushed cigarette packet called Sportsman. On either side of me, mesh fences, the flat grassed expanse of the airport, and wind. But I'm pleased to be walking again, finding my stride, feeling the bag knocking against my haunch.

The town's suburban edge is raw and midday silent, the newly planted gardens low, name-tags wrapped around the stems of baby camellias. Coming subdivisions are marked with string and pegs. In a kitchen window a woman is tipping something into scales. I smile. She waves from behind the glass with silent exuberance. Each new bungalow is fronted by a garage door the width of two cars. The names of the new roads are meaningless, bureaucrat-chosen noises. J.F. Kennedy Drive. Venus Way. Dunk Place. Development is outpacing any historical connection to the land.

The further into town I walk, the older the bungalows, the taller the camellias. A woman in her thirties with a heel-bouncing stride calls out to me. I don't catch what she says. She wears a flimsy skirt over trousers. She calls again in what sounds like a private language, comes up to me, cadges a cigarette, asks me where I'm going and announces that she'll come with me. Within half a mile I have learned that she writes on the walls of her house in big black letters, that everything's fucked, that her son cries tears that come from nowhere, and that Palmerston North's a dump. I can find little to reply to anything she says, but it doesn't matter. This is a monologue, spoken as much to the world and the wind as to me. It's hard to get a concrete noun out of her. I give up. It makes no difference. She talks. 'It's sort of all perception, don't you find that? It's all fucked up in the head. It depends on what they want, doesn't it?'

I ask her, though without much hope, who she means by 'they'.

'Yeah,' she says, 'right,' and she begs another cigarette. When she takes the lighter our fingers touch. Her skin is like glasspaper.

I foresee difficulty in shaking her off. All the way past the car yards with their flutter of plastic bunting, over the railway bridge, the road straight as a ruler, the businesses slowly smartening as we near the centre of this flat, plain town, I plan the moment of separation. Then on a bench in the central square I bunch my courage and tell her that I would rather be alone. She says oh, gets up, and stares at me for a second or two. I brace myself for a volley of abuse but suddenly she just turns and goes, striding bouncily through the traffic and off up a road chosen seemingly at random. I feel relief and guilt. Relief at being alone again. Guilt at having been given a glimpse into a screwed life, and wanting only to be shot of it.

The square has a clocktower of concrete disguised as concrete and topped with a white concrete cross. The lawns are hummocked and fountained and Milton Keynes-ed, scattered with benches and conversation pits and kiddie parks for the exclusive use of stick-figure citizens on an architect's plans. They swirl with a dusting of litter. And on the far side of the square there's an outstanding candidate, a pre-race favourite, for the world's ugliest building competition.

Amazingly, it turns out to be the Administration Building for the City of Palmerston North. To ensure that no one has a chance to miss its ugliness it spans the roadway. The wind sweeps round it, gaining 10 mph and a biting edge, whipping round corners to flip the skirts and jackets of the administrative workers.

How does such a building get erected? What makes architects think that rough concrete slabs will do as cladding? What makes them think that random bursts of primary-coloured paint and a clumsy concrete imitation of a turret will relieve the brutality of the whole? What makes them think that this concrete will not weep and stain and age, as every concrete slab in history has aged, to the colour of sick elephant skin? In short, what makes them think that stuff like this will do, that there are no aesthetic canons, that the architects of yesterday all got it wrong and that they can cuff aside the past and found a new aesthetic?

In the chilly shadows underneath the hideousness, a pleading notice: 'The Council has provided New Zealand's best skateboard park for you on the corner of Church and Pitt Street. Why not make use of it?' I could tell them why not, but they wouldn't understand. The planners' vision does not take kindly to how people are. It sees them as stick figures of reason.

Beyond the house of admin, a convention centre. It conforms to the architectural rule that covers all buildings with the word 'centre' in their title. It is newer than the admin paradise, and as ugly.

The only feature at the bleak heart of Palmerston North that could not be found in, say, Croydon in Surrey, is a statue 'erected in the memory of Te Peeti Te Awe Awe, Chief of the Rangitane Tribe, who served under General Hood during the Maori Wars. Presented by Her Majesty the Queen with a sword and a Union Jack "Tanenuiarangi" in recognition of his loyalty and valour.'

The Maori Wars, now politely renamed the New Zealand Wars, not only didn't happen in Croydon, they pretty much didn't happen in the South Island. The wars were a series of campaigns and stand-offs and occasional battles in various bits of the North Island during the 1860s between the Imperial troops and Maori. They were complex but the nub of the matter was always, as with all wars, land. Maori won many of the battles, but effectively the Crown won the war. What complicated matters was that the word Maori meant almost nothing to Maori. They did not see themselves as a race of people. They saw themselves, still see themselves, as tribes. Some of these tribes had feuded for centuries, so they found it hard to unite against the white man. And, as the statue confirms, many of them fought alongside him.

No doubt I shall see and learn more on this trip. Meanwhile I have Palmerston North to chew on. I am not salivating.

My motel, at the distant end of a drab straight road, is newish and painted baby-lung pink and smoker-lung grey. The proprietor beams at me, reaches under the counter and hands me a cold can of beer. And I realise that my smile is the first since I got off the plane.

On the wall of my room there's a print of Corot's *Ville*

d'Avray, presumably because it's hard to find a paintable bit of Palmerston North. Palmy's a university town but when I go back to its heart at dusk in search of an evening's pleasure I find no raucous students. Only raucous birds. They're homing in from everywhere to roost in the bare winter trees of the square, furiously gossiping sparrows, and a screaming plunging multitude of starlings, racing in silhouette across the pink-tinged sky like a tumult of arrowheads. Thousands, perhaps millions of them, drawn to a few dozen trees like iron filings to a magnet, jostling and bickering, cramming the branches, and shitting bountifully on the administrative cars underneath.

I try three pubs, all clearly designed to draw students like starlings, great barns of places with hoseable floors, but they're quiet and gloomy. Perhaps it's holiday time again. I find life only in an imitation English pub, low-roofed, with fake half-timbering, a fake stable door, fake roses in a hanging basket out the front, and fake pints, half a litre or less. But at least the young barman has real breasts. They're like giant slugs, pushing at the fabric of his polo shirt. The place is busy with cheerful middle-aged men in pastel sweaters, most of them moustached and saying fuck a lot, and all of them discussing golf.

On my way back to my motel, a shop selling 'the cheapest shoes in Palmerston North' has heavy metal grilles across the door and windows and an array of stickers advertising security companies and their 24-hour vigilance. The shop next door selling silver curios has none of these. Drizzle is falling.

My room's got a spa bath, the sort of white triangular thing invariably advertised with pictures of a couple in it drinking from champagne flûtes and smiling because they are about to shag. In the hope of wringing a little pleasure from the last of the day I step into the bath with a book, William Fiennes's gentle and honest tale of his pursuit of snow geese from Florida to Canada. But I can find no comfortable reading position in the triangle. The jets are judiciously placed so as to avoid giving merriment, and the motor that drives them makes a noise that ruins reading.

As I dry myself I wonder whether Palmerston North is truly dreary, or whether the fault is mine. Perhaps I have yet to adjust to being on the move once more, am still jangling with rootlessness. But I'm not going to give this place another chance. Tomorrow I'll head north-east, towards the coast.

I go out onto the balcony for a last cigarette, a towel around my waist, the concrete cold on bare feet. The drizzle's stopped but clouds obscure the stars. Somewhere far off in the darkness I can hear drunk young men shouting aggressive incoherence, like stags in rut. I'm sorry I missed them.

15

Hellebore to Deco

Hellebores, with their pale and ghostly flowers, are precisely the sort of plants you would expect to thrive on corpses. The Palmerston North cemetery abounds in them. They form my last image of the city.

I carry on past the headstone specialist, past a market garden where two men in what look to be coolie hats bend over what look to be cabbages, past the firewood yard where a man feeds logs to a vicious-looking diesel splitter, to a gravel layby where I lay down my bag opposite a paddock of black cattle, and I stick out my thumb for the first time in the North Island.

A boy racer stops. Even as he brakes I feel a gust of joy that the magic still works. It's like hooking the season's first fish.

John's from Eketahuna. His car's a low-slung growling yellow thing with an exhaust pipe as fat as a field-gun. The passenger seat is almost horizontal.

'Why have I heard of Eketahuna?'

'Piss probably, mate,' says John. 'That's all people do there, just go on the piss.'

He's never left the country. He'd like to go to Queensland, or perhaps follow his brother to Perth, but he's not interested in Europe or the States. 'There's too much bombing and that over there.'

Kiwis, he tells me, are hard-doers. 'That's why the Aussies want us. They're all cruisy, the Aussies.'

Dull flat land gives way to the Manawatu Gorge, the brown river below to the left. On the far bank, the railway line is little more than a ledge above the water, ducking in and out of tunnels hacked and blasted through the rock. It's a precarious nineteenth-century lifeline now threatened by the motor car, the shift to trucking, and the stealthy return of the bush.

We wind through the gorge then down onto the Tararua Plain. Until little more than a century ago, it was a vast and barely penetrable forest, thousands of years old and a hundred feet tall. Now it's dairy country, rich marshy paddocks studded with clumps of reeds like stands of knitting needles, and towns like Woodville where John drops me. The only living being I see in Woodville is a woman shooing three brown and white calves through a gate. Her gumboot sticks in the mud and comes off. 'Shee-yit,' she shouts with unrestrained ferocity, just as a car stops to take me to Dannevirke.

In the early 1870s there was no road here, no land link

between the port of Napier on the east coast and Wellington on the south. The government sent an emissary to Scandinavia with instructions to hire married men to build such a road. Each family would be given 40 acres. The emissary returned with 21 families, most of them Danish. Each family got its forty acres and a big surprise. Their land was dense forest. So was the road-route.

Apparently the authorities had insisted on married men because they were less likely to skedaddle. Wives and families were effectively held as hostages in Napier. The men did not skedaddle. They felled the forest. They built the road. There were grievances and strikes and delays but in the end the work was done. Hence the name of Dannevirke, meaning Danish work. At the entrance to the town the current city fathers want to erect a giant Viking, complete with horned helmet, beard and Popeye arms, and dignified presumably by the traditional rectal pole, to establish the identity of Dannevirke and lure the wallet-toting tourists. That Vikings with horns on their helmets aren't the most accurate representation of some nineteenth-century Scandinavian husbands who hoped to improve their lot, doesn't matter. This is tourism.

In the Dannevirke information centre I am the only wallet-toter. I ask where I can see remnants of the old Danish settlement. The sweet woman at the counter is a little abashed. Her answer is nowhere. The town centre has shifted down the road a bit, and the old shacks and cabins have long since been razed.

In the main street, the few shoppers I see don't look like Abba. The names above the local shops don't end in –sson. It's just another rural New Zealand town, honest, unsanctified by history, practical and a little rough at the edges. The one thing that would really draw the tourists to Dannevirke is the forest that used to be here. In other words, they'd come to Dannevirke only for Dannevirkelessness.

The old courthouse serves as the museum, a ramshackle

jumble of artefacts presided over by the standard-issue old man in a cold back room with a single-bar electric heater. 'Things were tough for the settlers,' he says, 'real tough. Want a coffee?' He shows me photos of twenty-strong bullock trains hauling massive totara and matai trunks through mud. The men don't look like Vikings. They look like tough working men. The terrain looks like the Somme circa 1917. 'This place was known as Sleeper Town. It cut the railway sleepers for most of the island.' He fingers a network of cracks in the plaster of one wall, like an aerial photo of the Ganges delta. 'Had another little quake here last week. 5.6 it was.'

One display board is devoted to black and white snaps of the Dannevirke Harriers road race on a wet day in the early fifties. You could date it from the raincoats. They've all got belts. There's a collecting box marked 'Food for Britain', a display of axes and double-handed saws, and two stuffed birds in a glass case. The birds are huia, a hundred years extinct. The size of slim magpies with long curved beaks, they had white-tipped tail feathers that Maori chieftains used to wear in their hair. These birds were apparently too fearless or friendly to survive the advent of the trigger-happy whitey. This pair was shot and stuffed in 1889 and given as a wedding present. Thirteen years later stuffed huia were the only huia left. On top of the case stands an empty bottle of Huia-brand Flavoured Beverage. 'Contains preservative' it says.

I hitch out of un-Danish Dannevirke beside a little cul-de-sac of pensioner bungalows called Elsinore Court. Their battlements are dank stucco. Two Maori boys in hooded sweatshirts come up the hill towards me, pitbulls straining ahead of them on leads. The boys lean back like water-skiers. 'You'd go better up the road, bro,' says one. 'Up by the pub there.'

I thank him and stay where I am. Clouds are darkening and bulging to the west. There's ample traffic but nothing looks like stopping. No driver even registers my presence. I look over my shoulder. The dogs have towed the boys out of sight. I head up the road to the spot they indicated which is marginally worse than where I was. I get a lift immediately.

Round-faced, Maori and a cheerful giggler, he's the youngest of nine kids. His mum was one of twelve, his nan one of sixteen. Now in his early twenties he's already father of three himself, by two different women. He does shiftwork in a dog-food factory at Waipukurau, is heading there now to go to work. But he'd like to go to the States. 'My brothers and sisters, lots of them have gone to Aussie, but I want to go more farrer.'

'Why the States?'

'It's fast, man, fast. And big, eh? Big buildings, big cars, big roads. We got one lane on the road. They got six.'

He speaks distinctively Maori English. It's neither an accent nor a dialect, but rather a manner. He raises the intonation at the ends of sentences to turn statements into questions, he tags them with 'eh?' and he calls me 'man' or 'bro'. And he giggles. The giggles rise through and around his words like the bubbles in Coke. He punctuates with giggles.

The rain has come. Like most cars I get lifts from, this one's small, messy and battered. The wipers are defective. He has to work them with the lever one flick at a time.

He points out a little town where several aunties live, the cemetery where others are buried. As we near Waipukurau where this lift ends, the sun returns, and the land is a brilliant wet green over small crested hills, like billiard cloth stretched over Cornish pasties.

At the café table next to me in Waipukurau's shopping street, three men sit in rural uniform: brown elastic-sided boots, cream moleskins, blue Guernseys. Each has a cellphone laid beside his coffee cup. They're talking money. The waitress has hiccoughs. A rest-home minibus draws up in front of me with a freight of six white-headed women in heavy coats. The uniformed nurse parks nose-first and leaps out and dashes into the chemist's, leaving the tail of the van exposed to the traffic and the old women cooking in the sun-streaked interior. Across the road a

Maori man in a muscle shirt lifts a huge and elderly television from the boot of a Holden Commodore and lugs it into Betta Electrical. He's got a facial tattoo, a moko, a device that traditionally told of a warrior's standing and genealogy. To me it looks threatening.

The sun slanting against my neck feels like an iron held close to the skin. This is central Hawke's Bay, though still some way from Napier and the sea. It's hot, dry, sunny land. Waipukurau is a one-street rural-services town, a Geraldine, but it does have a road junction. Turn right and the road will take you to Porangahau on the coast and then to a hill called Taumatawhakatangihangakoauauotamateapokaiwhenuakitanatahu and then to Wimbledon.Taumatawhakatangihangakoauauotamateapokaiwhenuakitanatahu means 'when Tamatea's brother was killed in a battle near here, Tamatea climbed this ridge and played a lament on his flute'. Wimbledon means 'place too small to have a public tennis court'.

Turn left and you'll get a lift from a self-aggrandising bore. Or at least I do. And as he drives me towards the coast, and as sheep farms give way to orchards and vineyards, I slide towards catalepsy.

This man even boasts about shopping. He buys everything in bulk, gets 25 per cent off retail. 'Who wouldn't want that? Old-fashioned shopping's a thing of the past. What do you pay for dish-washing liquid? Go on, how much for one bottle of dish-washing liquid? I'll tell you. Three dollars is what you pay, and that's on special. Now guess what I get it for? A dollar twenty-five, that's what. Forty-eight bottles for sixty bucks. That's a dollar twenty-five a bottle, delivered to your door by courier from this warehouse in Auckland. Mate, you've got to be a mug to pay retail. No one's doing it any more. The supermarkets are really hurting.'

But he's not just the king of shopping. He's the king of yarn-telling too. 'I said to him, I said ... and he just roared. Said it was the best thing he'd heard in years.' And he's the king of fishing guides. 'I told him to go to the third bridge. He was late back. "How was the fishing?" I asked. "Ten casts, seven fish," he said. "Told you so, didn't I," I said. "Too right," he said.'

Why do some men have to brag like children? Their lies are transparent. The status they achieve is a false eminence. No one believes such men, let alone admires them. Surely, we all just bite our tongues, grind our teeth, and go away as soon as we can. Don't we? Well, I do. But he gives me a good long lift.

I do the final hop to Napier with the help of two grinning German youths who pick me up on a bridge over a fat river, just as it's threatening rain. In the back of their ancient combi-van there's a stained and torn double mattress that I sit on, a poster celebrating fifty years in the US Navy, tattered floral curtains, and an arch of yellow plastic roses framing the driver's head .

The boys have found jobs for the winter pruning apple orchards. They have only good things to say about New Zealand. Kiwis, they say, are relaxed and generous. Unlike Germans, Kiwis invite you into their homes. I write down my address, saying that if they are ever in the South Island they are welcome to stay.

'Zanks,' says the non-driver. He turns to flash me a watermelon grin and tucks the scrap of paper deeply and carefully into his wallet. He has skimpy young man's sideburns. 'We will be zere in December,' he says, which is not what I meant at all. Don't Germans recognise an empty gesture?

The boys are from what used to be East Germany. I ask about unification.

'Some things have changed for the better,' says Herr Sideburns, 'and some for the worse.'

'Like what?' I say. 'What's changed for the worse?'

'Education,' he says. 'It used to be free.'

It is only after they have dropped me on the seafront in the heart of Napier that I realise that when the Berlin Wall fell, so very recently it seems, these boys were barely in primary school.

At 10.46 a.m. on Tuesday, 3 February 1931, Napier shook and fell down. A shallow earthquake, centred 16 kilometres to the north and lasting two and a half minutes, with a thirty-second lull in the middle, shook the town to bits. 258 people died, 162 of them in Napier itself. In the information centre on the promenade there's a photograph of the town centre the day after. All the roofs have gone, and most of the walls. The place is rubble. It looks like London in the Blitz, like Dresden.

The quake changed the very tilt of the earth. Over 2,000 hectares of seabed rose to become land. Napier said thank you and built an airport on it. Meanwhile architects rebuilt the city centre in the style of the day, Art Deco. It's a sunny style for a sunny place. The plaster porticos and pastel paint make the place architecturally distinctive, a rare quality in New Zealand. And Napier trades on it. It hosts Art Deco tours, Art Deco conferences, and an annual all-singing, all-dancing Art Deco festival that I'm glad to have missed.

My motel is not Art Deco. It's Bella Vista. My room is indistinguishable from the Bella Vista room I rented in Invercargill, except that this balcony offers a bella vista of the Napier Returned Services Association building, which is also not Art Deco. When I sign for the room the motelier cheerfully tells me that I have agreed to pay $200 if I smoke in my room. Outside my door there's a little ashtray with moss on it. I look along the balcony. Each door has an ashtray outside it. Each ashtray has identically patterned moss on it.

In the photograph of flattened Napier the only things undamaged by the quake are a row of Norfolk pines that front the promenade. They're still there, strange foreign-looking trees, more than halfway to being palms, their straight boughs spaced on the trunk as if by a pair of dividers, their tufted leaves or needles looking crudely artificial. Between the trees and the beach lies a sunken public garden where an empty wheelchair nudges back and forth in the breeze. I can see no nurse struck down by a heart attack, no ancient patient dragging himself through the perennials to fetch help. It seems that someone has stolen an invalid. For ransom? For medical experiment? For fun? For a bet? There's no one about. I lay a palm on the wheelchair's seat. Warm to the touch – warmer, I'm sure, than can be explained by the weak afternoon sun.

Sherlock leaves this conundrum to better minds than his, makes a mental note to get the local paper in the morning, steps through a gap in the concrete retaining wall and faces the Pacific. Pebbles, coarse black sand and a steep slope to the breakers that roll in fat and full, and hit the land with a roar. A prominent sign says 'Warning: the beach is dangerous'. It seems redundant, but it may, just possibly, explain the wheelchair.

The centre of town is largely pedestrianised. Plate-glass windows front the same chainstores as you'll find in every town in the country. But raise the eyes and the Art Deco façades with their stepped parapets, their curved corners, their flat roofs, their highlight motifs, give the place the feel of a jazz band, or a cinema organ, or one of Waugh's early novels.

And there's a fine second-hand bookshop. For once the proprietor is not a disappointed man with a shabby-genteel jacket held together by tobacco smoke and love of Labrador, but a bright and endearing woman who likes to talk books. And it seems that her tastes resemble mine. 'My heart leaps up,' said Wordsworth, 'when I behold a rainbow in the sky.' Mine does something similar when I catch sight of an elderly orange Penguin. And here's a wall of orange Penguins, ageing towards brown, their spines crackable, their paper wartime grainy, their printing faintly smudged. My heart does the hurdles. Orwell, Waugh, Greene, all the familiar culprits, and all the more desirable for being familiar. On the bargain table I find L.P. Hartley's *Shrimp and the Anemone* a gentle gem of a novel, the first of a trilogy and better by far than the two that followed it, as is the rule with trilogies. And R.H. Morrieson's *The Scarecrow*, a grisly comic loveliness written by a drunken Taranaki muso. Stolen

chickens, sly-grogging and necrophilia set in the rural innocence of sixties' New Zealand.

I want to buy twenty books, all of which I've read before.
Were I at home, I would. I'd lug them back to my house like
booty, stroke their covers, shelve them and forget about them,
content with the mere acquisition. I draw succour from their
cultural reassurance, I suppose, but I don't care. Here I am
acutely aware of their weight. I natter enthusiastically with the
proprietor until closing time and then leave with nothing but
farewells and hollow promises of returns, which presumably is
how the owners of second-hand bookshops get to look disappointed.

Having travelled a fair distance, survived a bore and eaten
nothing since breakfast but a roadside banana, I promise myself
a substantial dinner, preceded by a single whetter of Guinness.
The Art Deco hotel on the seafront does not serve Guinness.
The barman directs me to the Irish bar. It's the authentic fake
and it's early evening empty. Bar stool, ashtray, pint, book. I feel
tired, good, easy of mind. William Fiennes has just made
friends on a Greyhound bus with an ex-nun who has a passion
for laundry. And I make friends with a builder. It just happens.
A casual good evening when he enters, an unconsidered
remark or two, a weak shared joke, then fatally the acceptance
of the offer of a beer. I dog-ear a page in *The Snow Geese*, slide
the book back into my pocket, and change guise from the man-
with-a-book to the man-in-company. They are grossly different
beasts.

The man-with-a-book is a restrained sort, cautious, sensible,
polite, wary of danger, little more than warm and breathing
furniture, barely affecting the place he occupies. By ten o'clock
he's back in his motel bed, well-fed, content and still reading.
His adventures are the adventures of others, the word-made
pictures in his head. But the man-in-company, though similar
to the eye, is a boisterous buffoon, a man with a will as weak as
water, a man for whom a casual 'good evening' is a door that

opens on a binge. This man can crown an evening of beers with five last beers, and then with at least a couple, perhaps more, of categorically and incontrovertibly last beers.

The builder isn't a builder. In the best male New Zealand tradition, he's an amateur builder. He used to run a bar but at the same time he amateurishly built a house, sold it at a profit, found he'd enjoyed the process, so sold his bar and built houses full-time. He's now knocking up a modest little three-storey number on a hill section above Napier that was cheap because its view of the sea was blocked. Keen nevertheless on securing a sea-view and the price that goes with it, he is amateurishly cantilevering the whole building out from the slope.

'One day,' he says, sipping thoughtfully, 'I suppose I'll have to get my builder's ticket.'

DIY is in this country's blood. The traditional Kiwi house is a bungalow with wooden floors, wooden framing, wooden weatherboarding and a roof of corrugated iron. Acquire a dozen decent tools and you can fix most of it.

My first house was ramshackle throughout, but the bathroom was ramshackler. A friend said I should do it up. When I said I couldn't afford to get a man in, he said I should do it myself. Put in a new floor, build a partition wall, resite the lavatory, fix the plumbing and 'she'll be jake.' He'd give me a hand, he said. When I said that I wouldn't know where to start, that I had rented many a worse bathroom and that I could happily live with it as it was, he stamped a hole in the floorboards. 'Let's go to it,' he said and we went to it. We built a new bathroom in a week. We means he.

It was the same with cars. Men mended their cars. When I first arrived, the roads of the South Island were a museum: Morris Oxfords, Austin Cambridges, Ford Anglias, Triumph Heralds, all of them maintained by their owners.

It is no longer so. Most New Zealand cars are now imported second-hand from Japan. They are cheaper and more reliable, and so crammed wih technology that they are harder for the tinkerer to fix. At the same time, houses are being built in more complex ways and of more modern materials. Today's middle-aged Kiwi male may be the last heir of a tradition of technological self-sufficiency.

The builder and I move from the Irish bar to an establishment less than 100 yards away. To my surprise it's an Irish bar. Builder runs into a Maori mate who is short, wide, smartly dressed and passionate about rugby. The evening takes off its tie and rolls up its sleeves.

16
Snot snot Huka hooker

I wake at five in the position that corpses adopt for detectives to draw chalk lines around them. I am on the bed. By way of preparing myself for sleep I have removed one shoe. The door of my room is open to the world.

Immediately on waking I run the mental video of the night before, fast forwarding through the chaos in search of the clip that will make me yelp with embarrassment. It's an automatic reflex after a raucous night out. If I find such a clip I run and re-run it in my head, drawn to it as the tongue is drawn to an exposed nerve in a tooth.

On first inspection the tape of last night seems innocuous. Apart, that is, from the quiz night.

Strange things quiz nights, and very popular things. People flock to be tested on things that there's no point in knowing. Name the All Black who was also a professional juggler. What's the age of consent in Libya? What was the maiden name of the juggling All Black's Libyan bride? That sort of thing. Though people pay to take part, the prizes are rarely worth having. People just want to be acknowledged for knowing stuff. But no one seriously acknowledges anyone else for knowing the sort of stuff you need to know for quiz nights. So in the end, I suppose, contestants are just wanting to feel clever. They're kids raising a hand for teacher. 'Please miss, me, miss,' begging for the pat on the head and the smugness of being right. And when I say they, I mean we. I love quiz nights.

And I entered into the quiz last night with gusto and a belly-ful of Guinness. I don't know what had happened to the builder. Perhaps he went home to knock up a couple of dormer windows and mitre a few architraves before bed.

The bar may or may not have been Irish. An English lad with a Michael Jackson fedora and a Michael Jackson wrap-around microphone, and who was, indeed, distinguishable from Michael Jackson only by looking human, was strolling through the pub reading questions from a clipboard. Huddled knots of contestants consulted each other in exaggerated secrecy and wrote down answers. The knot I attached myself to uninvited included a girl with crimson hair done into spikes. She told me she was an artist.

'How many countries border Switzerland?' asked Michael Jackson.

'Four,' I said, because I thought I could name three.

'Three,' said the girl with spiked hair. She named them. I insisted on four, refused to name the fourth, said that she could either trust me or distrust me and that trust mattered more than the question, left the group in a mock huff, joined another, told them the answer was three, and named them. They wrote down three. The answer was four. I returned to the first group and crowed.

I've done worse. I have memories of things that happened twenty years ago that still retain the power to make me curl like a foetus, hug my knees and whimper.

I close the door of my room, undress, sluice myself with water and Panadol, get back into bed and drowse uneasily till eight. Hunger gets me up in the end. I can't remember eating anything last night.

On the sunny promenade a hugely hairy man and a woman in ill-advised shorts come jogging towards me, their faces the standard masks of self-hatred. I feel a stab of nausea at the thought of trying to jog. The world is fuzzy at the edges. My brain feels shrouded in sensitive gauze. It takes a while to find a café that isn't playing background music.

Shared hangovers are comic. Solitary hangovers aren't. My mind turns in on itself, sees nothing beyond its own distress. The smell of coffee promises relief, but the coffee itself fails to deliver. It goes gratefully enough down the throat but fails to reach the parts that need moistening. I chew for too long at an anhydrous croissant, find my hunger has evaporated, and order two more coffees. But what I really need is laughter, or at least company. I pull *The Snow Geese* from my pocket and wedge the gull's-wings of its spine under the rim of the croissant plate only to find that overnight the print has shrunk.

I had thought to spend the day pootling around Napier but now I just want to go. It's as though this hangover belongs to this town. I keep expecting to run into the girl with the spiked hair and I would prefer not to. I ask the waitress where I'd find the road to Gisborne, the next substantial town up the coast.

She shrugs. She's never been to Gisborne. But a man with a briefcase overhears and gives me directions to the one road north. Apparently, some 20 kilometres out of town it splits. 'Go left for Taupo, right for Gisborne,' he says. He looks like an insurance assessor, and has a Salman Rushdie face, all beard below and baldness above, as if his head were stuck on upside down.

When I go to fetch my bag, a dozen pensioner women are doing aerobics in the Napier Returned Services Association. Their instructor is young, breezy, sunshine-cheerful and supple as a whip. The old dears aren't. They do stiff parodies of her bends and stretches. When one of them sees me watching her trying to touch her knees, she straightens and looks flustered and I move on.

Dickens Street, Carlyle Street, Emerson Street, Another Unread Victorian Street, then the long straightness of Hyderabad Street. It's warm and too far. My armpits smell of Guinness.

Though Napier is new to me, the walk out follows a familiar pattern. The town centre, its shops well-kept, its footpaths peopled, gives way to residential territory and dying shops, dying because everyone now has a car. The undusted window displays, peppered with the weightless corpses of flies, are admissions of defeat.

Then garages, car yards, boat yards, and demolition yards with leaning rows of unwantable second-hand doors, like monstrous library shelves.

I hitch by the estuary where a stout woman repeatedly calls to a mongrel called Poppy. Poppy ignores her. The woman tries approaching calmly, but Poppy, all frolicsome energy and game for a game, waits crouched to the last second then leaps beyond reach and barks. The woman looks around. I look away. The woman chases Poppy. The woman is bad at chasing. Poppy is happy and quite uncatchable. I sneeze.

I sneeze again. It's the booze. Sometimes it does this to me, sometimes it doesn't. I presume it's an allergy, one of those intermittent allergies.

By the time a car stops for me, my sinuses are at peak production. The car is new, Japanese and forget-me-not blue. Peter offers me a lift to Taupo.

I was keen to see Gisborne and the East Cape but I am keener still for a couple of hours in an air-conditioned car. And conversation may take my mind, so to speak, off my head. 'Thank you,' I say, and get in. I sneeze.

'You got the bot?'

'I guess so,' I say. 'I'm sorry. It's come on really suddenly.'

But Peter's remarkably forgiving. I keep my handkerchief at the perpetual ready. By the time we've done twenty miles it's a sodden bulky horror. Thrown at a wall it would stick.

The Hawke's Bay vineyards in winter are just stakes and wires and shrivelled black things. As we climb into the ranges, the terrain beyond the cabin of the car grows slowly rougher and so does the conversation within. We start with formalities couched in maiden-aunt English. Then Peter drops in a 'bullshit'. I don't react, deploy a 'bastard' of my own. Soon Peter unleashes a 'fuck' and it's implicitly, semi-consciously, agreed that there are no linguistic taboos. I like that process of feeling out the territory. It's a type of courtesy.

Peter buys land for the government. Land for roads, for parks, for anything the government needs land for. Like so many jobs it is one that I've never heard of, never imagined imagining. For every day of the sixteen years I've been in this country, he's been on the road buying bits of it. I'm not sure that travel broadens the mind. But it does underline the narrowness of experience.

We pass through vast plantations of pine, cloaking the hills in dark green uniformity. They're like the wheatfields of giants, with a gap between planting and reaping of one hundred seasons instead of three. Where a distant stand of trees has been felled, it looks like a tear on a snooker table. Close up, the land is churned and mashed and littered with branches, bark and needles. Or it's replanted with knee-high seedlings, tufts of green with twenty-five years to live.

'The timber price is rock bottom,' says Peter. 'Apparently it's so mild in Siberia that the loggers have been able to get to forests normally frozen out of reach. There's a whole wall of cheap wood coming out of Russia.' He pauses. 'Or so I've been told. But it's probably bull.'

His wife rings him on speaker phone, calling from I don't know where. Before she can say anything, Peter announces that he's got a hitchhiker aboard.

'Don't be silly,' she says. 'You never pick up hitchhikers.'

Peter turns to me. 'Say something,' he says. He seems very keen that I should.

'Hello, er, Peter's wife.' My eloquence is cut short by a sneeze that rattles the windows. The sneeze convinces her. The conversation between husband and wife is reduced to a stilted series of questions and answers about the weather in Napier, the weather at home, where Peter will have lunch, what he's thinking of having for lunch, what time he's likely to be home.

When he hangs up I expect him to laugh and apologise. He doesn't.

Peter turns out to be a fisherman, his favourite river the Tongariro that drains into the southern end of Lake Taupo, and is perhaps the most famous trout river in the world.

Trout were introduced to New Zealand in the nineteenth century by groups known as Acclimatisation Societies who imported wildlife from Europe for reasons of sport or nostalgia or food. What they achieved was catastrophe. The rabbits, for example, bred like rabbits. Instead of the farmers eating the rabbits, the rabbits ate the farms. So in came the stoats and weasels to control the rabbits. They cheerfully tucked into the rabbits, until they discovered the native birds. They proved particularly fond of kiwi chicks. Just about the only exception to this catalogue of disaster was the trout.

Before the Europeans came the rivers held eels and several indigenous varieties of fish. But there was room for more, and in the wild fresh water that poured off the mountains, and in the great lakes like Taupo, trout flourished as nowhere else in the world. The first trout I caught in this country weighed four pounds. The second weighed six. In New Zealand these are respectable fish. In England they would be candidates for stuffing and mounting. Almost all fresh water in this country now holds trout. They have done little harm to the waterways and a lot of good to the economy. Fly-fishermen come from the world over to fish the Mataura round Gore, the primal rivers of Fiordland, the glacier-fed streams of the Mackenzie and the lake we're now heading towards.

Peter and I discuss the differences between fly-fishing in the South Island and in Taupo. They are differences of scale. In the south the flies are generally smaller, subtler. It is not a conversation to engross a non-fisherman, but it carries us 100 miles or more, through the ranges that keep the east coast dry, and then down into the huge volcanic basin of the central North Island, and the largest lake in Australasia, Lake Taupo. It's so big it's tidal.

I was last here fifteen years ago. I came to fish and I rolled my car. Nine in the morning and I was heading for the Hinemaiaia River in my monstrous Holden with its three gears on the steering column. The Hallelujah Chorus was on the tape deck. I tossed a cigarette out of the window, sensed that it had blown back into the car, turned to look, ran a front wheel off the road, flipped and skidded 100 yards on the roof. The car came to rest against a fence. All the glass was gone but the cabin was intact. The tape was still playing. I was pinned upside down. I lay there a while, my neck bent like a question mark. I just breathed and trembled, reordering a suddenly tumbled world. Then I wriggled out through the hole where a window had been.

Several cars had stopped. People had gathered at the top of

the bank above me. They watched with interest as a ghost-white figure crawled from the wreckage to a thunderous chorus of Hallelujah. The car was written off. Over the phone the insurance company told me what I would get for it. The garage had two cars that I could afford, a Mini and an old Peugeot that the proprietor was reluctant to part with. I persuaded him. It kept going for a whole week.

Peter drops me in downtown Taupo and I go straight to a chemist's shop. It's got one of those open counters where you describe your symptoms to the pharmacist and to twenty eavesdroppers who are feigning an interest in packets of corn-plasters.

'I think,' I explain snottily, 'I may have an allergy to booze.'

The pharmacist looks intently at me for several seconds. 'You write newspaper columns, don't you,' he says. It's not quite the sympathetic medical attention I was hoping for. 'Going to write one about this?'

He advises anti-histamines which come at the usual amusing price that they stick on medicines in the knowledge that people who need them will pay. Few non-prescription medicines in my experience afford much relief, but the hope of health still opens the wallet.

I ask for a cup of water to wash down one of my pills.

'No point,' says the pharmacist. 'It's too late. You need to take one straight after drinking or, ideally, before you start.'

I take one anyway. Then without even looking at the lake, I rent the first cheap room I can find and spend most of the rest of the day, in the scenic heart of the North Island, in bed with a box of tissues, William Fiennes and several hundred thousand snow geese.

When morning comes the snot has gone, and so has a 50-seater tour bus. The thing was parked and locked near a Taupo tourist attraction and somebody nicked it. It seems an unlikely choice for a joy ride and an even more unlikely choice for a get-away car. The theft is front-page news in the local paper.

Taupo is at the volcanic heart of the North Island. The lake fills the caldera of a volcano that blew 1,800 years ago. The eruption was remarked on in Rome. The sun in the east looked bloody and weak, wrote some scribe in a toga, and thus unwittingly made the first European reference to New Zealand.

In the distance to the south stand the peaks of two extant volcanoes, snowy, glistening, almost cornily scenic. Between them and me lies the lake, equally glistening and home to a million pink-cheeked rainbow trout. Anyone can catch them and anyone does. Boats supply tourists with lead-cored lines or down-riggers, and the tourists have simply to drop the things over the side and wait. According to the *Guide to Taupo* that I read over my breakfast croissants, and which is a strong competitor for the most illiterate brochure published in an English-speaking country, these crude methods of fishing are despised by 'purests' who prefer to fish with a nymph that 'imitates an insect lava or a fish row'. Either way, it's apparently 'a great adrenalin rush when it Strikes'.

What the brochure doesn't mention is that there are other purests who despise the nymph, who consider its use to be cheating, and who believe that the only true way to fish for trout is with the dry fly. Such people are mostly pompous Englishmen and I used to be one of them. The day before I crashed my car here in 1987 I spent a fishless morning casting a delicate dry fly to fat trout lying doggo on the bed of the Hinemaiaia River. Throughout the morning a man with manic eyes and Belisha beacon hair repeatedly irrupted from the undergrowth on the far bank looking more manic at each irruption, but with an ever-growing array of fish strung from a contraption at his side. Then he suddenly waded the river, sat me down, asked to see my fly box, scoffed, and showed me what was what in Taupo fishing. I remember imitation stone-fly nymphs an inch in length, glow-bugs like neon squash balls, and attractors like baby squid. Since then I've fished with anything that catches fish.

But I am not fishing today. I am off to the Huka Falls, which the brochure calls 'an icon attraction' but which I hope will be worth seeing nevertheless. The Falls lie on the Waikato River that winds from Taupo to the Tasman Sea and generates much of New Zealand's electricity en route. This morning the river has the black-green sheen of a mallard's head. It flows with the sinuous strength of big water, carving a gorge through the hill, then widening between banks of bush. And steam. There is steam rising from a patch of ferns and brambles. I scramble down the slope, kneel, and lower my hand into a little tributary. It's as hot as a bath.

There's a faultline running from the volcanoes in the south-west of the island to the Bay of Plenty in the north-east. It acts as a link between the hot heart of the planet and its cool skin. The heat below boils the aquifers above, the aquifers that feed this stream that steams into the Waikato River as if it were the most ordinary thing in the world to be doing. I find it bog-gling, exciting. This is primal heat, heat that lies underneath us everywhere we go as we strut the cooled crust of the globe. It's belittling heat.

Everything feels good. I am delighted by the sun and the hot water. I'm delighted to be snotless and unencumbered by a bag. I'm even delighted to say good morning to a German couple with faultless teeth and mountain bikes and young-people-being-healthy clothes. And as I stride along the track towards the Falls, I realise that what I had taken for straggling remnants of morning mist above the bush are all distant bil-lows of steam.

You can hear the Huka Falls before you see them. The gur-gling placidity of the river gives way to a roar that seems to be transmitted through the earth rather than through the air.

The Falls compress a 100 metre-wide river into a 15-metre gulley. They are more narrows than falls, a frantic turbulence, a thunderous mass of froth and churn, a murderously enraged washing machine, entirely white and daunting. A bridge spans the top end. To lean over the rail is to feel your stomach lurch. You don't want to fall in.

In February 1989 Peter Plumley Walker fell in. He was dead at the time. And thus began one of New Zealand's most entertaining murder cases, one that taught the great New Zealand public a whole new vocabulary.

Just as one would hope with a name like Plumley Walker, the man was of English descent, ex-RAF, and a cricket umpire. He had a moustache that would be deemed extravagant on a squadron leader. And one sunny morning fourteen years ago he was found floating below the Huka Falls, dead as a stick and with his wrists and ankles bound.

The investigation uncovered a sex-life that probably gave more joy to the prurient public than it ever gave to the poor man himself. Mr Walker, it emerged, paid young women to bind and humiliate him.

A fortnight after the body was found, a teenage woman appeared in court charged with his murder. She gave her profession as dominatrix. New Zealand wrote the word down and delightedly memorised it. The Crown asserted that she had dumped his body in the river after a bondage session had gone too far, after, indeed, it had gone as far as any session of anything but necrophilia could go.

During the case, details arose of whips, masks, chains, torture chambers and golden showers. New Zealand had never had such fun and was never so innocent again.

But no bodies in the Falls this morning, only a swag of tourists leaning over the bridge and taking photos. And the inevitable jet-boats nosing to the foot of the Falls with their life-jacketed cargo strapped in the back being told stuff. I'm glad I'm not among them. But I hope they're being told about Mr Plumley Walker.

On the far side of the bridge a large car park holds buses, rental cars, camper vans, a kiosk selling chocolate and postcards, four fractious Australian children and two aggressive

Australian parents. They are suffering the perennial tourist grief. They have been attracted to an attraction, driven there and found that after five minutes it's done with. That's it. Seen the Huka Falls. What's next?

Beside the kiosk and some earnest information boards, there's a toilet that even the men have to pay to use. During the smoking of a single cigarette I watch three blokes separately approach the turnstile, see that cash is required, pause, pretend to read the earnest information boards, then turn nonchalantly away and amble without apparent purpose in the direction of the dense surrounding bush. One of them even whistles a casual tune.

I enquire after buses back to Taupo, find I'll have to wait forty-five minutes, consider hitching, decide to walk and feel happy and virtuous and hot. I stop only to watch a bungy jumper. They're becoming hard to avoid in New Zealand. I join the crowd at the designated viewing point. As the man shuffles to the edge of the platform, he looks from a distance like the blindfolded victim of a firing squad. He pauses. You can sense him breathing in. Then he bends at the knee, launches, does a creditably graceful swallow dive, is hauled up short of the water, bounces somewhat less gracefully a couple of times, comes to rest, and hangs like meat on a hook. The crowd turns away with an air of disappointment, as if thwarted.

Taupo's growing. It seems twice the size of sixteen years ago. The lake remains its prime asset but Taupo now offers much more than fish. I consider visiting 'the world's only geothermal prawn farm' until I read that it is educational. Instead I spend an hour in a neat museum with exactly what you'd expect in it: stuffed fish, stuffed birds, geothermal stuff, logging stuff, Maori and Victorian stuff. Elsewhere in Taupo there are gardens, adventure activities, and also a well-equipped Centre for Natural Wellbeing. It advertises Bowen therapy, APS therapy, Biopton light, Reflexology, Reiki, clairvoyant readings and astrology, which seems to cover all the bases until I discover a little establishment near my motel that also offers Australian bush flower therapy and Hopi ear candles.

In comparison with this lot, Jasmine seems old hat. She merely channels an American-Indian spirit guide called Yellow Star although, if pushed, she is prepared to do a spot of magnetic healing or aura balancing.

In short, Taupo's got an abundance of things to keep you busy while your bloke's out fishing, and quite a lot of them are bullshit. But Taupo's also got, and this is a first in my experience, a women's hairdresser-cum-second-hand-bookshop.

Having finished with the good and gentle Mr Fiennes and his good and gentle geese, I need a book. What people do without a book on them I don't know. Well, actually, I think I do know. They toy with their cellphones. You can see them in any airport, any café, any place of waiting, cradling their gizmos like premature babies and doing engrossing things with them.

If I've got nothing to read I feel like an amputee. In earlier hitchhiking years I often found myself in foreign lavatories with nothing printed but my passport. I can still recite, more or less, that lovely piece about Her Britannic Majesty's Principal Secretary of State requesting and requiring, in the name of Her Majesty, every wop kraut dago mick and spick not only to let me pass freely without let or hindrance but also to bandage any wounds I may incur and lend me a fiver to get home. Or else.

The hairdresser is dressing hair with those deeply mysterious strips of tin foil that do I don't know what and I'm not about to ask. Instead I ask where the books are and she gestures to the room above. I scurry upstairs to find disappointment. I probably should have guessed. Rows of romances, and Jilly Coopers, and Jackie Collins and Georgette Bloody Heyers and a single shelf of other stuff, none of which seizes me. I spend $5 on *Jude the Obscure*, largely because I just have to have a book, but also because of John Arlott. When he read the passage in which the owl child kills the other children and then himself,

John Arlott apparently leaped out of bed and ran naked down the street screaming for company.

When I read that passage in bed at university a quarter of a century ago I stayed in bed. But I'm curious to see whether the passage of time has wrought a change. Given my flat and safe suburban life, I would be pleased to be as struck with horror as Mr Arlott was – indeed, to feel any emotion of that intensity.

It is illegal to sell trout in this country. If you want to eat trout you have to catch it. I don't want to eat trout – they taste of mud and have too many bones – but I do want to eat fish. So here, by one of the greatest freshwater fishing lakes in the world, and as far inland as it is possible to be in New Zealand, I go to a seafood restaurant.

This is the proper meal I promised myself in Napier and never got round to having. I prop *Jude* against the vase of flowers and order chowder and sole. The chowder comes in a hollowed loaf. You eat the soup then the crockery. Both are fine. The sole is finer. Most fish tastes of, well, fish, but sole is sweet. It requires only butter, parsley, and a fork to rake the flaking flesh from the bones. This is one of those rare moments of indulgence as good in the present as in expectation or retrospect. I wish you could be here to share it, but at a distant table. I am content with the company of Thomas Hardy. His prose is cumbersome, his dialogue profoundly unconvincing, his plots laboured, but there's an integrity behind it all that draws me to him. *The Mayor of Casterbridge* makes me cry. Perhaps *Jude* will make me scream.

The waitress is Hardy-esque. No one could call her performance polished or sophisticated. But it's honest. When she asks if the food's all right, she seems to want to know if the food's all right. When I ask after the wine I ordered, she puts one hand to her mouth, the other on my forearm. 'Cripes,' she says, 'I clean forgot.' It's better than getting the wine on time.

I tip her fatly. It's probably only the third or fourth tip I've given since I set out. In New Zealand tipping is as it should be, a voluntary act, an expression of particular gratitude, rather than what it has become when, say, taking a cab in London, to wit, a grudging unearned bonus given to a fat rebarbative aggressive semi-literate sneering racist thug.

I round off the evening in an ugly bar, half-listening to a man who tells me how much he prefers his dog to his wife, half-watching a Super 12 rugby match in which two former pupils are playing, and half-thinking that I'd rather be back in my room reading about Jude Fawley killing a pig. An hour later I am.

Arabella upbraids Jude for killing the pig too swiftly. It should, she says, have been left to bleed and squeal. She would have made a fine cabbie.

17
Sulphuric All Blacks

The car slows as it passes me and stops 50 yards up the road. I'm not sure that it's stopped for me, but there's no layby and it's not a place where anyone would choose to pull over. No one gets out. I pick up my bag and run in a manner that illustrates why few Olympic sprinters carry a bag. 'Please don't drive off,' is what my lumbering says. 'This is a tough road to hitch and I've been here too long.'

The car doesn't drive off. I reach it, panting, and open the passenger door. An elderly couple recoil from me with precisely synchronised horror. The woman screams and grasps her husband. His mouth opens wide, his eyes wider. A road map is spread over the steering wheel.

'Look, I'm really sorry, I thought you'd ... oh, it doesn't matter, I'm just really really sorry.' And I shut the door.

I think of opening the door again to explain precisely how the error arose, but something tells me I would only compound the situation. And besides, the driver is pulling away with great haste. A yellow van swerves round him in a squeal of wrenched rubber.

'My client maintains, Mr Bennett, that moments before the accident you opened the door of his car.'

'Well, yes, but I was hitchhiking and I thought the car had stopped to . . .'

'Hitchhiking, Mr Bennett, at your age? Were you impoverished at the time?'

'No, it's just that . . .'

'Furthermore, Mr Bennett, according to my client you were breathing heavily.'

'I'd been running.'

'I see. So, Mr Bennett, if we accept, for one moment, your story that you were both running and hitchhiking at the same time, is it standard hitchhiking practice to approach vehicles uninvited, wrench open the door of a car belonging to elderly people, and . . .'

In short, I am grateful that the driver of the yellow van has the skill to avoid a crash.

At the same time I am so swamped with embarrassment, guilt and genuine sympathy, that I burst out laughing. You don't laugh much on your own on the side of the road, or at least I don't. But I have only to picture those two faces frozen with horror and I find myself rocking with the sort of laugh that subsides and then suddenly redoubles.

Mr and Mrs Whoever, if you're reading this, I'm sorry. Send me an address and I'll send you an apologetic crate of sherry. Or a car alarm.

But I wish they had been offering me a lift. This is a bad road. It's been a long walk out of Taupo, relieved a little, but not enough, by the panoramic view of the volcanoes, the lake, and the little township parked decoratively at its northern end. Though that township is beginning to creep over the hills in a fungus of big holiday homes. Each home is designed to exploit the view, and each does its bit to spoil it.

The main road north is three-laned and fast. It offers nowhere to pull over. I round a bend. Another long fast straight and another distant bend. Fifteen minutes later, I round that bend and the view is repeated. This is vehicle land, land to be passed through. I doubt that anyone has walked it in a while.

It's sunny. My oilskin vest is pudgy to the touch. And I am rescued by a Maori boy going the wrong way. He's going the wrong way only because he's turned round to fetch me.

'Couldn't leave you there, bro, eh? No bugger's gonna stop for you there.'

He's in 'customer service' at a geothermal tourist attraction five miles up the road, but he drives a mile or two out of his way in order to drop me at an intersection. His car's a wreck, his conversation limited, but his demeanour is as genial as sunshine, and his smile's as wide as his face. When I ask him if he's ever been overseas, it's clear not only that he hasn't, but also that he has never thought of doing so. He's a good kid.

He drops me where the road splits. North to Auckland on State Highway 1 – the road I began on 1,000 miles to the south – or north-east to Rotorua. I set up shop by the road to Rotorua.

Every visitor to this country goes to Rotorua. I never have. I expect mudpools. I expect Maori dancing. I expect tourists. And I expect to dislike it. In less than five minutes I'm heading towards it in a gold-coloured rental car driven by a driven entrepreneur.

I've heard of his company. It makes emergency lighting for places where people gather, stuff to steer the panicking multitude to safety.

'September the eleventh,' he says, 'came about six months too early for us. Shitty thing to say, but it's true.'

His is a product for the times. What's more I've read newspaper articles about it and the prospects of big international contracts. The articles implied that here, yet again, is an archetypal Kiwi story. The backyard inventor outdoes the money-drenched multinationals. From the garden shed to the world. It's the sort of story that the national psyche sucks sustenance from.

But my driver makes it clear that that's not quite how it is, and that the little-battler-beats-the-big-boys story is no more true of New Zealand than it is of, say, the UK or Belgium, and probably less true than it is of the States. But he doesn't mind pandering to the myth. Myths can be stronger than truth.

What is typically Kiwi, however, is that I am sitting next to a man I have read about. With the population the size it is, the famous are at your supermarket, members of your tennis club, sitting on the next bar stool. It's a good thing.

A phrase you hear too much of here is 'the tall-poppy syndrome'. It implies that New Zealand has a unique propensity for cutting off its heroes at the knees. It also implies that that's a bad habit. Both implications are wrong. For one thing this country is neither more nor less delighted than any other when a rockstar is done for driving drunk or a newsreader for ogling kiddie porn. For another thing, it's not a bad habit (the tall-poppy stuff that is, rather than the kiddie porn). In an Andy Warhol world of cheap, brief, random and unmerited celebrity there needs to be a whole lot more cutting off at the knees than there is. And because of the small population and the accessibility of the people in the news, New Zealand is less given to bestowing unmerited admiration than some places I've lived.

While we're on the subject it should also be noted that those occasional sadsacks who moan that they are the victims of tall-poppy syndrome are always short daisies.

Anyway, my entrepreneurial driver is fresh of mind and forthright as a punch. He's come from a conference for businessmen such as himself, hosted by a government that is typically keen to associate with people who've succeeded without it. Or even despite it.

Like me he's never been to Rotorua, is going there now only to catch a plane back to Christchurch. Together we marvel at the land. We are driving through clusters of strange small hills like clutches of eggs, cloaked in a green so richly brilliant it looks false. And gouts of steam gush from unconsidered bits of nowhere, utterly remarkable and seemingly unremarked.

Rotorua smells like a school chemistry lab. Across the road from where he drops me there's a golf course, dotted with the usual men of indeterminate age pulling trolleys like field guns, and wearing pullovers that are patterned only on the front. Steam belches from holes in the fairways. It wafts across the greens. It looks like golf on Jupiter. And I'm the only one standing to stare. The golfers are hunching over their putts.

The two miles of straight road between me and the town centre are given over to accommodation. There's a Rob Roy Motel, a Geneva Motor Lodge, a Best Western, a Capri, a Baden Baden, a Palm Court, a 4 Canoes, an Any-emotive-sounding-nugget-drawn-from-any-marketable-culture-in-the-world, and a Grand Tiara Hotel that boasts a McLardy's Irish Bar and a nightly Maori concert.

With so many places available I unerringly choose the worst of them, a motel run – if that's the word, and it emphatically isn't – by a man who was born to be an morgue attendant. He has a motel to match.

I didn't stay in a motel till I was twenty-five when I hitched down the west coast of the States. Motels were the cheapest places to stay and the cheapest of them were seriously dire.

They resembled temporary porn studios – and some of them probably were, though rarely while I was in them. But they established my mental template for a motel room, a sort of Platonic ideal of grunge. It's this room.

Dark, humming with the noise of close traffic, a narrow sink, a leaking tap, don't-care joinery thick with paint, a tissue-thin pillow case with the ghosts of stains washed into the once pink cloth, a ceiling of stippled plaster, each stipple minutely tipped with dirt like a smoker's tooth, a dented kettle that won't switch itself off, and beneath it a laminated wooden tea-tray, bleached and buckled and chipped by time and chance and a thousand transient forgotten guests. Every one of those guests has left a molecule of self. The air's like gravy. And I'm allowed to smoke in it. I silently bet myself that the ashtray, when I find it, will be made of chunky amber glass. I find it in what the motel brochure doubtless calls the kitchenette. The ashtray is made of chunky green glass. The room is so authentically dispiriting that I like it. I head out to pootle in a good mood.

On the north-west edge of Rotorua, a school is surrounded by a playing field. Beside the playing-field, a road. Over the road, just a gentle chip of a rugby ball from the first-fifteen pitch, a park. On the edge of the park, a hole in the ground. Kick the ball into the hole, and it's time to buy another ball.

This hole is audible from 20 feet. It glugs, sucks and farts. When a gust of wind momentarily clears the steam, I get a glimpse of a mud-pool 10 feet down, rhinoceros-grey and boiling. This hole just begs for metaphor – death-pit, shaft to oblivion, gateway to the underworld. It's utterly forbidding. But it's nothing special. The park is pocked with these holes, no two the same. Some spit, some churn, and all steam. Viewed from the school playing-field, this neat suburban park looks like a field kitchen for troglodytes.

The mud can be as thick as foul ice-cream, or it can run like slurry. And there are pools of blackly translucent hot water that slant down and away into the earth to a depth you can only guess at. The depth you guess is unlimited. These pits, these holes, this blackness could stretch to the planet's red core.

Each hole is surrounded by blackened vegetation that thrives on hot roots and a diet of sulphur.

Under a little pergola the hot water has been tamed and channelled into a paddling pool. A young couple sit wrapped around each other snogging on a bench, their shoes beside them, their feet in the water turning pink. And people in every-day clothes walk among the pools, going about their business, heading home, heading to work, preoccupied, unenthralled, because if you live in Rotorua this is how things are. You don't notice that even the town drains steam.

Otherwise the town centre is ordinary as a sparrow, a grid-based place with architecture that draws no attention to itself except when it's bad. There are the standard shops for resi-dents, the standard shops for visitors, and the standard pubs for both. I check the Pig and Whistle for televisions, because tonight the All Blacks play Australia.

The Pig and Whistle sells beers with humorous names. Nevertheless it has a telly over the bar and a big screen hired for the night and set up in a canvas extension at the back that is also hired for the night. 'Be here early,' says the barman. 'This place will go off.'

It's two o'clock. Kick-off's at seven-thirty. One man's already installed. Long-haired, youngish, handsome, with a packet of rolling tobacco on the bar in front of him, two packets of ciga-rette papers, and the first of a day-long string of beers, he doesn't intend to budge. We discuss the prospects, agree that the All Blacks should win, and then he tells me he's a chartered accountant. I say that I wouldn't have guessed.

'I like it,' he says. 'I was fucking good at maths at school.'

A woman with remarkably snaggled teeth has come to the bar to smoke. The non-smoking friends she's left in the restau-rant are also non-rugbyites. They've come from Auckland for a girlfriend's fortieth birthday party this evening, and so she'll have to miss the game.

'Can't you pretend to be ill?'

'They know me too well,' she says. 'Back home my nephew's got Sky and a giant screen. He's become my favourite relly.' She takes a long drag of her cigarette. 'Though only on Saturdays.'

Between the town centre and the shore of Lake Rotorua stand immaculate gardens, the borders forked and weedless, the lawns shaved to regimental uniformity. A concrete wall surrounds the Rachel Spring. It's a clear hot pool of Tartarean depth that would be a wonder of the world anywhere but here. I give it a glance.

At the head of the gardens stands the most impressive building I've seen in New Zealand, and that includes Invercargill's water-tower. The Rotorua Bath House was built by the government almost 100 years ago to foster tourism. It was known as The Great South Seas Spa. Europeans travelled here by ship to take the waters, to be immersed in mud, to be benignly electrocuted.

Red-roofed, turreted, fronted with cream plaster and wooden beams, the building was modelled on German spa houses. But it feels distinctively New Zealand in a way that few buildings do. One reason is the colours. Whether it was intended, I don't know, but this place uses the primitive pigments of Maori decorative arts: white, brown, black and red. And then there's the timber. The baronial entrance hall is a temple to native timber, polished to a lustre and dark as the country's heart. And I've had only one beer.

Though built in 1908 the Bath House was not the start of Rotorua tourism. Fifty years earlier the Pink and White Terraces were already pulling in the punters. A natural tumble of stepped rocks, encrusted pink and white by the sulphurous waters, and offering bathing at assorted temperatures, the Terraces were said to be one of the world's great sights. Then, in 1886, Mount Tarawera erupted, taking plenty of lives and half a mountain with it. The Terraces simply disappeared.

I learn all this in the Bath House which is now the Rotorua Museum, a state-of-the-curator's-art place with audio-visual displays round every corner and an emphasis on storytelling. Most impressive, educational and all the rest of it and I've had enough in half an hour. I prefer jumbles of stuffed and dusty birds.

Half an hour to kick-off, and the chartered accountant's still in the Pig and Whistle, but down to one pack of cigarette papers. He was wise to reserve his place. The pub seethes. I worm to the bar and in defiance of a little printed notice I stay there, my elbows sticky with slops, my shoulders constantly jostled, my services called on to pass beer over heads to the back. But I've got an uninterrupted view of the screen. The barmaid is wearing an Australian rugby shirt and everyone calls her a brave girl. She isn't. The crowd may be fervent, but they're as ferocious as gambolling lambs. Rugby violence happens only on the field.

All Black games matter to the country's image of itself. The result of tonight's game will directly affect the population statistics. When the All Blacks are winning, New Zealanders are more likely to come home from abroad, and those who are already home are more likely to stay. When the All Blacks are losing, the money of London and the sunshine of the Gold Coast pull more strongly. The reasons are historical.

Rugby Union springs from the great British public schools, where it combined with cricket, the Church of England and militarism to form a four-pronged defence against masturbation. I doubt that rugby had any effect on masturbation in New Zealand either, but the game caught on throughout this country in a way that it never has in Britain.

New Zealand adopted the game more or less by chance. In 1870 a certain Charles John Monro organised a game in Nelson. He had to teach both teams the rules. Then he took a team to play in Wellington. The Wellingtonians enjoyed themselves, and chose to take up Rugby Union in lieu of 'Melbourne rules', the chaotic sport still popular in bits of Australia in which the umpires look like ice-cream sellers practising semaphore.

Here rugby is indisputably, to quote the title of a recent and popular book, 'The Game for all New Zealanders'. As early as 1888 a 'New Zealand Native Team' toured Great Britain. Native did not mean Maori, but simply anyone who had been born on these islands.

Today one of the most evocative of kiwi images is a small-town rugby field in summer. Skewed wooden posts, or rusting metal ones, stand in a field of knee-deep hay or thistles. In a far corner there's a changing shed like an gipsy caravan with boarded windows. Unpretty, unkempt, honest, to the ex-pat Kiwi it's the heartstring-tugging equivalent of thatched cottages and duck ponds to a certain type of ex-pat Brit.

To a ragged cheer from the packed Pig and Whistle, the All Blacks run onto the pitch. They are wearing their new body-hugging, futuristic shirts, like fifteen Captain Kirks, though without the sagging tits. The backs are mainly brown boys from the North Island, the forwards white boys from the South. And no one cares. It doesn't occur to anyone to care.

White liberals who wear greenstone fishhooks round their necks to illustrate their solidarity with Maori, tend to sneer at rugby. They see it as the image of the old New Zealand, with its white, masculine monoculture. But Maori don't. Maori took to rugby from the outset. And, by a neat irony, the All Blacks club is the one utterly colour-blind institution in the land, the one place where skin colour just isn't noticed, the one place where people are judged as Martin Luther King hoped that his children might be judged, assuming, that is, that his children took up rugby.

The team that did most to establish the importance of rugby in New Zealand was the 1924 'Invincibles', who played thirty-two games in Great Britain and won the lot. It was giddy stuff for a country that still held Great Britain in a sort of ambivalent reverence, and that still sent to Great Britain most of its agricultural products and its brightest minds.

So rugby became established as a field of endeavour in which New Zealand could achieve supremacy, could compete with and expect to beat anyone in the world. And All Blacks became athletic royalty.

There's no such thing as an ex-All Black. To play once is to be dubbed for life. Successful and popular All Blacks can spend the rest of their lives making after-dinner speeches and endorsing products on television. Colin 'Pine Tree' Meads, for example, who hasn't played rugby for thirty years, plugs fence-posts, life-jackets and investment plans. Significant All-Black deaths are noted on the evening news. And when, as today, there's a big game on, the newsreaders, those cultural mannequins, invariably solicit favour with the masses by smiling at the camera as the bulletin closes and saying, 'Go the All Blacks.'

The players are lining up now for 'God Defend New Zealand', sung in Maori then English. It sounds better in Maori, but not much good in either language. Few of the players do more than mumble and no one in the pub does even that. The anthem seems a dreary Victorian legacy, as irrelevant to the nation's modern sense of self as a school song. But then comes the haka. The haka belongs. It is unique to this country, and its ferocity and masculinity and bellicosity are entirely apt to the circumstances. It fires the blood.

Not even the most crimson of rednecks is bothered that the haka is a Maori thing. Here the two cultures fuse indistinguishably into one. The haka that the All Blacks perform was supposedly composed by the warlike chief Te Rauparaha when he was hiding from pursuers in a kumara pit. The early settlers feared and hated Te Rauparaha, but his haka is loved. In translation it goes:

> It is death. It is death.
> It is life. It is life.
> This is the hairy person

Who caused the sun to shine.
Abreast. Keep Abreast.
The rank. Hold fast.
Into the sun that shines.

They are wise to perform it in Maori.

The whistle blows to start the game, and now's the time to steal a car. The streets of the country are deserted. If you are unlucky enough to activate a car alarm you can just saunter away at your leisure because the cops won't come till half-time.

But no cars are stolen. The thieves are watching the game.

The All Black winger breaks away. He's a wild-eyed lad from Fiji who leans backwards as he runs. And as he runs the whole pub stands on tiptoe and purses, tenses, clenches fists as if striving to hold back an orgasm. He scores and the bar erupts with flung beer and whooping. It's a lot of fun.

'Who's winning?' The speaker's a young Englishwoman with ringlets. She quizzes me about the rules. I give her clipped over-the-shoulder answers, my eyes on the game.

'Sorry,' she says. 'I'll shut up,' and to my surprise she does.

At half-time I buy her an apologetic beer. She teaches PE in East Anglia, is here on holiday and wants to come here to live but is in love with a plumber back home who earns twice as much as she does and who's got a Prince Albert.

'Is that one of those metal bars through . . .?'

'Yes,' she says, with the sort of look in her eyes that most people reserve for kittens. 'It's lovely. Do you play pool?'

'No.'

'I do. I love it. I'm bloody good. But it got me into trouble. Do you want to hear about it?' And suddenly there are tears in her eyes. But the players are back on the field and I nod towards the screen. 'Sorry,' I say. 'Later.'

The game's a cracker. The All Blacks have the lead but the Aussies threaten a comeback and the crowd groans and oohs and cheers as one, and surges like a school of fish. The All

Blacks hang on and win. There's a spasm of celebration, but it seems prompted more by relief than by joy.

If the New Zealand cricket team loses a match, no one much minds. People do not expect them to win. But people do, emphatically, expect the All Blacks to win. It appproaches a national need. And now the right thing has happened. Things are as they should be. Within a minute or so the noise in the pub has dropped to a normal level and within half an hour the crowd has gone.

The PE teacher and I head off to find a pool table. On the way she divulges how pool led her astray. She kissed an opponent, kissed him long and deep and sexually and she is overcome with guilt. She's crying as we walk.

'I don't see the problem.'

'But what'll Ben say?'

'Ben in England? Ben with the Prince Albert?'

'Yeah. He'll go crazy, I know he will.' She's weeping with alarming vigour.

'Sorry, but I don't understand. For one thing, you haven't done much. And for another, how's Ben going to find out?'

She looks at me with wet eyes the size of Frisbees..

'I've got to tell him. I can't not tell him. I was going to tell him on the phone last night but I just couldn't. I've spent five hundred quid ringing him up this holiday.'

The pool-hall air is thick with smoke and hostility. A concrete floor, a rudimentary bar, an area for dancing with no one dancing, music you can feel through your feet, and half a dozen pool tables all in action. The end table is Asian – six small and deft young men in suits and open-necked shirts, their hair dyed red or orange, accompanied by girls in skirts that barely widen at the hip and T-shirts that would fit a six year old.

Shaven-headed Maori boys lounge against the walls, drinking Lion Red from the bottle, sunglasses propped on their scalps. On my own I'd feel uneasy here. I'm twice the age of all of them, and half the size of many. My companion picks the roughest-looking table and lays a coin on the cushion. Ten minutes later we're playing doubles against a pair of hoods. I'm no good at pool. The English girl's an addict. She chalks her cue fastidiously. She leans over the table till the cue-butt's rubbing the cleft of her chin. And she misses every shot. I sink quite a few. I rather enjoy myself.

But we both play English pool. We weigh up shots. We aim for snookers. We hit the ball softly. We're cautious. The Maori boys take half a second to size up a shot then give it a smack. They thrash us.

It's half-past two when I meander back to Motel Grim under a moon that's almost full and suspiciously tangerine. But this time it is the moon.

18

Lala lands

A tramping club has found the stolen tour bus. It was dumped in the Kaimanawa Forest Park, fifteen kilometres from anywhere. The thief had nicked the radio. 'Obviously,' said Detective Humphries of the Taupo police, 'it was somebody who knew what they were doing.' Indeed, Officer.

The front page of the only Sunday broadsheet is devoted to

the All Blacks. There are pictures of big men at the moment of victory, their bright white mouthguards like slices of joy.

I'm looking forward to a day of tourism proper. This being Rotorua I am overwhelmed with choices. I can visit Rainbow in Fairy Springs Road, which promotes itself as essentially New Zealand. 'Experience the essence of New Zealand's unique farming lifestyle. You may be asked to milk the cow, feed the lambs or sit on our champion bull inside our all-weather show barn.' – just as real New Zealand farmers do.

Like the geothermal prawn farm, Rainbow is touted as 'fun and educational'. And like the geothermal prawn farm, I'll leave it alone.

At Wai-O-Tapu Thermal Wonderland I can watch the Lady Knox Geyser erupt at precisely 10.15 each morning, or else I can toddle off to the Sacred Gardens at Tamaki Headquarters which comprise 'an indoor, all-weather, peaceful haven where you can escape the hustle and bustle of everyday sightseeing and touring . . . Featuring the amazing Water Organ and Maori Medicinal Garden.'

Unable to take quite that much excitement I amble up Accommodation Avenue to visit Whakawerawera Thermal Village to 'view bubbling mud pools and thermal springs . . . and feel the rhythms of our cultural performances'. The ad shows a woman in traditional Maori costume feeling the rhythms by reclining amid steam.

Entry to the tourist village is by bridge over a stream. It's drizzling. Halfway down the bank three chubby Maori boys in swimming togs are squatting in a warm spring. An Asian man is videoing them. I am unsure if the boys are there by their choice or by other people's design. If by their choice, there's something tasteless in stopping to stare at them. If by other people's design, there's something even more tasteless.

From a wooden hut beyond the bridge a woman sells me a ticket and a map, and tells me to assemble at a certain hot pool in fifteen minutes to join a guided tour. She also tells me that a joyous and not-to-be-missed concert party will be erupting spontaneously at eleven-fifteen sharp. If I miss it, there's another at two. Then she adds with emphasis, 'We're nothing to do with the Maori Arts and Crafts lot up the road. They're completely separate.' On the map she indicates where that alien organisation lives, with a fierce obliterating scribble.

The village is a village. People live here amid the hot pools and the geysers. It resembles a scruffy Cornish fishing village, if you can imagine a Cornish fishing village dotted with hot fountains and smelling of bad eggs. Footpaths wind among the pools and little notices tell you that this pool is traditionally used for bathing, that one for boiling weka prior to plucking, this one for steaming flax, all the frightfully informative stuff that you read, note, inwardly digest, nod your head at, and excrete within seconds.

Wooden houses dot the lanes, with washing flapping on the verandahs gathering hydrogen sulphide. In the graveyard the tombs have metal standpipes to vent the gases. Dinky wooden craft shops sell dinky wooden crafts and greenstone carvings and flax mats and poi sticks and all the other stuff that attaches to a pre-European culture. I shun the guided tour, take a cursory look at a gushing geyser or two, overhear an earnest Canadian woman asking a guide about Maori spiritual beliefs, give the carved bargeboards and the woven walls of the meeting house a quick once-over, and go. It's still drizzling. The boys are still sitting in the hot pools by the bridge. They seem happy to be there. And I'm happy to be leaving.

I hated the place. Or rather I hated what the place implied about both its inhabitants and its paying visitors.

The inhabitants of that village are living in the twenty-first century. They have televisions and cars. They watched the All Blacks play last night and they cheered like the rest of us. But the village as presented implies something else. It implies, and makes its money by implying, an untouched pre-European culture, a little native Eden for us to gawp at. It's dishonest and it's demeaning.

There is no untouched Maori culture. When the Europeans arrived, for better or for worse, the two cultures met and mingled. Though each culture was affected by the other, it was the Maori culture that inevitably changed more. The Maori became vastly outnumbered and they lost control of the islands. In the end they had no choice but to change.

Though European attitudes to Maori were often well-intentioned, many things happened in those early days that were indefensible. Nevertheless, both the New Zealand historians I have read have insisted that Maori of the nineteenth century were no mere innocent and gullible victims. Though the settlers brought firearms that did no one any good, alcohol that did a lot of Maori a lot of harm, and diseases to which Maori had no immunity and that threatened at one point to eradicate the race, they also brought an abundance of stuff that Maori willingly embraced. Maori adopted food crops, metals, cloth and other technologies. They adopted Christian beliefs. And in all cases they adapted these things to serve Maori needs in a Maori way.

They also proved to be keen and able traders, as evidenced still by the village that I've just visited. But this 'living village', with its concert parties and its native crafts that would barely be practised were it not for tourism, seems to me to do Maori a disservice. The place feels halfway between a museum exhibit and a circus performance, while pretending to be everyday normality. It seems to me regressive, distorting and exploitative. But obviously it doesn't seem so to the people who live there and run the business, so who am I to criticise?

Well, I'm a tourist. And what is it that draws us tourists to cultural exhibits, apart, of course, from the perennial need for something to do and the equally common delight in voyeurism? Behind it there lurks, I think, a nostalgia for pre-industrial simplicity, a search for a quaint Eden. It's a futile and patronising search. There never were any quaint Edens. And I am pleased to be away from this parody of one.

My mood lightens as I wander round the town for several hours looking for unconsidered bits of thermal activity to peer into. Just below the Bath House I find a little walkway round Sulphur Bay. It ducks through scrub and every now and then emerges on the edge of Lake Rotorua. Gulls, shags, scaup, black swans and a beach full of quietly hissing holes. Each hole puffs whiffs of steam. Mineral deposits form fragile crusts over the holes like bulging saucepan lids. The water of the bay is milky with dissolved sulphur. It's like one of the less credible planet surfaces in *Star Trek*.

But Lake Roturua's sick, and Lake Rotoiti, just over the hill, is in danger of dying. Neither sickness has anything to do with thermal activity. The problems are manmade. For years sewage went straight into the lakes. Worse still is the leaching of agricultural phosphates and nitrates, dumped on the land to promote growth but now sifting down to the water. As a result the lakes are prone to virulent algal blooms that starve the depths of oxygen and threaten all life within them.

With the drizzle strengthening to rain and my legs grown heavy from sightseeing, I take a spa. The menu outside shows an array of options – communal pools, private baths, outdoor shallows in a sort of concrete riviera. Inside I learn that half the pools are closed because the naughty underworld has been emitting hydrogen sulphide at levels above those permitted by law.

I rent togs and a towel and join twenty or so people in a chest-deep bath of steaming mineral water the colour of Denisovich soup. Though I can see no notices forbidding it, there seems to be a general agreement not to put one's head below the water. So there's nothing to do but lean against the rail, stare vacantly through the mist and pretend not to be studying the other bathers.

There's probably a German word for body-shame. There should be an Australian one. One Australian woman is so monstrous, with a whole tyre dealership stacked beneath her saucy-postcard bathing suit, that her skinny but pumpkin-gutted husband has to push from behind to get her up the steps and out of the pool. His hands sink up to the wrists in her buttocks.

Flat-chested girls scamper from the changing-room and slip into the water like slim seals. A slope-shouldered adolescent boy crosses his arms across his concave chest. At the far end of the pool stands a knot of Asian youths, not smiling, barely talking, apart and entirely hairless.

I've never been a bather. I do a couple of desultory widths of paddling on my back. On the second width, in the manner of a boat nudging a wharf, I headbutt a bulky matron. 'Oh,' she says and looks at me, then moves haughtily away down the pool. I apologise to the back of her head, which alone remains above water level, and glides away from me like a buoy hauled slowly by an unseen line. Beneath the water her legs must be working like a pair of duck's feet.

As a child I hated water. The burning panic of getting the stuff up my nose induced a terror of drowning. Primary-school trips to the Burgess Hill swimming pool were nightmares. I stood gingerly in a corner of the shallow end, gripping both rails, dreading that someone would duck me. But then my dry-land mate Dave Collier told me that girls looked wonderful underwater, and he taught me how to hold my nose and plunge and open my eyes. He was right. Through the stinging chlorinated water that, at a conservative guess, was 30 per cent urine, I watched fascinated as the larger girls shifted about in a weightless lumbering dance, like hippos.

But here such pleasures aren't possible. I get bored and get out. In the end, though people have been coming here to take the waters for over 100 years, a mineral spa is just a hot bath. And just like a hot bath it makes me hungry. I take three burgers back to Motel Grim and spend a contented evening on the bed, clean, tired and immersed in Hardy's Victorian gloom.

19

Towards bananas

'It's a rammer.'
  'What's it for?'
  The driver turns to look me full in the face for the first time.
I have a feeling that I know what he's going to say. He says it.
  'Ramming.'
  Shortly afterwards he turns up the radio. It's tuned to Classic

Hits FM, songs from the sixties, seventies and eighties. They're all British or American. I recognise most of them. The driver hums along with 'Pretty Flamingo' and I give up on conversation.

The rammer's a brute of a metal thing lying on the flatbed of the truck behind me, on its way to Tauranga for some jolly ramming fun. The ramming dialogue above is the final chapter of a conversation that lasted ten minutes and consisted entirely of banal questions from me and monosyllabic answers from him. He's a Maori guy in blue overalls, round-faced, with a goatee beard and fat black pony-tail. He's not hostile but he just doesn't want to talk. I'm not sure why he picked me up. With conversation out of the reckoning, the only possibilities are sex and sheer kindness of heart. I've seen no hint of a sexual advance, nor frankly do I feel in any danger of one. So I'm in a truck heading for Tauranga with a kind-hearted mute and a rammer. There's a first time for everything. Louis MacNeice would have made something of it.

I'm grateful for the lift. It was a long and dreary walk out of Rotorua. The road kept promising to emerge from scrubby suburbs into hitchability but every bend would reveal another little patch of settlement, or a series of further bends. I must have walked for an hour and a half as streams of logging trucks rumbled by, their cradles holding the peeled stems of pine trees like bundles of giant reeds, filling the air as they passed with flung grit and the smell of disinfectant.

The road takes us past the ink-black edge of the dying Lake Rotoiti and through unstartling ranges of hills towards the Bay of Plenty and its kiwifruit farms. At this time of the year they're bare as the vineyards, just miles of paddocks strung with pairs of wires, like head-high miniature railways.

The kiwifruit's a masterpiece of marketing. Formerly the Chinese gooseberry it's been grown here for only thirty years or so but has become a huge industry. Kiwifruit taste of nothing much and are awkward to eat. They sell because they look exotic.

My driver drops me with a couple of amiable grunts on the far side of the Te Puke which, to the disappointment of every English tourist, is pronounced Pookee. It's the self-proclaimed 'Kiwifruit Capital of the World'. It's got a giant plastic kiwifruit on a pole.

I'm on the edge of the suburban creep of Tauranga, the fastest-growing town in the country. In the distance stands Mount Maunganui, a small volcanic peak above a beach where happy young people gather every New Year's Eve to celebrate the annual tick of the global clock in traditional manner by getting stomach-pump drunk and biffing bottles at policemen.

I hitch just beyond a roundabout. The first vehicle to swing round it is an ambulance. It stops ten yards short of me. I'm delighted. I once got a lift from a police car in Wales, and on another occasion a taxi driver took me from Cambridge to London for free on condition that I talked every inch of the way to keep him awake, which I did. But never have I dared to hope for a lift from an ambulance. I make towards it, only to see the driver hurriedly unclip his seat belt and dart into the back. Through the gap between the front seats I glimpse a withered hand and forearm, gesturing with frantic weakness. There is only the one ambulanceman. I decide that I should offer to drive the vehicle to hospital while he ministers to the sick, and am within a yard of the cab when he vaults back into his seat, guns the engine, turns on the siren and takes off. It's all rather exciting but it doesn't get me far.

Five minutes later a real-estate agent stops in an archetypical real-estate agent's saloon with an impossible showroom absence of rubbish on both back and front seats and asks me where I'm going. I'm not sure where I'm going so I ask her where she's going.

'To a funeral,' she says. 'Get in.'

She's wearing real-estate agent clothes and a real-estate agent's badge and her hair is coiffed as a real-estate agent's should be, and she's charming. She's running late already and still has to change out of her being-a-real-estate-agent clothes into her going-to-a-funeral clothes but, having advised me that Tauranga is not really worth stopping for and that since the day's still youngish I should head for the Coromandel before the big storm hits it in a day or two, she then drives me ten minutes out of her way to put me on the Coromandel road. As we go she tells me that business is booming, that Tauranga's chocka, that it's hard to find houses to sell at the moment, and that there is a huge influx of Brits, Canadians and, in particular, South Africans. And sure enough, as we skirt the edges of the town, there are the subdivisions carving off slices of what once were farms, and before that bush. String, pegs and muddy avenues foreshadow the advent of the next human paw print on the land. Then she stops the car at a place called Bethlehem, wishes me luck, and does the sort of U-turn amid traffic that befits a woman heading for a funeral.

I have never been to the Bethlehem near Jerusalem. If it's anything like the Bethlehem near Tauranga it consists of road-works. I edge round diggers, tiptoe through mud, knock a bollard over with my bag, am assaulted by noise, mount a little summit and am relieved by the sight of a long sweeping green valley. At its foot a white wooden bridge and a little gravel layby and a hint of a bend to slow the traffic. It's a hitchhiker's dream. I stride down the hill on bouncing heels. I shall hitch by running water. When there are gaps in the traffic or when I simply fancy a break, I shall lean over the rail and smoke a cig-arette and scan the water for the camouflaged torpedoes of trout.

Sometimes, as happened to me outside Wanaka, I find such a splendid hitching spot that I feel reluctant to leave it. But this is the first such spot I've found but never reached. As I'm approaching it, my thumb in my pocket and my heart still warmed by Ms Real Estate's kindness, a station wagon stops in front of me. More elderly mapreaders? Or perhaps the same pair of elderly mapreaders, who have changed their car for one with central locking and a security alarm, and who are now cruising the country looking for me with their friend the neighbourhood hit-man in the back seat cradling his semi-automatic. But an arm that is neither a firearm nor an elderly arm has appeared through the driver's window and is urging me down the hill. An osteopath and his wife are offering me a lift to Whangamata on the Coromandel peninsula and so I shall go to my grave not knowing whether the stream that lies just beyond Bethlehem holds trout.

The Coromandel peninsula, that juts up like a thumb to the right of Auckland, has a reputation. I've never been there, but I see it as a place of cottages, bush, beaches, potters, painters, vegetarians, hippies and dope. And also as a summer playground for the urban tribes of Auckland, which is only a couple of hours' drive away.

The osteopath's in shorts and jandals* and a tattered shirt. He and his wife are eager yachties. They own a catamaran. Each winter they shut up their house and make a voyage of several months to a Pacific island. On calm nights at sea they often set the sails, then go below to sleep and wake up somewhere else that looks the same.

'Isn't that dangerous?'

'It's the great no-no of sailing,' he says, 'but lots of people do it. They just don't admit it.'

I say that on the few occasions I've been sailing I've been either bored or frightened, but nothing in between.

'There is that,' he says, 'but we like arriving places. And we like adventures.'

Which leads him on to safety. He considers that we have grown too safety-conscious, too timorous. He mocks the recently enacted law requiring anyone who owns a swimming pool to fence it. It is a rare pleasure when hitchhiking to agree with your driver's opinion. Too often lifts are full of dishonest

*Flip-flops

agreement, because the lift is too short and your acquaintance too shallow to permit argument. And you feel obliged. I offer Mr Osteo my hard-hat story.

I'd long wondered about industrial hard hats, the ill-fitting yellow plastic things that managers conspicuously don above their suits and thin-soled office shoes when they visit building sites to pick through puddles and look knowing. So in the Lyttelton Working Men's Club I once asked a boiler-suited wharfie whether he knew of one example on the wharf where a hard hat had saved a life.

'No,' he said, 'not a life, though I have seen them stop a few nasty blows.' But the nastiest business he'd seen concerning a hard hat happened when a bloke was working on a pile of three shipping containers. He knelt to attach a crane hook and his hard hat fell off. When he shouted to warn people below, one guy looked up. The peak of the hard hat hit him on the bridge of his nose. They had to rebuild his face.

Mr and Mrs Osteo are eager travel guides. They point out the active volcano of White Island just offshore.

'If it blows, we've got thirty minutes to get out of Whangamata. The tsunami will flatten the place.' It's a statement that seems to me to put hard hats into perspective.

At Waihi they drive me round the back roads to show me where the old gold workings are, and where one night a couple of years ago a disused mineshaft collapsed and some houses fell into it.

Mr and Mrs Osteo have lived on the Coromandel for years. In the garden of their old house they grew avocadoes and Ladyfinger bananas, 160 to a bunch. I feel I'm pushing seriously north, catching a subtropical whiff on the wind. And yes, they confirm, there's a big storm on the way, due in a day or two.

The road narrows and winds through increasingly lush bush before dropping into Whangamata, population in winter 4,500, in summer 45,000. They insist in taking me to see their boat.

The little harbour glistens in the sun, its ripples sprinkled with bobbing yachts, their sails furled, their hulls as white as gulls, and rising behind them a sheltering hillside of pohutukawa trees.

'It's beautiful at Christmas when they're all in bloom,' says Mrs Osteo.

It's beautiful now, the whole place squatting perkily on its haunches begging to be photographed.

They let me buy them coffee in the dinky main street, and suggest I stay the night, but I have made good time today, and with the storm looming out there in the Pacific I press on up the peninsula.

It's immediately evident that I've left the main road and am back in the country. Almost every driver acknowledges my presence in some way, waving, indicating that they're turning off, or, if they're women, simply smiling a smile that says, 'You know I'd love to, but . . .'

Pete's a buck-toothed plasterer. And he's yet another driver who's passed me, gone 400 yards up the road, been sideswiped by conscience, and turned round. Born and bred in Whangamata, he's nineteen years old and driving his boss's four-litre truck. For recreation he hunts pigs. He goes out at night armed with five dogs, a knife and a sawn-off Winchester.

The dogs divide into bailers and holders. When they sniff out a pig it is the bailers' job, oddly enough, to bail it up. Enter Pete, who somehow, and this bit is not entirely clear to me, flips the pig over. Then he sets the holder dogs onto it, with the purpose, oddly enough, of holding it, while Pete sticks it with his hunting knife. 'Sticks' means cutting its throat.

The pigs can run to 260 pounds, which in metric terms translates as a lot of pig. If the pig's so big that he doesn't dare stick it, Pete blasts it with the Winchester. But he doesn't like to, because it's easy in the darkness to hit one of the dogs, especially the black one, a pitbull.

Having killed the pig and gutted it, Pete then lugs it out of the bush on his back, its front trotters round his neck and its head bouncing on his shoulder, tusked, grinning and dead.

Pig hunting's popular throughout New Zealand. One boy in the school boarding-house where I taught had decorated every wall of his cubicle with photographs of stuck pigs. He was especially fond of his sticking knife. For superstitious reasons he never washed it. When his mother sent him a food parcel he used the knife to cut the string, and then to cut the fruitcake.

Pete would like to travel. 'My sister just got back from doing fifteen countries. You know, Canada, England, the UK – that's Canada isn't it? Me, I'd like to cruise round Amsterdam. Yeah, that's the place, eh, Amsterdam.'

'What do you do when you're not working or pig-hunting?'

'Go on the piss, eh. Not much else to do in Wonga.'

Wonga, obviously, is the local contraction for Whangamata, which raises a puzzle over pronunciation I have never heard explained or even addressed.

Television newsreaders and other linguistic authorities pronounce the first syllable of Whangamata as 'fung'. Apparently this accords more accurately with Maori pronunciation. Maori was an oral culture. It was Europeans who put the language on paper and they did so phonetically. And what I don't understand is that if Maori pronounced Whangamata as 'fungamata', why did the Europeans write down 'whangamata'?

The only explanation I can suggest, and I do so tentatively, is the number of Maori nouns and place-names that begin with 'Whak' – Whakatane, whakapapa and so on. Is it just possible that prudish Victorian minds were unwilling to begin these words with 'fuk'?

Anyway, Pete the pig-sticker is turning off, and he drops me at a junction where all I have for company is a bog, reeds, scrub, a couple of morose cattle, and deep in the bush, no doubt, a herd of 260-pound pigs. In short, it's the middle of whacking nowhere. And I'm there for a while.

It's not until late afternoon, with the light beginning to

thicken, and the pigs beginning to rise from their daytime slumbers and starting to think about breakfast, that the Tairua harbourmaster stops and drives me to his harbour. And not just to it. He insists on driving me around it, to show me what's what.

What's what is a pretty little resort with a vast estuary of mudflats, a conical mount at the harbour mouth, and holiday homes all over, creeping round the lower slopes of the conical mount, lining the estuary, and perched precariously on poles among the tree ferns. Most seem to be winter empty.

'In summer this is the jet-ski capital of New Zealand,' says the harbourmaster. 'You'll get a good meal at the pub there, that's the old people's home, that motel next door is the one to stay in and down here by the wharf, this is the Sports Fishing Club where we drink. Visitors are welcome. See you later, perhaps.'

My motel room, with a Rembrandt print and a coffee plunger, has pretensions to posh. The pub doesn't, but it serves me a meal of deep-fried bits of fish that's enough for three. And that happens to be exactly the number of people in the bar, if you include the barmaid and the man reading the news on the television. When I leave, I hear the door lock behind me. It's half past eight and the town is smothered in silence.

Down by the bridge a heron stalks the mudflats in the dark, its grey body a mere shape of lightness against the black water. Outside the wooden community hall, there's a smattering of tall and narrow old people's cars. Through a gap in the curtains I see two rows of stackable chairs, strips of baize laid out on the floor and a dozen pensioners playing indoor bowls. Along the shoreline all but a few houses are empty, their curtains drawn like closed eyes. The lights of televisions flicker in one house in ten. I spy on a bearded man sprawled on a sofa with a flat glass of beer on the table beside him, watching the screen and ferociously picking his nose, his finger probing towards his brain.

Back along the foreshore to the Sports Fishing Club. It's

closed. Outside my motel room I have a final cigarette beneath the stars. The only constellation I have ever been able to identify with any certainty is Orion. In New Zealand he's upside down, his sword, instead of dangling from his three-star belt, stabs upwards into nowhere.

A car with flashing amber warning lights moves slowly up the road, followed by two wooden houses. They're lashed onto monstrous trucks.

From the old people's home comes a sudden single wail. Then the silence surges back.

20

Holiday money

'Does anyone here know how to cook couscous?'

The speaker is a man at the check-out of the Tairua supermarket, which is not particularly super, but it is small-town friendly. He's addressing everyone in the shop, which is five of us.

'Yes,' I say. 'You mix equal quantities of water and couscous, simmer it gently for about an hour, drain it, then throw it away. It's dreadful stuff.'

There's a momentary pause and then the man, the check-out woman and both the other customers fall about with laughter. I can't remember ever having had such total comic success. For a few delirious seconds I believe that I'm actually not going to be charged for my cigarettes and bananas (which are disappointingly imported from Ecuador). Economic normality prevails in the end, but I set off to hitch feeling absurdly like King Wit of Coromandel.

It's already been a good morning. I woke early and walked an hour or more round the harbour fringe, sharing the place only with herons, myna birds, a tui in a pohutukawa, and more kingfishers than I have ever seen in one place. Then over the sand dunes by the conical mount and down onto the postcard beach where the rising sun threw the standard blinding path across the water. A man in white gumboots fished with his rod set vertical in a holder, a single finger crooked over the line as if taking the ocean's pulse. A woman power-walked along the sand with a shamblingly happy retriever, and two wet-suited surfers bobbed and waited for waves 100 yards out to sea, like seals.

The real-estate agent's window in town advertises a small bare section on the conical mount overlooking this beach. It's priced at $495,000.

The Sports Fishing Club is open. A dozen women are doing aerobics in the bar with giant plastic balls. And a couple of old people's cars are still parked outside the community hall. I peep again through the window, hoping to catch the oldies sprawled snoring over chairs in attitudes of dissolution, their teeth jutting out and sucking back with each shuddering passage of old-person breath. But there are only neatly stacked chairs and neatly rolled bowling mats.

One good thing about small quiet towns is that it takes only ten minutes to walk out of them. Soon I'm stationed by a paddock in which strut half a dozen pukekos. Pukekos have adapted well to living round the fringes of human habitation. Because they're common they receive no attention. Were they rare, they would be considered endearing. Sleek as bullets, with electric-blue breasts, a black-green sheen on the wings, and a big scarlet bill and nose plate, they step high over the wetlands on their huge splayed feet as if studiously avoiding dogshit. But they are poor pedestrians. Their corpses are a common sight on the verge, bowled, disrupted by death, their sleekness all gone, like wrecked umbrellas.

There's nothing like half an hour's fruitless hitching to shake off the mantle of King Wit of Coromandel. Except, that is, for an hour's fruitless hitching. But this is rural New Zealand and I am confident the lift will come. Beside me in the paddock there's a tree that looks dead, or that would look dead were its leafless and apparently lifeless branches not sprouting vermilion flowers. On the north-east horizon I can see the first distant smudge of frontal cloud.

The lift comes from an old man. He played rugby round here in the days when all the roads were merely gravel. 'We travelled by bus and stopped at every pub,' he says. 'Great days, they were. I loved my footy.'

He played at wing or full back, and the acme of his career was his selection for a regional team to play the 1956 Springboks.

I've heard a lot about the '56 Springboks, the consensus being that they were the hardest team, the most physical team, and therefore the most admirable team ever to tour this country. The tales of what went on in the murky world of the front row of the scrum during the test matches of that year are the New Zealand equivalent of Arthurian legend.

'How did you go?'

'Lost seventeen-six.'

'Any tries?'

'Two penalty goals. I kicked them both.' And the inside of his Mitsubishi RVR becomes suffused with the warmth of nostalgia.

He's seventy-three. I can picture him almost half a century

ago in shorts that we would find comical, thick woollen socks
and boots that laced up over the ankle, digging a mound of
earth with his heel, laying the ball on it like a missile in a silo,
stepping back one, two, three paces, feeling the big hat-wearing
crowd fall silent, then stepping smartly up and toe-ending the
heavy leather ball between the posts, hearing the cheers and
running back to his place, trying not to smile while the heart
inside him leaped like an impala.

'Yeah,' he says more to himself than to me, 'I loved my footy.'

He played the game until he had kids. Now he has grand-
kids. The current light of his life is two years old.

'I've done all sorts,' he says, 'paper-hanging, selling, driving,
anything to make a buck. Used to drive an old Leyland artic. I
learned how to take corners on these roads. You ease off
coming into them, then accelerate out.' He demonstrates the
art, letting the RVR slow as we approach a thickly wooded
bend, then putting his foot down. The bend is tighter than it
seemed. He struggles to hold the lane, drives straight at an
oncoming logging truck and I've suddenly got my arms
crossed over my face, as he wrenches the wheel back to safety.

'Sorry,' he says and grins like a guilty boy and drives on
towards Whitianga with the caution of a nun.

Whenever the winding road climbs to a ridgeline it reveals a
vista of hills folding behind hills, all of them bush-covered, the
near ones green as lawns, the further ones darkening with distance to purple and then to black. And in between them
glimpses of inlets, flashing like fish. Then down a final hill into
Whitianga which the driver refers to as 'Witti'. He'll never read
the news on television.

Whitianga is booming. If you own land overlooking the
wharf you can name your price. Huge diggers are carving out
new subdivisions well away from the harbour, and new canals
adjoining them, so that owners can moor at their back door.

'Some of these places are going up by fifteen thousand dollars a week,' he says. 'It's Auckland money. Everything's

changed. It used to be just baches here,' and he drops me at a petrol station in the centre of town.

You can see how it's changed. At heart it's a small place with a jewelled and winking harbour, sunk among hills and bush. But there's enough flat land to expand on and the expansion's happening. Half-million-dollar holiday homes are rising everywhere, raw and crude and angular, dwarfing the low-built wooden prettiness of downtown. There are restaurants with names that took some thinking up and menus that take some interpreting, and every third building in the main street is either a brasserie-cum-café or a real-estate agency.

The new holiday mansions here and in Queenstown and Wanaka and Taupo are rising from the rubble of the traditional Kiwi bach. And as the old man's tone implied, the bach is dear to the Kiwi heart.

A bach is a shack in nowhere. It belongs to a family and is handed down through generations. By definition it is rudimentary. The archetypal bach has no electricity, a wood stove, a wooden floor, a sagging veranda, a tin roof, bunk beds with cruddy mattresses, and it is close to water so that the kids can drown unsupervised.

The bach represents much that was at the hub of the traditional Kiwi self-image. It was the holiday home that was not exclusive to the rich. Few people were rich in New Zealand. The rich belonged to the class-ridden old world. This new world was founded in an egalitarian spirit. Simply by being a Kiwi you shared in a different form of wealth, the wealth of living in a wide and sparsely populated land that, with its mountains and lakes and 18,000 kilometres of coastline, had space and beauty in such abundance that anyone could afford to own their little bit of it.

The bach was also a sentimental reference back to the pioneering days and the settlers who made do with little. At heart even the most urban Kiwi saw himself as rural. He might be obliged to live in town to feed himself and family, but for a few weeks every year he could shake off the fripperies of town like a dog shaking off water. In the heat of January he could discard his city clothes and he could pootle about in shorts in a dinghy and catch fish and cook them on an open fire and play beach cricket with his kids who went barefoot in paradise.

But that world is changing fast and the ramshackle bach is threatened. There are more people here now. There is more money too, and a greater disparity between the rich and the poor. And foreigners are sniffing about as well, foreigners from the over-rich and over-crowded northern hemisphere, foreigners who are buying up land at prices way beyond the reach of locals. And the land they want has a view of water, be it salt or fresh. Shania Twain, it's said, has just offered I don't know how many ridiculous millions for a view of Lake Wanaka. In short, the world is coming and the baches are going. You can see the change in the diggers and dozers and the mounds of fresh-turned earth around Whitianga. And you can see it in the clothes of the people at the café where I'm sitting now. They are not beach-cricket clothes or fishing clothes. They are smart clothes, rich clothes, city clothes.

Two loud and jolly older women beckon me over to their table. They want to know where I'm from.

'Oh, the South Island!' says one when I tell her. She makes it sound like a foreign country. 'I'd just love to do a few weeks down there, touring around. But the hubby doesn't want to. Says he did that before with his first wife. That's a real turn-on,' and the two of them explode into laughter.

One of them tells me she lives in Opito Bay. 'You've just got to go there,' she says, and offers me directions. 'It's the most beautiful place in the world. And we've got lots of millionaires.' And again the pair of them roar.

A sparrow perches on a chair back, waiting to make a raid on the crumbs of my carrot cake, waiting for me to go. I go.

'Don't forget,' says the woman. 'Opito Bay. Most beautiful place in the world.'

Somewhere round here is the Mercury Bay Yacht Club. It was from there, a no-account nothing of an outfit, that New Zealand first challenged for the Americas Cup. It sounds like the essential Kiwi story, but once again looks deceive. One man was behind the challenge – Sir Michael Fay, a multi-millionaire merchant banker, who had done very nicely indeed, thank you, from helping to sell the railway network of New Zealand to the Americans. He lives abroad now.

I get a lift out of Whitianga from Don. His van looks as though he's deliberately pelted it with rocks. Forty-eight years old, bearded and single, he lives high on a hill in a wooden house half-hidden by tree ferns. Well-educated and quick of mind, he's a man of the bush. He hates towns, hates what's happening to Whitianga, and is leaving soon for the wilds of the South Island and a job at a lodge in the mountains beyond Queenstown.

'New Zealanders,' he says, 'handle money badly. We use it to ruin the best things we've got.'

Don goes out of his way beyond the turn-off to his house, offers me advice on picking up young foreign women at back-packers' hostels, and drops me in a deserted bay. Only a couple of holiday homes here, but bulldozers are marking out a new sub-division. 'Paradise Found', it's called. 'Hurry. Only 1 section left.'

What looks like a discarded retread on the roadside turns out to be a penguin, tyre-marks across its carcase, its flippers flung out at agonised angles, its head turned to one side and flattened like paper. The beak is open as if to squawk, and there are flies in the sockets of its eyes. I nudge it into the grass with my toe, get a short lift from a man delivering a 29-inch television to a house in the wilderness, spend a cooling hour by a field full of spur-winged plovers and paradise ducks and a single hen pheasant and then am invited to climb aboard a post office delivery van.

'I've seen you several times,' says the woman.

'And I've seen you,' I say. Perhaps half a dozen times in the last few hours I've idly watched her van driving up tiny gravel

side-roads and re-emerging ten minutes later presumably one
parcel lighter.

'It must get lonely by the road,' she says, 'just waiting.'

I reflect that lonely isn't quite the word. Hitching can feel
dull and flat at times, and worrying too when night is
approaching or when, as now, the weather is darkening
towards a storm. But there is always a post office van to watch,
or a spur-winged plover, and a headful of memories to mull
over, memories that I've forgotten that I own, memories that
make me chuckle or wince in the middle of nowhere. 'No,' I
say, 'not lonely. Not quite.'

Next to me on the seat lie 100 furled copies of the *Hauraki
Herald* and a scattering of parcels.

'Just a few more stops,' she says and we turn down a dank
drive to deliver two ominous official envelopes to a woman
with a swarm of children at her knees, then cross the road to
stuff a letterbox without leaving the cab. The road winds up a
hill that I'm glad I didn't have to climb. At the summit there's
a designated scenic look-out. Thick bush steeples down to the
township of Coromandel and the Hauraki Gulf beyond. It's
the aerial photograph of a billion brochures, the idyll of blue
and green, primeval and apparently benign.

On the descent we pass a man in a bush shirt, a rifle broken
over his shoulder and three pig dogs fawning at his heels. They
are thin, short-haired dogs, free of all inessentials, just legs and
body and jaw. I swivel in my seat to get a better look at them
and him. He's got a face like a crag, deep-set eyes, two lines of
shaved moustache running down to his jawbone, and he
flashes me a look that's one part suspicion, one part contempt
and five parts withering malice. I don't think he'd have
laughed at my couscous joke. Somehow I doubt that he's heard
of couscous.

The one main street in Coromandel township still smacks of
the place's past. The shiplap shopfronts would look at home in
a spaghetti western, for this place began as a gold town. When

the gold ran out it became a logging town. Now there's neither gold nor logging. The Assay Office is a wine bar. The 12-gauge railway that winds up the hillside carries only cargoes of tourists, and duck-boarded trails have been carved through the bush to lead visitors to the few remaining examples of the kauri trees that covered the peninsula before the loggers came.

The information centre recommends a hostel round the corner. The place is funky with eco-sculptures, windchimes, and no-nuke rainbows, and so plastered with aggressive No Smoking signs that I do an about-turn before I encounter the no-doubt kaftan-wearing proprietor. I dump my bag at the pub and walk down to the wharf.

I'm a sucker for wharves, especially when they're as battered as this one. Its pitted sleepers are runnelled and fissured, the gaps between them widening with age. Seaweed hangs from the piles like rubbery rags, and stinking clumps of shellfish are clamped tight against the air. And what boats there are alongside, blunt-nosed, orange-netted, salt-stained trawlers and mussel boats, each one magnificent with rust. For me such boats are the stuff of romance. They make me want to run away to sea, to stand on the deck, my face streaming with water, hauling on the lines. At the same time I know with absolute certainty that I'm no trawler man. My hands are soft landlubber's hands, my stomach's weak. I'd be at sea at sea.

It's going to rain. The sky is darkening and lowering like a press. The air is fattening, ripening, preparing to burst.

'It was,' writes Hardy on page 110 of the New Wessex Edition of *Jude*, 'a louring, mournful, still afternoon when a religion of some sort seems a necessity to ordinary, practical men, and not only a luxury of the emotional and leisured classes.' Emotional and leisured myself, I duck into St Colman's Catholic Church. I want to know who St Colman was. The place is small, the pews few, the altar a humdrum table. Photocopied hymn sheets. Walls of tongue-and-groove timber painted cream, single-bar electric heaters mounted at head height, and a little red tabernacle light like something from a cheap gift shop.

St Colman it seems was the Abbot of Lindisfarne, who died at Inishbofin in 676. He lives on here because he was the patron saint of Irish gold-miners. By the door a stoup of presumably holy water. I dip my fingers and vaguely cross myself – for reasons that I don't think I could explain even if I wanted to, which I don't, but which have nothing to do with religion – and go to the pub.

The pub I'm staying in is at the bottom of the street and known to the locals, with their flair for imaginative metaphor, as 'the bottom pub'. This one's at the top of the street, and is known as 'the top pub'.

You can tell the nature of a New Zealand pub from the way it drinks its beer. Rural and working-class New Zealand drinks brown beer by the jug. Urban and professional New Zealand drinks yellow beer by the bottle. The brown beer is brewed in cities by one or other of two monopoly brewers, but it is branded to seem local. The yellow beer is brewed in the same cities by one or other of the same two monopoly brewers, but it is branded to seem European.

Until the late sixties the pubs closed at six. The freezing worker would leave work at five and have to get as much down the neck as possible in an hour. The pubs sprouted bars of extraordinary length so every man could get to them, and they dispensed the beer by hosepipe. And because there was no time to waste, drinkers left their cash in front of them on the counter for the barman to raid. Old men still do.

This one's a rural, working-men's pub. The severed and stuffed heads of boar and stags look down on the drinkers from dark plaques of timber like honours boards, the boar all tusked and snarling, the stags faintly smiling. The drinkers wear work boots, shorts and check shirts, except for two who are old and in slippers. One of the oldies coughs, sneezes, goes apoplectic red, clutches a hankie to his face, splutters, takes half a minute to recover and then says loudly, to no one, to everyone, to the world that has made him old, 'cunt'.

Two beers and a chapter of *Jude* then out into drizzle. The craft shops are closing for the day, the clouds seem low enough to touch, the bush on the surrounding hills lends a dank and brooding oppressiveness, and I transfer my patronage from the top pub to the bottom pub and its upstairs restaurant.

'Mushroom sauce or onion jus with your steak?'

The waitress is a pretty girl who flirts at every opportunity with the understandably cheerful chef.

'Onion jus,' I say, 'so long as it's not drizzled.'

She starts to write it down.

'No, no, sorry. It was sort of, well, a joke.'

She looks at me uncertainly.

'It's just that any menu with the word "drizzled" in it is bull-shit.'

And to my surprise her professional manner tumbles off her like a nightgown, and she laughs. It's a good laugh. I decide she's a very bright girl.

'So how would you like your steak?'

'Well done,' I say. 'Seriously well done. Like a running shoe.' I hope the simile will cause another laugh, but it doesn't. The waitress moves to a table where three Australian men have been listening to our dialogue. One of them orders a steak.

'Medium rare,' he says loudly for my benefit. 'That should please the chef.'

Instantly I hate the man. Why should it matter to him how I like my meat cooked? And who decreed that blood was virtuous? Did Jesus order rare?

Anthony Bourdain, the chef and author, who claims to revel in drugs, offal and sleeplessness, and who also scoffs at food snobs, says that chefs traditionally reserved the worst steaks for the boofheads who ordered them well done. Fuck them.

My steak is excellent.

21

Familia blues and trees

Patio furniture wakes me. A balcony runs along the top storey of the pub and outside each bedroom there's a wooden table and a cluster of aluminium chairs. Or there was. The chairs have all blown south to my end, and are piled outside my window, upside down, on their sides, tilted, their legs meshed together at spastic angles and rattling. The rain is horizontal. The trees are thrashing like a rock concert. It's weather to stare at. The *Hauraki Herald* tells me that it's meant to set in for three days.

I breakfast on pancakes, butter and syrup in a little café with half a dozen mournful tourists and the rain drumming in waves against the iron roof, drowning the splutters of the coffee machine. The windows are curtains of water. Occasional blurred figures leap from cars in the wild dark world beyond and sprint for cover, inadequate newspapers clamped over their heads. As with all extreme weather, I find it mesmeric.

The two women behind the counter are discussing the possibility of being cut off. A friend of one of them has to get to Auckland tomorrow and is wondering whether to leave now. In storms like this the road between here and Thames is often blocked by slips.

When I hear them say that, I make a decision, pull on my beanie, zip my oilskin vest to the chin, pull my hands up into the sleeves of my sweater, open the café door and run. I try to sidestep the deeper flows of water in the street, hit one, give up and just run. A minute later I'm standing dripping and panting in the office of the Coromandel's only garage, being laughed at by a woman.

'I'm sorry,' she says unconvincingly, 'but you look like a drowned rat.'

My jeans are black with wet, steaming at the thigh but cold against my flesh. I tell the woman that I'd like to rent a car.

She makes me a coffee and rummages for the phone. Like every garage office I have seen, this one's chaotic. A tank-grey filing cabinet, the bottom drawer open because it's too crammed to close, teetering box files heaped on top of it, each with its own unique set of black thumbprints, and a desk so strewn with papers that while she makes the call, some of them sneak up over the cradle and when she finishes talking she puts the receiver down on top of them.

'There'll be a car for you at midday,' she says, 'if the road stays open.'

'Any suggestions on things to do in Coromandel for the next three hours?'

'Yeah,' she says. 'Keep dry.'

There are three cafés close together in the main street. In each I have two coffees and a piss. And though *Jude* is open on my table I do a lot of staring at the rain. It brings to mind the scene from *Tess of the d'Urbervilles* where the church gargoyle spews water onto the grave of, is it Tess's mother? It's vintage Hardy.

My car's a Mazda Familia. I can't think of a more depressing name and I feel like a cheat for renting it, but I'm delighted to be on the move. And I make a vow to myself that I will not drive past a hitchhiker.

Twenty years ago Tim and I tried to go to Iceland. We were both rich at the time, he permanently, I temporarily. On a bright Monday morning we walked from Tim's flat in Notting Hill to the first travel agent we could find.

'Two tickets to Iceland, please,' said Tim, 'leaving this morning and coming back on Sunday.'

There were no flights before Wednesday. We went to two other travel agents and were told the same story. We went to the pub to think. Tim left the table and came back with a rental car.

'Where are we going?' I asked as we headed west out of London. Tim shrugged. I don't remember whose idea it was to navigate by hitchhiker, but I do remember the first one we picked up. He had a lot of hair and was going to Rugby.

'Whereabouts in Rugby?' said Tim as we drove away with him in the back.

'West Rugby.'

'Where exactly?'

At this point I could sense our passenger's sudden nervousness, but he named a street.

'What number?' said Tim.

He told us and we drove him to the door. He didn't ask us in.

We spent the whole week in this way. It was the best holiday of my life.

But there'll be no one hitching today, and even if there is I'll be unlikely to see him through the mist on the inside of the glass and the rain on the outside, rain so heavy at times that it makes the wipers falter under its weight.

If you want to know if the road between Coromandel and Thames is a pretty thing you'll have to drive it yourself. All I can tell you is that it winds a lot and for much of the route it runs beside the sea. Today, the first fifty yards of that sea are camel-coloured with run-off from the land. The next fifty million yards are invisible.

I can see no point in stopping. And besides, there is one place that I have resolved that I must visit on this trip. And now, in impossible weather and with a car of my own, I may as well cover the miles between here and there. That place is the very tip of New Zealand, Cape Reinga. The man who drove me from Woodville to Dannevirke last week told me that it was the only place in the world where you could see two oceans meeting. I want to see two oceans meeting.

Driving isn't travelling. Driving demands your attention, and a car is hermetic. I spear through something resembling Act III of *King Lear*, weather that would threaten me with hypothermia, yet I am warm, dry, seated and listening to the radio. As I pass a paddock of drenched and huddled sheep, two women in Wellington are gabbling about fashion week. An earnest man follows them, keen to change my opinion on the invasion of Iraq. Now that I've been on the road a while, I barely have an opinion to be changed. Travel is solipsistic. It snaps the threads of the news. And it teaches that any news you need to know will reach you somehow. The rest is mere titilla-tion. 'If we read,' wrote the notable hermit and occasional dingbat Thoreau, 'of one man robbed, or murdered, or killed by accident, or one house burned, or one vessel wrecked, or one steamboat blown up, or one cow run over on the Western Railroad, or one mad dog killed, or one lot of grasshoppers in the winter – we need never read of another. One is enough.'

I change station to a music channel, tire of that and silence the thing. Nothing but the hissing of tyres, the rain like a million fingers on the roof, and the swish-click-swish of the wipers, for mile after grey and sodden mile. The hills of the Coromandel level off. I cross a long skinny bridge over a river the colour of effluent, and follow a ruler-straight road across the flat Firth of Thames. The road widens into State Highway 2, then widens further into Highway 1, the country's single artery, drawing me on and up to where the Manukau harbour bites into the land from the west and the Waitemata harbour does the same from the east. On the isthmus between the two lies this nation's only metropolis, the big smoke of New Zealand, the city that the South Island slightly fears and loves to resent, Auckland. I drive straight through it.

The weather deters me from stopping and so does the sheer size of the place. I have been here numerous times and never seem to have found the same part of it twice. Apart, that is, from the surprisingly small city centre where the tower blocks grow and Queen Street runs down the hill and into the harbour.

Though Auckland houses more than a quarter of the country's population, that's not much over a million people, a number dwarfed by the world's major cities. And yet Auckland occupies an acreage larger than either Paris and London. It lies draped over the land like a flung garment, from the wild surfing beaches of the west coast to the gentler bays of the Pacific to the east. There are suburbs to the west where the houses are so buried in bush that the place seems barely inhabited. Dotted here and there about the city are a clutch of dead volcanic mounds like the pointed ends of eggs, mounds that Maori used for centuries as fortifications in their inter-tribal wars.

Auckland's a haphazard place. Unlike the planned settlements of Christchurch, Dunedin, Wellington and others, Auckland simply grew like bacteria on a petri dish. With its two harbours and its northern setting it was the natural port of contact with the rest of the world and a natural place of trade. It still is. Auckland dominates the economy. And there is a sense of business urgency about its streets that makes it feel more like Sydney or even Hong Kong than the rest of New Zealand. Part of that is the racial mix.

As well as people of Maori and European descent there are people here from every Asian country. And Auckland has the largest Polynesian population of anywhere in the world, including Polynesia.

In other words, and quite simply, Auckland's a city as the world knows cities. It's got pimps and fashion queens, helicopters and derelicts, no-go areas and suburbs so affluent that they smell nice. And the rest of the country isn't quite sure what to make of it. Southern people speak in fascinated wonder of its traffic jams. And Auckland just doesn't care. It has business to do.

I see no traffic jams. The road fattens like the barrel of a pipette and sucks me through. The needle on the Mazda barely drops below 80 kph. Over the harbour bridge, past the vast marina where the sleek yachts jostle, their sails furled bleakly in the rain, on through the thinning suburbs and out onto the northern neck of land that looks like a single-finger gesture to the Pacific, the final sliver of this country that ends in Cape Reinga, and that is officially and imaginatively known as Northland.

I try the radio again. A talkback jock is inviting his listeners to tell him what happiness is.

'Well, Garry, I just want to say that what makes me happy is love. Like the Beatles said. That's all. Bye bye.'

'It's all about following your dreams, isn't it, Garry. I mean if you haven't got a dream, what have you got?'

'What's your dream, Peter?'

Click, buzz. 'Ah well,' says Garry, 'I guess we'll never know what Peter's dream is.'

Caller after caller offers banalities so predictable that I clench the steering wheel. And each trumpets his kinship to Mother Teresa by insisting that money has nothing to do with happiness. Then an old man rings in with a voice that squeaks like polystyrene. He sounds inches from the grave.

'I'm eighty-three, Garry, and I just want to say that all your other callers have been talking bullshit.'

'Really, John, what makes you say that?'

'Try telling one of them he's just won Lotto, and see if he smiles or not.'

'I see. So, John, money makes people happy, does it?'

'Put it this way, mate, whenever I've had a dollar in my pocket I've always stood a sight better chance of being happy than when I haven't.'

Talkback radio is voyeurism for the ear. Plus solace for the lonely, I suppose, and a vent for outrage, for second-hand opinion, for the bores who can't find an audience in the pub. And to think of all of us on this drenching afternoon tuned in like a disparate family to this stilted conversation led by the facile Garry – well, it doesn't make me happy. I turn the radio off and realise I am bored. A sign says 'Turn right for Kauri Park' so I do.

The road climbs over a little hill, down a lane and ends in a deserted car park. The rain is hitting the tarmac hard enough to bounce. To my left a paddock of sodden sheep. To my right a little museum with a sign saying shut. In front of me a tall wall of bush. And in front of that, encircled by a wooden walkway, a monstrous tree. I pull on my beanie, zip up my vest and step out into the weather's instant assault. When I look up at the tree the rain drills my face.

When Chaucer was born this was a sturdy young tree. When Shakespeare was born it was 300 years old. It predates most of the great cathedrals of Europe. Its trunk is sky-rocket straight and sky-rocket bulky, limbless for half its height. Ferns sprout from its crevices. Its crown is an asymmetric mess, like an inverted root system. I lean against it, give it a slap. It's like slapping a building. This is a tree out of Tolkien. It's a kauri. Until the white man came, Northland was covered in them.

A boardwalk leads into the bush. It's dark as a cave. The canopy turns the torrent into a billion audible drips. There are labels on the tree types and designated spots for sitting to look at them. But it's too wet. I give the kauri a farewell pat as I pass and drive the Familia into nearby Warkworth, a puddle gathering under the pedals.

To arrive by car is to arrive dissatisfied. I've done nothing to get here but twiddle my arms and feet a bit. For perhaps 250 miles, I've ridden an armchair, cocooned by glass and steel. No contact with the harsh road metal, no sniff of the air, no glimpse of the birds, no shivering with the wind, no stamping of feet, no shoulder sore from lugging my bag, no elation, no doubt, no hope, no horror. I just sat and arrived. I gained no sense of transition. The emotional graph travelled flat across the grid. I met no one. I learned nothing except what I read on a sign about a tree in the rain. And the motel's dreadful. Not comic dreadful, not nostalgic dreadful, just bad-motel dreadful. And the rain's still coming down as if trying to dent the road.

I eat in the first place I find, a swanky brasserie with bi-fold doors that could open up the front of the building onto the stone veranda. No one will be opening those doors this evening.

The place is midweek empty. I eat a small bowl of giant mussels. Each shell's the size of a dinghy. And each mussel has a frilly fringe of flesh attached to it, the biological purpose of which I can't tell you, but it looks like a pensioner's gumline.

When I ask for more bread to mop up the liquor, the waitress charges me $2 for one slice. Probably because it's raining.

22

Giants

The damp morning newspaper tells me that the government has decided to improve the quality of life in New Zealand. It's a modest notion, and here's how they're going to do it.

'The government will establish an inter-agency steering group to co-ordinate policies that promote a work-life balance. The group will ensure that research and policy development on the issue by government agencies is co-ordinated.' It is sure to bring great joy.

Overnight the clouds have risen from ceiling height to roof height and are dropping only a drift of drizzle. Warkworth turns out to be modest and sweet. It draws few tourists and is the better for it. Five minutes will take you round the whole tri-angular centre of Warkworth and they are five minutes well spent: several fine colonial frontages, a family butcher that's been slaughtering since 1922, a Masonic Hall with columns and portico, a weatherboard pub with an ornate veranda, and the Queens Street Café Bookshop which has few books but which does me the best bacon and eggs of my trip, despite a puzzling bowl of what may be tomato relish but which looks, frankly, menstrual. And right beside everything, just where it should be, runs a substantial river, chocolate from the rains, rat-tling fiercely under the bridge and over the weir. Every town should have a river. Gloomy old men can lean on the bridge to stare at it, cheerful little children can feed ducks beside it, dogs can be swept away by it, and from time to time people can drown in it when trying to rescue their dogs. The dogs, by the way, always survive.

Just north of Warkworth the road splits. You can go left up the west coast or right up the east. I go left. It's green-hill coun-try, cattle and sheep country, rich-looking pastureland, sparsely populated – and today it's wet as misery. The Familia and I sweep on. At one point I slow down for a couple of women on foot in the heart of nowhere, hoping that they might stick a thumb out. They hear my slowing wheels, turn round and peer through the rain at me with what looks like fear.

How many varieties of tree have a museum devoted to them? I can name one. The kauri museum sits on what may or may not be a pretty hillside – it's hard to tell in the rain. Inside the building there are logs the size of whales, dioramas of saw mills, austerely beautiful old steam engines, endless black and white photos of working men in braces, and an example of the first Caterpillar tractor dating from 1929. Whenever one of these tractors arrived in the forest it threw 112 bullocks onto the dole.

There are specimens of swamp kauri, trees that fell into bogs up to 35,000 years ago. The timber remains workable. And there's a room full of gum.

Kauri gum was once big business. Secreted by the tree, it hardens into translucent amber nuggets and was used to make varnishes and polishes. Alternatively it could be carved into decorative sculptures, all of them, if this collection is representative, hideous.

Outside the museum stands a single living specimen of the tree itself. It's not very big. To see a remnant of true kauri forest you have to travel to Waipoua, an hour or so north of here. The man who did most to save the Waipoua forest, a Professor W. McGregor, is recognised in the museum with a commemorative bust. It's carved from kauri.

The hills drop to the coast and the flatland kumara farms, looking mournful under cloud. Dargaville looks even more mournful. A Maori busker squats in a doorway knock-knock-knockin' on heaven's door as women scamper by him with pushchairs and umbrellas. A little stationery store in the main street offers me postcards of lambs, penguins, kauri, beaches and whales, but no shots of Dargaville. There should at least be one of the Northern Wairoa Hotel, where I have lunch. Within its grand weatherboard exterior, painted a colour that perhaps I wouldn't have chosen myself, it enshrines both past and present. The spacious lobby ends in a staircase that, with its width, curved balustrade and magnificent dark timber, just begs to be called sweeping. But the reception desk at its foot is shrouded in security mesh. The whole hotel has a long-stewed smell, a hotel smell of forgotten Rotary meetings, and smoke and dance bands and old carpet and travelling salesmen and leather suitcases and prawn cocktails and brilliantine and beer and yesterday.

To one side of the lobby a door opens onto a formal dining room, its tables laid not for lunch, but for luncheon. It's luncheon-time now. The room is empty.

The bar where I have a pie and a pint is almost empty too. I join only half a dozen silent, gentle, but impressively committed drinkers. But just off the bar there's a darkened room, its windows blacked. All four walls of this room are lined with bleeping pokie machines, their fluoro screens alive with colours never found in the bush. At each machine there's a hunched attentive player seated on a stool. And behind each stool stands a knot of silent spectators, all intently watching the machine win.

With no belief that I have done justice to Dargaville but with no desire to stay and do it, I power the Familia up again – its toytown engine seems nothing if not eager – and head north once more.

On the fringe of the Waipoua Forest a road sign tells me to 'Watch Out for kiwis', which is quaint, but a bit of a puzzle. Do the signmakers imagine that if it were not for the sign I would run the birds down? And if it so happened that I was a committed runner-down of kiwis, do they imagine that the sign would dissuade me? In the end, I suspect, the sign exists to please tourists.

As the forest closes in on either side of the road the radio fades to static. Mist hangs in pockets. It's hard to tell if it's still raining or just universally wet. The greenery is multi-layered, and dense as sofa stuffing. Rising above it all are the totemic trunks of the kauri, straight as masts and limbless for at least half their height. Their crowns are so ragged they seem like prototype trees, pre-tree trees, trees that the creator drew in his infancy when he was just beginning to get the hang of things.

A gravel lay-by and a modest sign tell me that I have reached a place I learned about in the museum. I get out of the car. Nothing but dripping vegetation and a pervasive smell of sweet rot. I follow a little path through the bush that takes a turn to the left. A swathe has been cut through the under-growth in front of me. At the end of the swathe stands a tree with a name. This is Tane Mahuta, Lord of the Forest. It's big. It's very big. It's the biggest kauri in the country and therefore in the world. At roughly 2,000 years old, it's also the oldest. It and Christ were seeds at the same time. I'm not sure what to do.

You're not allowed close enough to climb the tree or even touch it, not that I feel any great urge to do either. Tolkien would no doubt start scribbling a story. I feel nothing but a vague sense of awe, that keeps me there staring at a big, wet, mute, insensate vegetable giant for perhaps three minutes. Then I go, feeling vaguely as Larkin felt when he put his cycle clips back on in the early fifties. But I'm glad, like Larkin in church, to have had the place to myself.

The forest ends, the road climbs over a crest and below lies the Hokianga harbour, a postcard view with a non-postcard sky. Van Gogh might have painted this sky in one of his less cheerful moments. The rolling green flanks of the inlet are dotted with little white villages, the first of which is called Omapere. The only living things in Omapere are a couple of damp goats and a policeman holding a device like a hairdrier, which he is clearly delighted to have learned how to operate, so delighted indeed that he flags me down to show me the dinky little LCD display announcing that I was doing 64 kph in a 50 kph zone.

'Sorry,' I say, and gesture mutely to the carnage I haven't wrought, the mangled pensioners, the weeping orphans.

'We've had complaints about speeding round here.'

Who from? The goats?

'You're not local, are you?'

I sense the possibility of charity. 'No, from the South Island. I've heard so much about Northland. Pity about the weather, but what a place, eh.' I gesture expansively at the sodden empty landscape, while taking care to keep the trowel I am laying it on with out of the constable's sight. 'What's the best way to get to Kaitaia? I'm heading there this evening.'

The constable becomes a very nice constable. He directs me to the ferry across the Hokianga, advises me to take the back roads from there to Kaitaia, wishes me a happy holiday, hopes that I'll take good reports of the place back south with me, tells me he's always wanted to visit the South Island, and fines me $80.

The ferry's a drive-on barge that carries up to twenty cars between Rawene and Kohukohu, which the big and merry ticket-seller on board calls Koko. On the far bank a white steeple scratches at the belly of the clouds. There are only two cars aboard, my embarrassingly urban Familia and an impressively battered ute with a battered dog box on the back and three battered men in the two-man cab, all of them wearing bush shirts and drinking Lion Red from cans that aren't at all battered. When I get out of the Familia in the rain to do some touristy prow-standing and scenery-appreciating, all three of the men stare at me with affectionate amusement that they disguise as contempt.

For reasons that I have never understood, the weather forecast on the evening news devotes some of its time to telling us about the weather that's just happened. And on three days out of five Kaitaia wins the competition for the warmest place. But it won't today. Rain strafes the subtropical main street. Wind screams past the huge Work and Income shopfront, and flattens the sign advertising coach tours of Ninety Mile Beach. As I check into a motel I make a mental note to catch the six o'clock news, to see if the forecasters tell the truth.

The perimeter fence of the motel is topped with razor wire. The single main street has an air of dilapidation that the weather does nothing to relieve. A gaggle of youths in sweatshirts shelter in a side alley beneath crude murals. The first two pubs I peer into don't appeal. Nor does the third, but it's the last one in the street. The windows down one side have been bricked in and painted violet. There's a crude stage, a small dance floor, a small mirror ball, and a chunky cheerful barmaid playing pool with an elderly Maori giant.

'Do you play?' he says. His voice is soft and low, an excellent thing in giants.

'Badly,' I say, and go on to prove it. The barmaid beats me. The giant thrashes me. Each of his hands is like the scoop on a digger. While thrashing me for the second time he reveals that he played a bit of rugby in his time.

'Who for?'

'The All Blacks.'

He tells me about an All Black tour to Australia in the sixties. One of the players, whom I had better not name but who is now a prominent businessman, had a lovely time at a party and wangled the hostess into bed. Her brothers grew suspicious. The business ended with the prominent businessman hiding under a bed, while my giant companion fought the brothers. And it was my giant companion who took the rap in the morning.

The following season the prominent businessman and the giant met in a domestic match.

'At the first line-out I smacked him one on the nose. "You wait, you Maori cunt," he said, so I smacked him again and he was stretchered off. Shall we have one more?'

I fetch a couple of jugs as a down payment on more stories. And perhaps as a provisional nose-guard.

The giant is one of nine children, three boys and six girls. The eldest girl died of leukaemia the night before an Auckland game. 'I played for her that day,' he says. 'Played out of my skin.'

His All Black career was brief. Rugby Union was an amateur game. Rugby League paid money. He took the money, changing code for a thousand down and twenty quid a game. In the New Zealand of the sixties that was apostasy. His name was expunged from the records. Meanwhile he raised a family in

Auckland, spent twenty years in the freezing works, then
retired back to Kaitaia where he was brought up.

I tell him that first thing tomorrow morning I'm driving to
Cape Reinga.

'I'll come with you,' he says. It's a statement rather than a
question. 'Haven't been up there for a while.'

I'm delighted. I've had enough of driving alone and have
despaired of finding a hitchhiker. He gives me directions to his
house. Before I leave to find something to eat, we go for a piss
together. He's sixty-four. He pisses like a horse. He dents the
stainless steel.

I find a little restaurant working hard at being upbeat in
what seems a downbeat town. On my table a folded brochure
dares me to drink a scorpion. 'Each bottle of Skorppio vodka
contains a real scorpion,' as opposed, I suppose, to those fake
scorpions you keep coming across. 'The scorpion's telson
(stinger) is still attached and contains full venomous glands,' as
opposed, I suppose, to those empty telsons you keep coming
across. 'Should you feel a tingling sensation in body extremities, seek medical attention.' But no word on what to do should
you feel a sense of nauseous outrage and fist-clenching frustration at an advertising campaign that depends for its success
on an appeal to an entirely spurious virility test and that . . .
forget it Joe.

My meal is excellent, and enhanced by the joy of watching a
keen South African father on the next table. He has two teenage
children that he is frantic to be on good terms with. But he
addresses them as if they were still ten. All he gets from them is
grunts. Then when he goes to the bar to fetch them yet more
elaborate soft drinks, they erupt behind his back into animated
conversation. I expect they'll drive him to scorpions.

Not yet ready for bed I go to see Dion. Fat, funny and
ensconced on a little stage, Dion is the resident entertainment at
a bar that seems to have been built, furnished and opened in
the hour since I last walked along the main street. From his

stool behind an electronic keyboard Dion seizes on me the moment I walk in, asks me questions about my life, improvises songs based on my answers, delivers monologues about his and my schooldays that make me chuckle in a way that few entertainers manage to make me chuckle, and bids me a generous farewell when I leave three beers later. I feel a little guilty for going because I am his entire audience.

The gaggle of sweatshirted youths I saw earlier, their hoods pulled up over their heads, are blocking the dark pavement ahead of me. 'Hello Kaitaia,' I bellow, and fling my arms wide in greeting. They laugh and cadge a couple of cigarettes. It's good to reflect that these young people will soon have their quality of life boosted by an inter-departmental steering group.

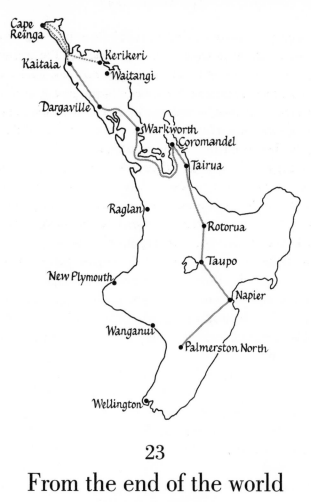

23

From the end of the world
to grapefruit

Having missed the weather report on the evening news I watch it on breakfast television. Kaitaia yesterday was 10 degrees. The forecast for today is 11 degrees. With rain. They're not wrong. The main street looks no more prepossessing than it did yesterday and the only place open this early for breakfast is McDonald's, which is run by Indians and empty but for me.

Front-page news is an earthquake near Te Anau. Big bits have fallen off mountains, and medium-sized jars of jam have fallen off a supermarket shelf in Queenstown. There are no photos of the mountains, but several of the jam. And there are interviews with residents, most of whose jam seems to have survived. But they are wary of aftershocks.

At the petrol station I ask the woman checking my oil what's happened to the weather. 'It's supposed to be hot up here,' I say.

'Something's gone wrong for sure,' she says. In a beanie and a Caltex jacket buttoned to the throat, she looks seriously concerned. 'I reckon we got global cooling up here.'

The giant is waiting outside his gingerbread house in the country, a couple of miles out of town. We shake hands and I point the Familia north just as soon as I've regained the feeling in my arm. We're heading for the end of the land. I'm not much given to geographical excitement but for once I feel a zing of expectation.

The country hereabouts seems grim, but it would be hard for it to seem otherwise. Dead-person clouds slice the tops from every hill. We pass patches of swamp, ponga, mangrove and, to my surprise, bamboo. And there's an abundance of the dead-looking trees with scarlet flowers that I first saw on the Coromandel.

'Flame trees, Joe. They're a bloody pain. Just shove a twig in the ground and it grows like a weed.'

A string of small settlements line the road, each just a sprinkle of houses and sheds, with a petrol pump and a vowel-laden Maori place-name. Herds of cattle stand dumb and immobile in the wet, waiting. A man on horseback in oilskins, his face clenched against the weather. At the heels of the horse, three dogs as thin as whips.

'My brothers and me,' says the giant, 'we used to ride up here for the muster on my uncle's station. A day and a half it took us.' It's taken the Familia an hour and a half.

To the west there are signposts to Ninety Mile Beach that runs invisibly beside the length of this road for I don't know how many miles. Apparently the beach is officially a road. Back in Kaitaia the Sand Safari Co invites you to 'experience the solitude and magnificence' of the beach, in the company of like-minded devotees of solitude and magnificence aboard a 41-seater bus that drives the length of the solitude and magnificence with the air-conditioning on.

As the land approaches its own extinction it narrows. I catch glimpses of inlets to the east, nosing among the hills, the mud-flats reflecting the grey of the sky, fishing boats beached by the tide and lurching on their keels as if shot.

We pass the last pub in the country, the last shop, the last petrol pump. All fuel now behind us we're on our own, civilisation dropping away like rags. The tarseal gives way to gravel, running through stands of what looks like blackened manuka, its foliage stunted and combed by the winds. At the top of each rise the air seizes the Familia and shakes it like a rattle.

To the west, the Tasman is white-ribbed and forbidding. To the east, the Pacific, sheltered by the land from the westerly, looks pacific.

And then, just as we top the final rise, by some meteorological freak about which it would be easy to say silly things, the sun comes out. It's the first sun I have seen for three days. The road ends abruptly in a car park. It's deserted. I'm oddly excited.

The giant has been here many times. He says he'll stay in the car. When I get out, the wind snatches my cigarette and tosses it instantly miles away. The car aerial hums like a plucked string. There's a blockhouse toilet, a letterbox with a flap over its mouth to protect the tourist postcards, and a signboard telling me worthy stuff.

A track leads down to the lighthouse. Names and dates are scored into the wooden handrail, names in German, English, Maori and the hieroglyphs of Japanese, puny scribblings in a limitless place. Beyond the squat whitewashed bulk of the lighthouse a few metres of boggy turf suddenly become cliff. The wind is such that I daren't go within five metres of the edge. Beyond that edge, just sea. Sea for ever and in every direction. To my left and far away, Australia. To my right and impossibly further still away, Chile. And straight ahead of me, the whole of the vast Pacific. If you sailed north from here and were unlucky enough to miss Fiji, the next land you'd see would be arctic Russia.

This is the place where our element ends. Here is rock, sea, wind, all of it dwarfing and wordless. There's nothing to do here, nothing except to stand a while and gawp.

And just as the man said, I can see two oceans clashing. Two differently angled lines of waves meet like ribs on a fish. At the point of coincidence the water churns hugely.

Off to the east lies Spirit Cove where, according to Maori legend, the souls of the dead began their journey back to the homeland of Hawaiki-a-Nui. Hawaiki-a-Nui may be mythical, but the myth is founded on fact. The Maori came here from Polynesia. No one knows exactly when they arrived in New Zealand but it was probably around the thirteenth century.

And New Zealand wasn't the only place they went. When they arrived here, they brought the kumara or sweet potato. They'd got that from South America. (In exchange they'd given South America coconuts.) So, at a time when Europeans had barely gone beyond the Med, Polynesian navigators had explored the Pacific. And they'd done it all in outrigger canoes.

I stand and stare at the fierce and seemingly limitless water in front of me. If I had a hat, I'd doff it to those extraordinary explorers. But I haven't got a hat. And if had, the wind would have whipped it off by now and flung it halfway to Samoa. I turn round and go back to the Mazda Familia.

'What do you reckon,' says the giant as I open the driver's door, holding it with both hands against the wind to save the hinges.

'Yeah,' I say. 'It's OK.'

'Let's go get a drink,' he says.

The Houhora Tavern is the country's most northern pub. It's just opening. Two Maori women beat us to the bar by a short head. 'Kia ora,' says the giant. The older of the women, a gaunt but spritely thing, replies in a stream of Maori. It's the first time I've heard Maori spoken other than at official events or on earnest Sunday morning television. The giant shrugs his shoulders and says, 'Sorry, love.' She smiles, lights a cigarette, sips her beer, sighs and says in English, 'I needed that.' It's half-past ten.

The walls are hung with stuffed snapper looking pinkly synthetic and running to 33 pounds. There are alien-like moonfish, a monstrous marlin, a boar's head, a piglet, and a series of bloody photos of a white pointer shark that was caught nearby and strung up for general delight. It's as long as a kayak and fat as a rowboat. Signs above the bar announce that 'Fighting brings a three-month suspension for both parties', and that 'The first bell means no more jugs, second bell, drink up, third bell, good night.' I have a Coke, and a magma pie. The giant doesn't so much drink his jug as inhale it, and orders another.

Back in the Familia I ask him about the recent Maori claims to own the foreshore and seabed under the terms of the Treaty of Waitangi. 'Bloody Maoris,' he says, and that appears to be the end of that little cultural discourse. Half an hour later he has me pull over at a second pub, run by a mate of his, another former All Black. 'You'll like him, Joe. He's a dag.'

The dag's wearing slippers, track pants and a v-necked rugby-club sweater, watching horse racing, pouring beer for half a dozen impassive all-day drinkers and being funny. Even at sixty something he has the impertinent twinkle of a good fly-half. I order a jug for the giant and a twelve-ounce beer for me. The dag refuses to take my money. Above the bar hangs a black and white photo of the giant in his playing days. He was a black-haired Adonis.

'Tomahawk, we knew him as,' says the dag.

I ask why, though I can readily guess.

'He'd smack you down from behind soon as look at you.'

The giant hides his delight behind a look of pained innocence.

'Wouldn't you, you big Maori bastard.'

'Steady,' says the giant happily. 'I'm tangata whenua, you know.' Tangata whenua means the people of the land, the original ones. 'I own the land this pub's standing on.'

'Oh, tangata whenua are you, well then I've got an account for you,' says the landlord.

At the end of the bar, a Maori guy in a Rugby League shirt who has said nothing, snorts with pleasure.

'We'll have one for the road, eh Joe,' says the giant.

A stout man marches in, orders a small beer, plays the piano on the bartop with impatient fingers while the beer is pouring, sinks half the beer in a gulp and complains about a problem with his pancreas. 'My guts were just rumbling and burning like there was a volcano down there, like they were boiling. Jeez, I was clean off my tucker for three days. Doc said I had to cut down on my drinking. I'd only been having half a dozen stubbies a day, and a couple of gins to help me sleep. How am I supposed to cut down on that?'

We have two for the road. When I drop the giant back at his little house it's well after midday. Two dogs in the yard strain on their ropes to greet him with fawning delight. He ignores them, waves to me, goes inside. The low clouds have closed back in to clamp down on the day. I point the Familia through the mist towards the east coast and the Bay of Islands, and drive the hour or so to Kerikeri feeling, well, feeling like the low grey sky.

The vegetation in Kerikeri testifies to the climate that prevails here but that I'm not getting any of. The place is like Torquay on steroids. Roadside stalls offer avocadoes, tangeloes, persimmons, oranges, lemons, all plump as pregnancies and fresh from the tree. The gardens are dense with fat-leaved sub-tropical rubber-plant-like things that if you sit awhile you can actually see growing. Even the meanest bungalow has a dozen bushes out the front that are studded with mandarins like Christmas baubles. Neglected grapefruit swell, turn brown, fall and burst to a slush. Tread on one accidentally and your heel slides instantly from under you and you teeter a moment on one foot and just manage not to fall. You look down expecting to see dogshit and are pleased to see grapefruit, but less pleased to see two nine-year-old girls in outrageously sexual Britney Spears get-ups giggling at you.

Kerikeri boasts the oldest stone building in New Zealand. For once the verb 'boasts' is accurate. The Stone Store erected by the Church Missionary Society in 1832 appears in every brochure in the town. It's square and it's made of stone, and it's respectably proportioned and frankly, well, anyway, it's shut. But over a small footbridge and five minutes along a track are the remains of the Kororipo Pa, a Maori hill fort. Grassed and buildingless now, it still shows the patterns of its ditches and ramparts, and brings sharply to my mind the neolithic hill forts on the South Downs of Sussex. I spent much of my childhood sliding down their grassy terraces and whooping.

Chief Hongi Hika of the Nga Puhi tribe held this pa. In 1820 he became one of the first Maori to go to England, where he helped professors at Cambridge to compile *A Grammar and Vocabulary of the Language of New Zealand*. He was presented to a lot of curious bigwigs who gave him a lot of gifts, and to George IV who gave him a suit of armour. Hongi decided that he would like to become King of New Zealand. On the way home he sold all the gifts except for the suit of armour. With the proceeds he bought muskets, and then, according to the sober information board erected at the pa, went on 'an orgy of conquest'. He wore the armour into battle against rival tribes. More because of the muskets than of any great military prowess he wrought carnage throughout the upper North Island, defeating tribes in, among other places, Rotorua, Thames and the Waikato. He and his warriors ate many of their victims. But he got on very well with the missionaries.

I am no historian and this book is certainly no history. But if it were, I think I would begin my research round here in the Bay of Islands, because it was here that so much of the early contact between European and Maori took place, here that such integration as has happened began, here that conflicts arose that fester today, and near here that the Treaty of Waitangi, the founding document of New Zealand, was signed. And if they'd known that people like me would be writing about it 160 years later they might have taken a little more care with what the bloody thing said.

But Waitangi can wait for tomorrow. In Kerikeri now for the night I reach the internet café in time to look up the giant on a website devoted to the All Blacks. A French rugby writer of the sixties described him as a 'magnificent animal' who could and did win games 'practically single-handed' and who 'could change the course of a match with a couple of effortless long-range penalty goals or with a characteristic gallop through a cringing mob of would-be tacklers'.

I take a monstrous seafood pizza back to my motel. On most Saturday nights in this country in the rugby season it is possible to spend the evening watching three consecutive live rugby matches on Sky Television. Prone on the bed and sticky with cheese, I do. I while away the barren wilderness of half-times by picking the prawns off my chest, and the stringy bits of mussel from between my back teeth.

24

Bungleville

It's the last of four days with the Familia. I'll be pleased to be rid of it. Though it's enabled me to reach the one place I felt impelled to reach, and though it has lugged me through the weather, and though it's allowed me to stop at will, I have felt imprisoned by it, and sheltered from chance.

On a train from Paris to Dieppe some twenty years ago, I

overheard three English lads on their way home after a few
weeks travelling around Europe. 'That wasn't a holiday,' said
one, 'that was a fucking endurance test.' I thought then, and I
think now, that that is how travelling should be.

God knows I'm no adventurer. I'll never Laurie Lee my way
through Spain on foot with a wedge of cheese and a fiddle. I
identify rather with the cringing would-be tacklers of the
world. And that may partly explain why I want travelling to
put me on my mettle, to test me a little. I resent, for example,
the ease of air travel. It seems like cheating. So I'm keen now to
ditch the car, lay my bag beside the road and indulge once
again in the vanity of feeling like the little boy alone under a big
sky. And besides, it's stopped raining.

Low clouds are still fatly loitering over the citrus groves, but
the Familia's wipers are stilled as I point its bonnet down to the
road towards the birthplace of a nation.

In the car park at Waitangi a substantial notice urges me to
lock my car. Beyond a bit of tended bush there's a good-looking
timber visitor centre. A video backed by spooky music supplies
a scrupulously balanced potted history of the birth pangs of
New Zealand. A gentleman of advanced years, whose unfor-
givable shorts suggest that he may just be Australian, has a
palm-sized Handycam to his eye. He is videoing the video. And
in the shadowy corner of the theatre there's a student from the
Media and Cultural Identity department of the local polytechnic
who is videoing the Australian videoing the video. Instantly I
whip out my Handycam to video the student videoing the man
videoing the video, but suddenly he arches his back, like Olga
Korbut on the beam, and disappears up his own arse.

A walkway takes me down to a sort of carport sheltering the
Ngatoki Matawhaorua, a 76-man war canoe. It's a Viking long-
ship of the South Pacific, exquisite with carving. On days of
celebration, numerous such waka (there is no 's' in Maori so
plurals are troublesome to the English speaker) are put to sea
around the country, and hugely impressive they look too,

except when they capsize. There has been considerable debate in these safety-obsessed times over whether the bare-chested warrior paddlers should be obliged to wear fluorescent life-jackets. At the time of writing the debate is unresolved.

Below the canoe-house there's a tiny cove like a children's play-beach, where the newly appointed Governor Hobson stepped ashore 163 years ago with a treaty under his arm. He climbed a grassy knoll. Today it's a sodden grassy knoll, so sodden that my shoes make sucking noises and the moisture seeps over the soles and through the leather. A flagpole at the top flies three flags, the New Zealand flag, the Union Jack, and a flag I don't remember seeing before, but which my explanatory brochure tells me represents Maoridom. The flagpole marks the spot where, on 6 February 1840, Governor Hobson, representing Queen Victoria, and forty-three Maori chiefs signed the Treaty of Waitangi.

When the Treaty was signed, Hobson said, 'He iwi tahi tahou' – 'We are now one people', which was an appropriate sentiment, but I think it would be fair to say he jumped the gun a bit.

The Treaty of Waitangi was a necessary thing. The place was a mess. Settlers were arriving in growing numbers, many of them from Australia, and there was no effective authority to control what they did, though there were several people willing to assume that authority. An outfit called The New Zealand Company was planning to establish settlements and create its own laws to govern them, and a splendid nutter called Baron de Thierry, a Frenchman born in England, wanted to annexe New Zealand personally. He had already appointed himself King of a small Pacific island and was keen to do the same here. It was clear that the situation demanded some sort of constitution and quickly.

(Baron de Thierry did make it to New Zealand in the end but he didn't quite become King. He became a music teacher in Auckland.)

London didn't want another colony. It already ran half the world and didn't see much profit in adding these islands. But it seems that what eventually induced the Colonial Office to dispatch Hobson was, at least in part, philanthropy. They wanted to ensure that Maori got a fair deal.

It could be argued that the fairest deal would have been to go away and leave them alone, but it was too late for that. Grog-sellers, musket-traders and land-grabbers were already swarming over the country.

The Treaty gave Victoria sovereignty over New Zealand, made Maori into British subjects, and guaranteed them 'full, exclusive and undisturbed possession' of their lands, forests, fisheries and so on. Or at least that's what it did in English.

The Maori version, hurriedly translated by a missionary, gave Victoria 'governorship', and Maori 'te tino rangatiratanga' which translates as 'the unqualified exercise of their chieftainship' over their lands. Naturally the Maori chiefs saw only the Maori version. The debate continues whether the British and the Maori signed the same deal. And I'm not going to contribute to that debate.

But it is clear that the intention from the outset was to guarantee rights to Maori that had never been guaranteed to any other colonised people. In sum, the Treaty of Waitangi was, and remains, both well-meant and a bungle. And the bungle's ramifications are still felt daily a century and a half later.

At the place where the bungle was signed, there's no one but me and the birds. A fantail parks briefly at my feet and looks up at me. Tuis chuckle and gurgle in a Norfolk pine. Four small red-headed parrots pick over fallen leaves. Native pigeons swoop and whirr, and a terribly English thrush scampers across the turf, then stops and cocks its head as if listening to Elgar.

The knoll looks out across the inner bit of the Bay of Islands. Despite the clouds it's a pretty place. A ferry burbles across the dark water between Paihia and Russell.

Behind me stands the Treaty House. Though originally the British Residency it's nothing much, a prefab shipped in numbered pieces from Sydney in the 1820s. It was allowed to fall into disrepair, before being renovated in the middle of last century. A short distance away, and far more impressive, is Te Whare Runanga, a meeting-house built for the centenary celebrations of 1940 and dedicated not to any particular tribe but to all tribes. I take off my shoes, step over the lintel and stand among carved bargeboards, woven wall mats, fierce wooden faces, squat bodies, paua-shell eyes, a host of dramatic Polynesian forms familiar to all New Zealanders.

The back of the Treaty House has been turned into a museum. There's a facsimile of the original Treaty in Maori, beginning 'He Wikitoria te Kuini o Ingarami' (which tells you most of the sounds the Maori language hasn't got) and ending with the signatures of the chiefs. Those who couldn't write made a mark representing their facial moko.

There's also a copy of the first document to come off a printing press in this country. It's a notice calling a public meeting to establish a Temperance Society in Russell. And thus began the great tradition of New Zealand wowserdom.

A boardwalk takes me through regenerating native bush – fern fronds curling, spindly saplings striving for the light – and returns me to the visitor centre with its shop full of the standard memorabilia. I buy a postcard.

The bubbly and motherly woman who takes my money asks me where I am sending it. 'To my mother in England,' I say.

'Oh, you're a good son,' she says, and shows me a painting of the signing of the Treaty. She picks out a seated chief, his back to the painter. 'My great-great-grandfather,' she says (though I may be a great or two out there).

I ask if she'll write a note to my mother in Maori on the postcard. She does, then translates it as, 'Greetings and the greatest respect to our old people.' As she writes the translation, she asks if my mother will mind the word 'old'.

She signs the note. Her surname is Smith-Gibbs. I raise my eyebrows at the name.

'Marriage,' she says, and chuckles.

Which invites me to deliver a little homily on the subject of current race relations in New Zealand, taking into account the views of the aggressively red-necked and the equally aggressively brown-necked, the debt that each Treaty partner owes to the other, the colonial guilt often found on one side of the divide and the sanitising nostalgia on the other, the muddying of the waters caused by a century and a half of cohabitation, and the impossibility of returning to the past coupled with the equal impossibility of ignoring it. But I'm not going to. I lack the knowledge.

All I will say is that New Zealand has done a sight better than the States, Canada, South Africa, Australia – anywhere, indeed, that has ever been colonised, a category that includes, if you go back far enough, pretty well every nation on the planet. That doesn't mean that it got things right. It means only that it got them less wrong.

But I do feel qualified to make two observations arising from this trip. One is that I've had a disproportionate number of lifts from Maori drivers. The other is that I have no doubt that if I'd had a brown face, I would have spent one hell of a lot longer waiting by the road. End of non-homily.

Paihia, just down the road from Waitangi, is a quaint resort with motels, fat real-estate prices, ice cream, craft shops, burger bars and aimless visitors disconcerted by the weather. I eat a lamentable pie, then take the ferry across the bay to Russell.

Russell used to be Kororareka, a name meaning, and I am not making this up, 'just about the sweetest blue penguin broth I have ever tasted'. And 'just about the sweetest blue penguin broth I have ever tasted' was the first capital of New Zealand. But it wasn't a success. In the lawless years of the early nineteenth century the place became known as 'the hellhole of the Pacific'. European sailors and whalers drank and swore and whored and swapped diseases and let their dogs off the lead. The modern equivalent would be the squalid no-go areas of any large city, South Auckland, say, or the dark barrios of Barcelona where lowlifes lounge with gold in their teeth and knives in their pockets. The bits of town, in other words, that tourists don't visit. Hellholes aren't popular.

But ex-hellholes are terribly popular. Russell's naughty-naughty past acts as a magnet. It provides a whiff of safe danger. The brochures inevitably call that past 'colourful'. The ferry I catch is loaded low in the water with a party of plump Englishwomen in leisurewear, and their bored, anoraked husbands. In 1830 the women would have been moving in the opposite direction as swiftly as possible. And the men would have been a lot less bored.

There's not much for us ferry passengers to do in Russell. We disperse at the wharf but over the next half-hour keep coming across each other as we wander the few, and not especially quaint, streets, peering at the first licensed hotel in New Zealand (1827), the battered 4-Square supermarket, the closed-for-renovations museum and Ye – do they really have to? – Olde Grog Shoppe.

I go for coffee in a beachfront tearoom and find most of the English already installed with coffee and fudge cake. Half an hour later I'm back in Paihia, watching a woman in a polo-neck sweater leaning out of a back window of the information centre surreptitiously feeding a doughnut to a fat duck. She's smiling. The duck's in neutral. And I've got driving to do. By ten o'clock tomorrow morning, I have to get the Familia to Hamilton, a couple of hundred miles south.

An hour or so down the road, somewhere near Whangarei, a swarm of motorbikes passes me, hundreds of them, like revving bluebottles, black leather riders in World War Two helmets. I hate them, the bikes and their riders, that is, not the helmets. No, I hate the helmets too.

The car in front of me is waiting to turn right. A bike has to brake and swerve to the left to pass him. The pillion passenger stretches a gauntleted arm and smashes the car's near-side mirror. Shiny bits bounce on the road. Fortunately I am right there and see it all, as if in slow motion. My heart floods with a surge of loathing and indignation, with a righteous sense of what is and is not fit, the bedrock sense of the nice middle classes, we people who are so hard to rouse from our torpor of civility, but who, when we are roused, strike fear in the devil himself. 'Fuck you, you shithead,' I mutter to the steering wheel, and slow down to let the other bikes past, hoping they won't hit the Familia or me, wanting them to go away.

Twenty minutes down the road I see them all gathered in a car park, like flies on a carcase. I drive past, hating them, hating myself.

The further south I drive, the more I see of the sun. I pull over briefly in Orewa for coffee and an urban beach scene: a hairy man swinging his minuscule daughter round him like a helicopter, a tiny Maori boy chasing a vast orange beach ball, a toddler jumping up and down to make splashes in the shallows, then suddenly jack-knifing, sitting and crying, and a team of the body-proud young training with boats and oars for a surf life-saving competition. It seems to me typically Australasian to make life-saving into a sport. It won't be long before there's competitive hip-replacement. Every hospital will have a trophy cupboard.

Below the Auckland Harbour Bridge the water is sparkling like crinkled foil. Is there, I wonder, another major city in the world where the harbour invades to the heart of downtown, and where moored yachts jostle within a few hundred yards of the poshest department stores? Well, there's Wellington, I suppose, and Sydney and Barcelona and Marseilles and Vancouver and, well, maybe it would be easier to list the cities where the harbour doesn't invade to the heart of etc., but it is all rather pretty on a sunny Sunday afternoon, though not pretty enough to make me stop. For the second time in four days I zip through Auckland with barely a touch on the brakes.

At Huntley a road turns off towards Ngaruawahia (pronounced 'not far from Hamilton') and fifty metres down that road there's a hitchhiker. I'm past the junction before I can react, but I pull over, turn round – amusing the driver of a petrol tanker so much as I do so that he honks me a five-second blast of appreciation – turn off and stop at the hitchhiker's feet.

'Where you going?'

'Raglan,' he says, only I have to get him to repeat it because he's got a South African accent so thick it approaches a speech impediment. His A's sound seriously odd.

I've heard of Raglan, or rather I have heard of the surfing at Raglan, but had no idea it was near here. He tells me he's always wanted to come to New Zealand.

'So, what do you make of it?'

'Too early to tell,' he says, 'but everyone seems pretty laid back. Haven't got around much yet, though. I've been in Raglan since I arrived. That's six weeks.'

'How long are you in NZ for?'

'Twelve weeks.'

The dull rolling land of northern Waikato has given way to rich steep downs, so green that for a moment I'm tempted by the word 'verdant'. Fortunately at that moment the road suddenly drops into Raglan and stops at the sea.

'Thaarnk,' says the South African and he's gone.

I immediately like Raglan. The old dear in the information centre has lived here all her life but says she preferred it when it was just a village. It still seems like a village to me – with a row of palm trees down the middle of the one significant street, a scatter of shops and eateries, and as handsome a pub as I've seen, weatherboard, well proportioned and with exactly the right wrought-iron balcony. And Raglan is full of the young.

One of them greets me from a café table. He's a constant grinner, no more than seventeen years old, and deeply attached to God. 'I work with youth,' he says remarkably early in the conversation. 'It's the most important thing in my life.'

Three hundred of the seven hundred kids at the high school attend the Assembly of God youth programme.

'Do you try to convert them?'

'That's our second aim. Our mission statement says the first aim . . .' he breaks off to wave delightedly to a minibus packed with kids who all wave back . . . 'where was I?'

'Your mission statement.'

'Oh yeah, the first aim is to provide a safe and friendly environment for them. There's a whole bunch of us in on it. We're a team.'

He tells me that the local high school has a surfing academy, a phrase that I make a mental note to remember for when I need to illustrate the meaning of oxymoron. It's up there with Happy Christmas and responsible drinking. 'Rich spoiled kids, from all over,' he says, 'coming to "our school". They tend to look down on us, but I guess they're all right, inside. And Raglan's a friendly place. A bunch of us did this sort of survey where we just sat beside the road in various places and waved at drivers and counted the number that waved back. Auckland scored three out of twenty, Hamilton seven, Raglan ten.'

The minibus returns and kids pour out and throng around the youth leader, telling him things, happy as chimps, noisy. 'I promised them some hang time,' he says. 'Sorry.'

The front room of the pub seems to have become a restaurant, but there's a barn of a bar at the back with a TV screen at one end and a burly man with a jug at the other. He's spent most of his life as a shearer.

'I've shorn all over. Been over your way a few times. Shore in Inverness, the Borders, Kent. In Kent they were amazed how much we drank. Used to come in just to watch us drink. First night there we drank nineteen pints each, and no putting it in the armpit to warm it up like you Poms.' He's a great laugher. As he laughs he hugs himself and rolls and unrolls the right sleeve of his battered shirt. 'I loved the Borderers. Great people. They've spent centuries getting rooted from both sides.'

On the wall of the pub there's a photo of Raglan in the thirties. The main street's dirt, and there are only a couple of stately-looking touring cars parked on it, but otherwise it looks much as it does today. The palms seem the same height.

I point at the photo. 'Are those Nikau palms?'

'Dunno, mate. Ratsnests, we call them.'

New Zealand, he tells me is 'a smalltown country'. 'The cities are all shit. Round here it's like the West Coast. No one cares too much. Down south's the same. We used to shear down Invercargill way. There was this pub the boys from the freezing works used to use on Saturday mornings. The Flying Jug, we called it. There were the guys from the Mataura works and the guys from Alliance. Us shearers used to just sit in the back and watch. They'd be playing pool, then bingo. Eleven-thirty, regular as clockwork, the jugs'd start flying. Eleven-thirty in the morning. The Flying Jug. Shit, it was funny.' He's hugging himself again, furling and unfurling his sleeve.

The stories come in a torrent. I try to buy him beer. He insists on getting me one, levering himself off his stool and chuckling across to the bar in track pants and jandals, still telling me stories over his shoulder.

A barefoot surfer comes in. Wet-suit and towel, one arm encircling the shoulder of a shy-looking girl. He buys six cans to take away.

'The surfies used to be good. They came in here and we beat them up. It was what you did. We've got the best left-hand surf in the country here, but I bet everyone's told you that. Where you heading for next?'

'Taranaki, I expect.'

'The Naki. Used to be dry there, you know, no booze. Who was that Maori chief, put his hat down on the map and said everywhere under it would be dry? Wanker, whoever he was.'

I ask him where I should eat in Raglan.

'Shit, mate, you'd better bloody get a move on.'

'It's half past seven.'

'Yeah, and it's Sunday night.'

He's right. I can find only one restaurant open and I'm their only customer. While I eat, the waitress cleans the tables and the inside of the fridge and then reads a magazine.

8.45 and the pub's shut. Up the road the Raglan Club Inc is shut, the bar stools upside down on the leaners. I wander a while through the now familiar silence of suburbs. A few televisions glow. I disturb a pair of young Labradors, one black, one golden, nosing round dustbins. They shy away, then approach. I pat the fat hollowness of their chests and they lean against my legs for more, then follow me. I've read somewhere recently that Mars, or perhaps Venus, is closer to earth than it has been, or will be again, for I don't know how many thousands of years. I can't see it. Or rather I can see it and a trillion other stars.

Down to the silent beach with the dogs still in tow, then along and back up the deserted main street and round the corner towards my motel. The door of a parked car opens.

'Just fuck off out of here,' says a male voice with undisguised venom. The dogs look up, stop, turn and amble affably away.

In my motel I turn on the sports channel. Jet-ski racing from Indonesia. I watch a man call Thenettrahool win. He is very excited.

25

Where war began

It's a fresh-born morning with all the trimmings – chill air, chirruping birds, no one about, and a Cambridge-blue sky as clear as a nun's conscience. I drive a mile or two south to where I've been told I'll see the wet-suited young, lured from their beds by the call of the swell, ride the best left-hand surf in the world.

I've never surfed and I doubt that I ever shall, but I can see how it appeals. There's the thrill of the free ride. Like skiing it is movement without expenditure of effort. And it comes with an edge of danger. The sea is huge, the surfer tiny. He's flirting with the abyss. And whatever happens, the wave will break. However skilled the surfer, however elegant and masterful his reign above the shifting wall of water, that reign will not last long. Every surf ride is the human span in miniature. It's elemental, precarious and doomed. And you get a lot of sex.

Or at least you know that other people think you get a lot of sex, which is every bit as good.

I stop the Familia on the bluff that overlooks the most renowned of the surfing beaches. The horizon's impeccably definite and as wide as the world. To the north, a line of folded hills melds gently into the sea. Seagulls mew and wheel on the bright air above a sea that's as flat as an iron. There's not a surfer in sight. Presumably they've all got up, drawn the curtains, surveyed the water and gone back to bed for more sex. But it's very pretty.

There's a Children's Bible Camp out here and a sign saying *Life is a Gift from God*. In faultless sunshine I breakfast on croissants at an outside table on Raglan's main street, head through the hills to Hamilton, and do an involuntary and unenchanting tour of the city while trying to find the Rent-a-Dent depot. The Waikato River is pretty enough, but the prettiness wears off when I pass it for the third time by the same bridge.

Hamilton is unique in being New Zealand's only substantial city that's not on the coast. Otherwise it seems short on uniqueness. Its civic motto is *Hamilton. More than you'd expect* which is less a motto than an admission of defeat. It doesn't make you expect much. Essentially Hamilton's a plain, flat market-town that exists to serve the rich dairying land of the Waikato. And having tired of driving its streets I shelve my masculinity and seek directions from a garrulous Indian pharmacist. He not only gives me impeccable directions and insists that I write them down, but also throws in abundant news about the state of the New Zealand economy, All Black rugby and Indian cricket.

Half an hour later when I hand over the Familia's keys I feel as I imagine pious people feel as they shed their burden of guilt in the confessional. At the car yard a doleful Jack Russell is wearing a bucket round its neck, like an Elizabethan ruff. Apparently the beast's got lupus. I bend to pat it and it cowers.

I catch a bus to the city's southern fringe, walk past the last houses with the sun hot on my neck, then drop my bag on the gravel of a lay-by, turn it, by superstitious habit, so that it is end-on to the traffic, and stick out my thumb. It feels like pulling on an old pair of jeans.

Garry drives barefoot. He's heading home to Hawera in Taranaki. Apparently the two most important people in the country come from Hawera and he asks me to tell him who they are. I can't.

'Craig Norgate,' he says, 'and John Mitchell.' Norgate is head of Fonterra, the dairy conglomerate that takes 90 per cent of New Zealand's milk and turns it into twelve billion dollars a year. And Mitchell's the coach of the All Blacks.

Garry's off shortly to South America for several months of adventure. When I fail to ask him why, he asks the question himself. And answers it. 'Because I've never been there,' he says.

He manages events for a living, and takes a detour to show me Mystery Creek, a complex of buildings and paddocks that for four days every year hosts the biggest agricultural exhibition in the country. He parks on a hill overlooking the site.

'So what do you think?' he says.

I say I think it's big.

Further down the road, a prominent gauge identifies itself as a 'Facial Eczema Risk Monitor'. Facial eczema is a disease of cattle. At present the risk is agreeably low.

Garry's an enthusiast, a positive thinker, with no time for the moaners of the world. 'It's amazing,' he says, 'what just a bit of energy can do for a place,' and to prove his point he stops the car in Otorohanga. It's the standard-issue one-street country town, the sort of place that has been in decline for a generation or more, as New Zealand has become more urban. But Otorohanga has chosen to arrest that decline by theming itself. Its theme is kiwiana. The main street is lined with large wooden facsimiles of the symbols of Kiwidom – a pair of jandals, a buzzy bee toy, a pavlova. A shop window is devoted to the history of sheep breeds.

'Brilliant, isn't it,' says Garry. Apparently it has worked. The tourists have flocked. No-account Otorohanga is thriving. Some slightly negative comments float into my mind but I say nothing. I don't want to be a moaner.

We pass the Waitomo Caves where you can ride an innertube along underground streams, or abseil 100 metres down through rock, then wriggle, blinded by the dark, through subterranean crevices and other things that I, as a world-ranked claustrophobe, shrink from even describing. I am grateful when we don't stop. But we do in the Awakino Gorge, where Garry urges me to scramble up a boulder for the view, and it's just dandy, a vista of river, bluffs and bush that in many parts of the world would have a car park and a designated viewing area and a stall selling ice-cream and postcards. Here, nothing.

This is the region known as King Country, named after the Maori King movement that arose in the 1850s.

In 1858 Europeans outnumbered Maori for the first time. In the same year the first Maori king was elected. This was not a challenge to the British Crown, but rather an attempt to unite Maori in opposition to land sales. Tribes held land in common, but many individual Maori and subtribes and people with grudges and drunks and profiteers could be persuaded to sell parcels of land, against tribal wishes.

In order to stop such sales, the tribes across the belly of the

North Island came together as a loose federation. It was effectively the first time that Maori had ever seen themselves as a race. The word maori simply meant normal. Furthermore they had no word for New Zealand. Today any schoolkid of any colour will tell you that the Maori for New Zealand is Aotearoa. The word is indeed Maori, meaning more or less 'land of the long white cloud', but it was never used to mean New Zealand until Europeans decided that it should be, early in the twentieth century.

What arose from the King movement was a stalemate. What collapsed were the good intentions of the Treaty of Waitangi.

The settlers wanted land. Maori wouldn't sell it. Things inevitably came to a head. A disputed land sale in Waitara in Taranaki led to shots being fired and the New Zealand Wars began. They lasted on and off for over a decade. And the government, instead of acting as a buffer between the two peoples, sided with the settlers. Read Michael King or James Belich if you want the details. They aren't pretty (the details that is. I've never laid eyes on either historian).

After the war the Crown confiscated a lot of land, supposedly as punishment. But it paid more attention to getting the land it wanted for settlement than to any sort of justice. From some defeated tribes it took little. From others who had barely fought it took a lot, especially in Taranaki and the Waikato. And thus it opened wounds that were to suppurate for over a century. Only in the last twenty years has the Treaty of Waitangi Commission done anything to salve them.

Disillusioned by the land confiscations a community of Maori developed at Parihaka in Taranaki, under the leadership of two prophets, Te Whiti and Tohu. They were Gandhis before Gandhi. They preached non-violent resistance to pakeha settlement of disputed land, pulling out survey pegs and removing fences. On 5 November 1881 over 600 troops and 1,000 settler volunteers descended on Parihaka. They were met by singing children who offered them food. The soldiers flattened the place. Te Whiti and Tohu were arrested for sedition and then sent without trial into exile in Otago.

Taranaki protrudes into the Tasman Sea like a wart. And it's a wart that has wormed its way into Tom Cruise's heart. He was here for six months to make a movie.

'He just loved it,' says Garry. 'No one pestered him, you see. They treated him as just one of the boys.'

The reason Tom Cruise was here is framed by the windscreen. Mount Taranaki is an extant volcano, textbook conical and topped with snow. It looks just like Mount Fuji. The film they've been making, a film that stars an American pretty boy and a New Zealand mountain, is called *The Last Samurai*.

New Zealand is as star-struck as the rest of the world. When Gwyneth Paltrow or Nicole Kidman or any other Hollywood idol sets foot here, the country switches off its brain and lets its lower lip sag. The star has to wade through puddles of saliva. But at the same time Hollywood is becoming New Zealand-struck. The remarkable scenery comes with a benign climate, low overheads and film crews that speak English. And then there's Peter Jackson, director of *Lord of the Rings*. He could scarcely be less Hollywood. He's fat. He doesn't seem to own a comb. He wears jandals, mauve shirts, and shorts you could run up a mast. He's his own man. He doesn't slap backs. He doesn't use hyperbole. He sees film-making as a job. And he makes films that people want to see. The first two parts of *Lord of the Rings* have bagged a few Oscars. The third part is touted to bag lots of them. Hollywood loves him. He's their pet troll.

Look at the map of Taranaki and the minor roads all stream from the volcano's flanks, radiating like crinkled spokes on a bicycle wheel. At the hub of the wheel the map's as blankly white as the snow it represents. Garry drops me where the road to Hawera veers off to skirt the volcano's base and I get a lift into New Plymouth from a cheerful painter and decorator who is married to a Venetian. He's worried about house prices.

'The Naki's got trendy. Rich Americans are buying up

anything with a seaview. They're pricing ordinary Kiwis out of the market. Personally, I blame Tom Cruise,' he says, and then he bursts out laughing.

He asks me where I want to go in New Plymouth. When I tell him I've no idea, he turns off the main road, drives down the hill through the town centre and stops opposite a backpacker hostel. 'There,' he says, 'that's where you're staying,' so that's where I stay.

I have avoided backpacker places. They conjure images of young people being earnest and wearing sandals and saying 'cool' and boiling rice in communal kitchens and sleeping in dormitories where the bunks are stacked three high on the wall and the air at midnight is loud with gasps and snores and ragged mutterings, and rank with feet.

But this place isn't like that at all, or at least the bits of it that I penetrate aren't. The proprietor, to be sure, has shaved his scalp while retaining a beard, and he's just returned from hiking in self-imposed discomfort round India and Sri Lanka, where he particularly admired the elephants, but he rents me what is effectively a motel room for half the price of a motel room. In addition I have access to a roof-top balcony painted orange, on which a young woman in flared jeans swings gently on a hammock smoking roll ups and reading *Valley of the Dolls*. She looks up and says, 'Hi.' It's like being addressed by 1973. She goes back to her book and I go down to the beach to look at the Wind Wand.

The beach isn't much of a beach, and the Wind Wand's a stick. But it's a seriously big stick, standing 45 metres tall with a little red light on the top. When the wind blows – and here on the promenade the wind blows unimpeded from the Tasman Sea – the stick bends. It can bend up to 20 metres from the vertical. I'm leaning back crook-necked and thinking this is actually a strangely pleasing stick, when a voice asks me if I'd be willing to answer some questions.

She's young and pretty and a journalist on the local paper,

and do I believe that Taranaki should declare itself a GE-free zone?

'No.'

'Why not?'

'You mean apart from it being a futile, uninformed, feel-good gesture?'

'Slow down,' she says. 'I'm not very good at shorthand.'

When we've dealt with GE she asks me if I knew that Tom Cruise had been here recently to make a movie. Apparently Tom just loved the place and it just loved Tom. Furthermore, according to a recent survey, New Plymouth is officially the most optimistic town in the country.

'Why do you think that is? Tom Cruise perhaps?'

'Perhaps,' she says.

The central township rises to Pukekura Park which the journalist told me I had to visit. It holds a delightful sunken cricket ground, the terraces grassed and stepped to create an amphitheatre. Behind it stand I don't know how many acres of landscaped grounds, set with lakes and bush and little patches of lawn, a fernery, a drinking fountain of dribbling lions built to commemorate Victoria's Diamond Jubilee, bridges, walkways, tots feeding ducks, and an ancient couple whose spines have both turned into question marks. They are holding hands, and shuffling with tiny steps and staring at the ground, fidelity in crumbling bodies. On a lawn named after some dead conservator, a young couple roll in damp oblivious embrace. Ponga, pines, rimu, a few kauri, and two schoolboys in shorts pushing bikes, eating ice creams and saying fuck loudly.

I wander back into town. True to form, the District Council has built itself the sort of charmless building it wouldn't give planning permission for to anyone else, but otherwise the town has a solid and self-contained provincial feel, and I can well believe its optimism.

I let the gentle slope ease me back down to the Wind Wand, now doing its stuff with more vigour as the breeze builds off the sea. I visit the museum, a recent building in glass and steel looking a little like a spaceship and packed with good stuff. Surprisingly there doesn't seem to be a Tom Cruise Gallery. Perhaps it's under construction. Or closed for a service of worship.

I learn that Mount Taranaki has blown itself out of existence half a dozen times in the last hundred thousand years and risen again each time. It last blew a couple of hundred years ago, and could go again whenever it felt grumpy. In New Zealand you are never far from a bit of geography that lends perspective.

The natural history displays include a species of giant worm-eating snail found only on the slopes of this volcano. And there's a giant weta. Weta are members of the grasshopper family. This particular species had been thought extinct until a kid from Mahoenui School took one in to show his teacher. It's got feelers and mandibles and jointed legs and it's the size of a thrush. I bet teacher was thrilled.

Among the usual stuffed birds there's a kakapo, a green, fat and flightless parrot, now gone from the mainland. In the late eighties, conservationists used the feathers and droppings of captive birds to train a Labrador to sniff out kakapo in the wild so that they could be removed to sanctuaries. The dog swiftly found a kakapo and equally swiftly killed it. That represented a decline in the total kakapo population of more than 1 per cent. So before they sent the dog out again they muzzled it. The dog promptly sniffed out a second bird, and the bird, equally promptly, died of fright. They gave up on the dog.

The reason I recall this story is that when it happened I copied it almost word for word from a local paper and faxed it to a friend in Fleet Street. She paid me thirty-five quid for it. I've thought well of kakapo since. But no bird more typifies the defencelessness of so many of the indigenous species. It's wingless, it waddles, it mates only in years when the food supply is good and then, when it does finally feel like mating, it advertises its whereabouts to one and all by booming.

In the gallery of Maori history I have time only to note a dogskin cloak and some grey-brown photos of the razing of Parihaka, before I am politely told the place is closing.

For all its optimism, New Plymouth on a Monday evening doesn't exactly fizz. Perhaps it's the residual influence of the Maori chief with the hat, to whom I've not been able to find any reference, but it takes me a while to find a pub. And when I do it's inevitably Irish or, if there is such a word and if there isn't I'm coining it, Irishish. Hanging above the bar is an honours board of darkly varnished word with names stencilled in gold – Tee Man, Thommo, Turbo – all of them members of the Guinness 100-pint club.

The All Black squad for the World Cup has just been named and the barmaid's worried. 'They've left out Mehrts,' she says, 'and given the kicking duties to Carlos.'

'Carlos is all right, isn't he?'

'Mate,' she says, 'he's only kicking at sixty-three per cent. The big games are going to hinge on penalties. This is going to lose us the World Cup.'

By the time you read this, she will have been proved right or wrong*. And she will also, as it happens, have graduated from Waikato University with an honours degree in psychology.

The barmaid goes out the back so I turn to the only other drinker at the bar and offer the most sure-fire conversation-starter in New Zealand at this moment. 'So what do you reckon about Carlos?'

'Carlos who?' he says.

Though born and bred in New Zealand, Peter has no interest in, or knowledge of, the national game. But he has plenty to say about the nation.

'We're heading for Third World status,' he says. 'Anyone living outside Auckland is stuck in a rural time-warp. But they can't afford to go and live in Auckland. So they're stuck. And

*She was right.

anyway, Auckland is becoming just a branch office for Sydney. The best and brightest are simply leaving the country. And those who stay behind subsist on myths.'

'What myths?'

'Oh, you know, the can-do Kiwi attitude. The number eight wire practicality. It may have been true once, but not any more, or at least not in the towns where nine tenths of us live. The average urban Kiwi can't open the bonnet of his car without professional help. He's confused and rootless. Do we have any sort of urban culture?'

I shrug helpfully.

'And the rural mythology that everyone trades on, it's all so hopelessly masculine. The beer ads and the rugby and "good on yer, mate" stuff – it's past its use-by date. The rest of the world's moved on. We're getting left behind.'

'So why do you stay?' I ask, noting at the same time that he has said all this quite cheerfully.

'Fair question,' he says. 'Habit, I suppose, and because this is home, and anyway I'm getting a bit old to shift now. But if I was twenty, I'd be off like a shot. Sydney first, then the world.'

On a screen behind his head a panel of former All Blacks are analysing the World Cup squad. The television is muted but you can tell by their faces that they're worried about Carlos.

Peter's got work in the morning. He leaves. I eat a plate of something with chicken in it that tastes of mushrooms. The woman who cooked it comes to ask me if it's all right, and stays to tell me how badly she suffers from vertigo. 'I can't even look up at the Wind Wand. My husband once took me to the Sky Tower in Auckland. I stood at the bottom. The whole thing was swaying. "You've got two chances of getting me up that thing," I said. "No chance and shit chance".'

A woman comes in towing a vast young Maori guy with a beard and the sort of Hawaiian shirt that you have to speak over the top of. He's from Waitara down the road, the place that sparked a war 140 years ago and is still a predominantly Maori town. She's from Lancashire. 'Oooh,' she says when she learns that I'm English, 'I love it here, don't you? I feel so free. Back home there's all this pressure to do this, do that, to conform. Here I feel I can do anything. Don't you think so? I want to start a café.'

Her enormous man keeps his own counsel, swaying slightly on his stool, humming to himself and leaving the talking to his woman and his shirt.

26

Mars in Sin City

'It's official!' says the front-page headline of the local paper. 'New Plymouth people most optimistic in NZ.' I'm sipping necessary coffee on the rooftop balcony at a rough wooden table sprinkled with potted cacti and paua shell ashtrays. Miss 1973 has gone and her hammock is damp from overnight rain. Clouds mass out to sea like grey-black cauliflowers, and the

Wind Wand is flexing. Down below me a schoolboy gets out of a Subaru station wagon, grunts a thankless thank you to his father and slams the car door. The crotch on his shorts is so skateboarding low that his feet are splayed like a duck's feet and he takes the short steps of an old man. Council workers in green overalls park their truck on a yellow line and unload trays of bedding plants. A high-stepping young woman in black drops library books through a slot. Bald men march briskly towards offices, their briefcases swinging like pendulums. It feels good to be standing outside it all. It's one of the boons of travel. By nine o'clock, the daily displacement of people from home to duty is done. The street settles down.

Because there are no roads over the volcano I go east to go south. The snowy cone has sucked clouds around it like a wig from a drag act, and the air is heavy with the threat of rain. Up the hill opposite the white-railed race track where a single trotting horse is training, I find New Plymouth Boys' High School. Some time ago a lad I taught English to, and who must now be considerably more than a lad, wrote to tell me he was teaching English here. On a whim I push through the heavy swinging door. I am assaulted by the smell of boys' school, a smell of gym shoes, edginess and floor polish.

'Sorry to bother you,' I say through a sliding window of toughened glass, 'but does George Penlington teach here?'

'Did but gone,' says the secretary in the manner of one accustomed to dealing succinctly with schoolboys. 'Went to England. Sorry.' The 'sorry' emerges on two differently-pitched notes, like the ding-dong of a doorbell, only here it closes the door of the conversation.

I'm sorry too. I'd like to have been shown to his classroom, seen every head turn as I entered, gestured to him just to carry on, sat at the back and watched him gradually regain order and spend half an hour doing what I spent too many years doing.

On the wallboard in the lobby the usual notices with too

few drawing pins. When the door opens they flutter like leaves. 'Year 8 Health Studies p.5 go to THE GYM. Bring towels'. 'Nepal Tour Brief Meeting E2, 11.05'. 'Year 11, 12, 13 students of Maori descent go to Boarders' Lounge period 1'. The apostrophe in Boarders' is, well, so very school.

On up the straight hill, over a bridge, and out to the edge of town. A battered hatchback brakes severely and stops at my feet with a squirt of gravel.

'Hey bro, wanna go to Inglewood? I'm having a really good day.'

I want to go to Inglewood very much.

'The missus has been in labour for nineteen hours. They're going to do a Caesarean. I'm just fetching her sister.'

A rap tape's playing, its beat strumming through the springs and vinyl of my seat, through the whole chassis of the car. The only word I can make out is 'motherfucker'. I make it out quite often.

'It's going to be a girl. A daughter, eh. I'm going to have a fucking daughter. In about two hours. Wicked, eh,' and he grins at me shyly. He tells me he belongs to the Pariata tribe. In his early twenties, I'd guess, and nervous of silence, he talks incessantly above the motherfuckers. 'You know the story of the three mountains, bro? Centuries, centuries ago, way back, Ruapehu, Tongariro and Taranaki were all together in the middle of the island. Ruapehu wanted one of the others as a boyfriend but couldn't choose between them. Tongariro and Taranaki fought over her and then they decided it would be best to scatter, so they went off to different bits of the island. That's why Taranaki's up there, eh. Even now no tribe will live in the middle between the mountains 'cos that spells trouble.'

I ask him what he does for a living.

'Painter-skater, man, a painter-skater. Skateboarder, you know. I'm a gun, eh. Go in for these competitions all over. Can't make much out of skating here, but in the States they got like full-time pros. That's got to be cool, eh.'

The mix of fierce black music, skateboarding, Maori mythology, nervousness, Anglo-Saxon swearing, American slang and radiant delight at fatherhood says more about the swirling and inseparable currents of the New Zealand brand of Western culture than any of the sociological treatises I haven't read. And it illustrates the folly that is generalisation, especially generalisation about race, a folly that I am constantly guilty of, as are thousands of others. Any observation about, say, Maori attitudes to pakeha must, if they are to be true, reflect the attitude of this complex man who stopped to pick me up on the day that he was to become a father.

It isn't far to Inglewood. 'Hey, have a good one, bro,' he says as he stops the car. I wish him good luck with fatherhood and skateboarding. 'Thanks, bro,' he says, and he powers away, the primitive scary chanting of the rapper audible above the engine.

There's a plaque on a chunk of stone. 'This plaque commemorates the arrival of the first Polish settlers in Taranaki and is erected by their descendants to mark the first hundred years of endeavour, 1876–1976'. In Dargaville I saw a similar plaque to the Dalmatians who came to dig kauri gum. In Dannevirke to the Scandinavians. In Dunedin to the Scots. The Dutch are everywhere and in Akaroa, near where I live, the French heritage is nurtured with signposts directing tourists to Le Mini-golf. In short, there is barely a European country unrepresented here. And yet one and all are lumped together under the term pakeha. It's a Maori word. There is debate over whether or not it was originally an insult. Translations range from 'angel-faced visitor and bringer of technological wisdom' to 'invader who tastes similar to pork'. Culturally-sensitive white people are fond of calling themselves pakeha.

It's a convenient label for New Zealanders of European extraction, but like the word Maori it covers so wide a spectrum that it is effectively without meaning.

I'm an hour or more at Inglewood. As often I drift into a

sort of reverie, similar to that period between wake and sleep when the mind watches itself drift. Perhaps it's the railway beside me but I slide into a memory from twenty-five years ago when I was teaching at a school for foreign children in Surrey and we were taking them up to London by train. The woman who ran the school was Spanish and shy. Her name was Dorita. She and I and a clownish colleague called Peter were walking up the train in search of a buffet car. Outside a first-class compartment in which there sat a single commuter in a suit doing the *Telegraph* crossword, Peter suddenly stopped. He slid open the door, pushed Dorita through it, pointed at the solitary gentleman and bellowed, 'Was that the man, Dorita?' The memory makes me chuckle. A station wagon goes past, stops and reverses to my feet.

'You're a lucky bastard,' says Richard, as we head south. He's middle-aged with merry eyes. 'I don't normally pick up hitchhikers. "Get a bus you mongrel" is what I usually think. But when I saw you I thought, "Well, at least that feller's got a half-smile on his face." So I stopped and came back.' Thank you Peter.

Richard's some sort of agricultural consultant with a small farm of his own, a big family, and the standard gripes about bureaucracy and political correctness. He also loathes litter, and he tells me a story.

He was stationary in a queue of traffic at a red light. The occupants of the car in front wound down a window and tossed out the detritus of a burger meal – the wrappers, boxes and drinking cones. Richard got out, picked the stuff up and offered it back to them through the window.

'Shit me. Up goes the window and then this big guy – one of our tangata whenua friends, of course – gets out the other side and comes up to me, his chest against my chest, and I think hell, I'm no fighter. I look round and there's all these people just sitting there in their cars, watching and doing nothing. Anyway, this big guy, he just sort of pushes me out the way and then tips a can of Coke all over the bonnet, gets back in the car and drives off. I'm just standing there shaking. There's this one driver winds his window down and says "good on you, mate," but the rest of them, they do nothing. The stupid thing is,'says Richard, 'I was still shaking half an hour later,' and he laughs.

I am acutely aware that I would have been one of those who stayed in his car to watch. I tell him my story of the motorbike and the wing mirror.

We pass through the remains of ancient lava flows, now smoothed into hummocks and clothed in grass and cattle. Then down the coast to Wanganui where Richard was taken as a seven-year-old to watch Peter Snell run on the grass track at Cook Gardens and break the world record for the mile.

'Dad told me to go and get Snell's autograph, but I was too shy. It'd be worth something now, I suppose.'

Wanganui's had a bad press. For the sophisticates of Wellington it defines provincialism. I'm surprised to find a sturdy Edwardian main street prettified with hanging baskets and wrought-iron lampposts. Astonishingly the council has managed to build itself something startlingly ugly, but overall the town feels like a woman who knows she's no beauty but has taken care to accentuate such charms as she has.

'Give me one good reason,' I say to the girl in the information centre, 'why I should stay in Wanganui tonight.'

She pauses to think, a finger at her lips, weighing Wanganui's many and varied sweetmeats in order to find the one most likely to excite my particular palate. 'Mars,' she says.

I'm impressed. I had expected bush walks or floral gardens.

'It's closer tonight than it will be for the next six thousand years. They're opening the observatory at seven-thirty so you can have a look at it.'

'I'll stay.'

'And then there's the in-ground lift. There are only two in the world and the other one's in Portugal.'

'I'll definitely stay.'

She recommends a backpackers' hostel where again I find a proprietor who inhabits the left-hand fringe of the political spectrum, and who does me a good room for not much. Then I set off to find out what an in-ground lift is.

It's a lift in the ground. To reach it I follow signs that lead me into a tunnel that burrows 200 yards into a hill. The tunnel's deserted. My footsteps echo. The arched ceiling is low enough to scratch the blisters of whitewash. Halfway along I involuntarily look over my shoulder to see if I'm being followed. It's a pointless action. If I were, I'd have nowhere to go. The tunnel ends in a wall where a notice tells me to ring the bell. When I do there's an immediate clanking of metal deep inside the hill, and the sound of a lift approaching.

It's the perfect place to film a thriller, with the embodiment of evil lumbering up the tunnel complete with malicious intentions and a grin on its face, music of the something-bad's-going-to-happen-very-soon variety, and me, as hero, looking square-jawed but taut, muttering, 'Hurry up, damn you, hurry *up*,' to the lift as the embodiment comes within grappling range and tosses its McDonald's wrappers over its shoulder and its grin widens and it says, 'So, motherfucker . . .'

The lift attendant is a woman. I gesture down the empty corridor. 'What a great place to make a horror movie.'

'Yes,' she says, and something in her voice suggests that I may not be quite the first person to have said this.

She shuts the door, which looks like the door on an old-fashioned lift, presses a button and the lift goes up like a lift. Through a little window in the side of the lift you can see you're moving up a concrete-lined shaft not entirely dissimilar to a lift-shaft. Then the lift stops and you emerge on top of a hill that you've just caught a lift through. And all for 50 cents! I realise that I'm in danger of boring any Portuguese readers, but I found it all rather charming.

The lift was built in 1919 to provide easy – and cinematic – access to a new hill suburb. The suburb's still there and so is a stone tower built as a war memorial and looking like a corner turret from a medieval castle, complete with arrow slits in the side, battlements at the top and a winding internal staircase. The interior walls have been painted orange, presumably to cover graffiti, but they didn't paint the underside of the steps. The 'Fuck you' in thick marker pen is anonymous and recent, as is the 'Erica gives good hed'. But on 8 October 1929, A.H. Smith of 65 Pitt Street, Redfern, Sydney wrote 'A.H. Smith, 65 Pitt Street, Redfern, Sydney, 8/10/29'. A cursory survey conducted as I climb confirms that these examples are essentially typical. Yesterday's louts were inhibited and unimaginative, but they could spell and they had neat handwriting. The exact opposite is true of today's louts.

From the top of the tower I can see Cook's Gardens, scene of Snell's record, the grass track now all-weather red. Out to sea, a mass of sombre cloud is lit golden from below by the late afternoon sun, and a defined and distant shower of rain falls like a haze of iron filings. To the east an endless recession of hills dissolves into sooty distance. Out of those hills comes the Whanganui river, passing through the town and curving into an estuary like a fishhook. Richard told me you could walk across the Whanganui on the turds. From up here that's impossible to confirm, but the water's the right colour.

Avoiding the risk of over-stimulation by elevator, I take the steps back down to town and a bridge over the river – no evidence, and I look carefully, of turds – and I feel I've earned a coffee. I am joined at my pavement table by two garrulous women. One gestures at the street. About eight cars are moving. 'Rush hour,' she says. 'This place is like an old jersey with holes in it. It's a comfortable place, easy. Everyone brought up in Wanganui can't wait to get out of it. But then they come back. They used to say that the city motto was "Wanganui – why bother?" but . . . oh, no, please don't write that down!'

In the Rutland Arms along the road, she tells me, there's a

photo on the wall of the first man to make a sword in New Zealand. 'He's my great-great-grandfather. You see, we're like nesting birds here.'

The women delightedly tell me stories of wife-swapping in the seventies that saw sleepy Wanganui nicknamed Sin City, of a couple of high-profile murders, of a suicide bomber who tried to blow up the police computer, and of the Motua Gardens occupation a few years ago, when Maori protesters barricaded themselves inside a small local park for a couple of months and for reasons that the women don't explain.

'I like to go running in my lunch-hour,' says one of the women, 'and I always go through those gardens, so one day I thought bugger it, hopped over the fence, and ran through. They were all too surprised to do anything. I just jumped over the fence the other side and kept going to the police station. The cops wanted to know if I was going to do it again and I said "too right, I am" and they said "when?" and I said "tomorrow" and I did. The protesters were expecting me this time and Ken Mair – he was the guy running the whole show – he calls me "a shit-stirring pakeha bitch". I just looked Ken Mair straight in the eye and I said "we're both Scottish".'

'Were you frightened?'

'Not really, I was just pissed off with the whole thing. I wanted to bring it to a head. And anyway, there were lots of cops there.'

In the Rutland Hotel there's an abundance of nineteenth-century photos – riverboats steaming on the Wanganui River, Maori settlements, Wanganui prison where the warders are soldiers with rifles and the prisoners Maori in blankets – and sure enough, there's the swordmaker. He's got the standard issue pioneer beard. He was called Armstrong and looks it.

Bang on seven-thirty I'm at the Cook's Gardens observatory, along with several earnest parents of bespectacled children, a shambling amateur astronomer, and 100 per cent cloud cover. 'Doesn't look too promising,' says the astronomer happily.

Under floodlights in the stadium below, the Wanganui District rugby team is training, grunting into tackle bags, side-stepping cones, gathering sweatily to hear instructions from the coach. A million moths zig-zag towards the floodlights like incandescent motes.

'Maybe we'll try again in a couple of hours,' says the astronomer. The parents take their children home and I head round the streets. Behind sash windows on the second floor of the United Friendly Societies Building 1923, a karate club in white pyjamas bellows in unison and kicks the air.

I return to the Rutland and drink with Scotty, an old Maori shearer, long since retired. 'I'll tell you what you need to be a good shearer,' he says, 'a good back and no brains,' and he giggles to himself and shouts me a beer.

It's after midnight when I get back to the hostel. I go to the garden for a last cigarette and a game of tug with the resident mongrel. As I haul him up growling onto his back claws, his teeth clamped round a cabbage tree frond, I notice a clear night sky and a reddish star bright in the east. That'll do me.

27

Both and each

John Ballance was an Irish-born politician. In Motua Gardens there's a statue of five-sixths of him on a plinth. The missing sixth is his head, sliced off, I presume, during the occupation. The statue of a high-born Maori chief known as Major Kemp is intact, even though he fought for the Crown.

I cross the river under clouds that are touching the treetops.

In fewer than 200 years this river has attracted a lot of New Zealand's history. Somewhere upstream is Jerusalem where the Catholics founded a mission and set about converting the Maori, and the poet J.K. Baxter founded a commune and set about growing lice. I stop at the hillock called Korokata, which is apparently Maori for Golgotha. In 1829, the rampaging te Rauparaha took on the local tribe and slew four hundred. Only a few strides further on, a plinth commemorates the death in 1865 of Hoani Wiremu Hipango, killed when leading Maori forces in defence of Wanganui. Wanganui then was mainly settlers. Hoani Hipango and his men defended it against rival Maori. The history of pakeha-Maori relations is no black and white story.

I hitch beside a paddock of hens. A single rooster lords it over the flock, strutting and preening, arrogant with beauty, his comb as crimson as sunset, his tail an armorial arch. He exists only to crow, eat, inseminate and rule, an avian dandy. I've kept a few roosters. They've all been cowards.

The rain is gently insistent, not so much falling as drifting, as if the sky has simply come to earth, the intervening sandwich-filling of the air gone. It's perfect weather for a sympathy lift. I get it from a man who works in something financial that I don't understand. He also collects books on the Nazis, which neither of us understands.

'I've had to build a garage to house them all,' he says. 'And most of them I haven't read. I've got to be nuts.'

He drops me at Sanson where the road splits. If I went straight on I'd be back in Palmerston North where I began this little jaunt, and where, at this very moment, if God's in his heaven, a disenchanted aesthete is crawling through the sewers beneath the council building, clamping a bundle to the concrete piles, pausing to quote Sydney Carton on the scaffold, then lighting the fuse.

But God isn't in his heaven. And he emphatically isn't in Sanson. One-street Sanson sits amid land as drab as a bad

Sunday, but less drab than Sanson itself. I'm sure Sansonians have a strong sense of community and vigorous sex-lives, but they can keep both. In the café, a pie-warmer holds two deep-fried drumsticks on a saucer. If you beat a drum with them you'd drown it in grease. And my coffee is stewed. I give it to the drains without the usual intervention of the kidneys. Outside the primary school a sign implies that the place is sponsored by McDonald's. An image of Ronald the clown capers in the rain and grins his fixed commercial merriment to nobody but me.

And it's here in unenchanted Sanson that I decide I've had enough. I can sense my curiosity dissolving in the rain. Without curiosity there's no point in travelling. I can think of only one place I'd like to see between here and Wellington – Kapiti Island, former stronghold of Te Rauparaha and now a bird sanctuary. With luck I'll spend the afternoon there then carry on to Wellington and fly home tomorrow. The word 'home' sounds good in my head.

I'm keen to see my dog of course. But I'm also suddenly keen to quit the constant nowness of moving, and the demands it makes. The mundane things swell when you're travelling. Things like eating and finding a bed and having clean clothes take too much of your time and thought. At home they're so easily dealt with. At home you're more free.

A young couple pick me up. The back of their van is crammed with diving gear and commercial-size cans of paint. The side window is missing, replaced by a real-estate sign cut to fit. 'The dog,' says the driver. 'He locked himself in. I had to break the window.'

They're both about twenty. He's got black eyes and pianist's fingers and he loves scuba-diving. When he gets his instructor's licence, he'll give up his painting job and go work on the mussel farms for $25 an hour. Or else the pair of them will emigrate to Aussie. He explains the bends to me, and describes how you can drift down a river without frightening the fish.

I say I'd like to do that. He says he'd like to hitch aimlessly round the North Island.

'Why don't you?' I say, reflecting even as I say it that this youth is seeing romance in the unromantic. He sees me as free.

'Can't mate. Got a fucking family now, haven't I,' but he smiles at his woman as he says it. She has dyed hair and a wide smile.

They've got two kids and they share private jokes. 'She's a Ford fanatic,' he says, gesturing to her. 'She wants to burn my Holden T-shirt. But she's not going to get it. I've hidden it.'

'Bastard,' she says with a delighted grin. The key-ring swinging in the steering column says 'My sexual preference is often'. She tells me they've got a waterbed. He wants to let the dog sleep on it, but she won't have it. I feel intrusive.

I ask them to drop me in Paraparaumu. 'Mate,' says the driver, 'I wouldn't bother. I was brought up there. It's the shits.' But it's also the nearest place to Kapiti Island.

It's hard to tell whether it's the shits or not. The rain is too dense. I scurry to a pub which is one-third pub and two-thirds pokie machines. The machines have all got names – Hollywood Dreams, Queen of the Nile, Show Me the Money, Spring Carnival – and every one of them, this weekday lunchtime, is manned or womanned. No one speaks. 'Only the hands are living,' wrote Auden in a poem about a casino that I used to teach, but from which I can remember only one other line: 'To a last feast of isolation, self-invited.' Most of the players are over forty. Their faces are the faces of cattle in the rain.

The coast is a mile or two away. I set out half-heartedly to walk there, am drenched after 100 yards, turn back to the main road, am tempted by the train to Wellington, decide to hitch for a few minutes, and get an immediate lift from a strange bearded man in a worryingly clean car. He repeatedly tells me that he's done a lot of hitching and I don't, for one minute, believe him.

Down through the Ngauranga Gorge, the road widening,

the volume of traffic swelling, in through the hilly suburbs, and he drops me at the top of Cuba Street in Wellington. I find a travel agency and book a flight home for tomorrow.

Like Ottawa, say, or Canberra, the capital that is Wellington exists to be a capital. It took over the role in 1865 from Auckland which in turn had taken it over from Penguin Broth. Wellington is a third the size of Auckland. It got the top job only because it's central.

In the rain, people are wearing the sort of overcoats I didn't think were made any more, three-quarter length, with belts and muted tartan linings, and all of them bureaucrat dark. They are the overcoats that sensible people remember to drape over one arm in the morning after listening to the weather forecast on the wireless.

But as if in reaction to its bureaucratic image, Wellington has also sprouted a grungy counter-culture. Here at the top end of town there are vegetarian restaurants and shops selling crystals, and young things in torn jeans walking the wet pavement in bare feet on their way to practise making noise in a garage with guitars and like-minded counter-culturalists. And every one of these counter-culturalists dreams of being signed up by a nice big American record company owned by filthy capitalists.

Most New Zealand settlements are surfeited with land. They spread like something spilled on the floor. But Wellington is compressed by geography, its centre occupying a narrow strip of sloping land between the harbour and a seismic fault. It's a city of gossip, cellphones and inter-departmental memos, a squashed boiling of people. After weeks of small and spacious places I feel crowded by this one. Taking refuge in a bookshop on Lambton Quay I see New Zealand's Minister of Finance. He's fingering spines in the history section. He does not appear to be shadowed by security.

A couple of years ago I watched a rehearsal for an investiture of some sort. It was taking place in front of the steps of

Parliament. Half of New Zealand's armed forces were there, and all of its bigwigs – Prime Minister, Chief Justice, Governor General, the lot. They were being guarded by a single policeman, and protested at by a single happy drunk. The policeman seemed to know the drunk well, and the drunk the policeman.

What was also noticeable was that all three of the bigwigs mentioned above, the three biggest bigwigs in the land, were women. Of what other country has that ever been true?

For obvious reasons I've met more men than women. I've had only two lifts from women on their own, and I have met few solitary women who were keen to chat in the pubs and the cafés. In a way that's apt. New Zealand has a superficially masculine image, and for much of the nineteenth century there were a lot more men than women on these islands.

Those men were often secluded in womanless societies for months at a time, in gold mines, forestry plantations or deer-culling camps, doing the pioneer work of an unbroken land. Hence the emphasis on mateship, on physical durability, on beer. Hence too perhaps the controlled ferocity of All Black forward packs, and the successes of Kiwi troops in British wars.

But alongside all this there has always been another side to New Zealand and it is appropriate that I should be reminded of it in Wellington. It's the liberal tradition. A tradition of social progress. New Zealand was the first country in the world to give women the vote. New Zealand established old-age pensions and a welfare state while other Western nations remained almost feudal. New Zealand is prominent in international peacekeeping.

These are governmental matters. They are the legacy of the spirit in which this country was colonised. It was a bid to establish fairness and harmony, in keeping with the evangelical spirit of the early Victorian era, the era that abolished the slave trade. And in the case of the planned settlements like Wellington, Christchurch and others, it was a bid to found something better than the old world. It was a bid for Utopia.

New Zealand is no Utopia. But down here in the remote Southern ocean, despite inevitable lapses, despite the wars and the crimes and the follies and the rape of the land, despite injustices and many a wrong turning, New Zealand has retained a Utopian streak. It persists in the promotion of the country as 100 per cent pure. It persists in its recent adoption of the role of Middle Earth. It persists in Whakawerawera Thermal Village. It persists in the common but false assertion that this is a classless society. And it persists in a reforming and improving zeal at the heart of government.

But this Utopianism has its flipsides. One is an urge towards bureaucracy and social engineering. You can see it in the compulsory fencing of private swimming pools, in the government's happiness policy, in the suburbs of state housing, in the very design of the Palmerston North administrative building. And along with this comes a puritan streak. It's there in the publessness of the once-dry Invercargill, in the Temperance Society pamphlet of 1832, in the fact that next year I won't be able to smoke in pubs, and in the Prime Minister's earnest holiday slogs through wet bush. The Prime Minister's a fine, strong and clever woman, but there's an I-know-what's-good-for-you-and-it-isn't-a-barrel-of-laughs puritanism even in the downturned corners of her smile.

And so we reach a contradiction at the heart of this place. On the one hand, it's a settler country, a land of rugby and beer and hunting and hard work, a land where men stamp holes in bathroom floors to force Poms to learn DIY. The father of a former pupil once slit open his thigh when blade-shearing, told no one, sewed the gash with baler twine, drove himself to hospital in a tractor, had the wound stitched and returned to work without fuss.

But on the other hand this is a liberal nation that aspires to fairness, a land where the greater good prevails over individual ambition.

A country can't be both of these things, but New Zealand is.

It has been from the start. Perhaps it is no wonder that it frets over its identity.

I work my way down through the scurrying streets to a pub opposite Parliament where I have arranged to meet the mother of a former pupil. Promptly at five o'clock the governmental workers begin to arrive, standing briefcases carefully on the floor, shedding their overcoats, shaking them and folding them over chair-backs, ordering wine, water, bottled beer, and using handkerchiefs to rub rain from their spectacles. As they drink I watch them loosen their ties, one after another.

On the walls of the pub, the caricatured heads of politicians are mounted on plaques. I have been here long enough to recognise them all.

Liz arrives. We talk about my trip, our dogs, her son, New Zealand. She tells me that she was recently stuck between floors in a lift. She picked up the emergency phone and it was answered in Australia.

Back at Liz's house her son turns up with his fiancée and a takeaway Chinese banquet. At school he was charming but forever in trouble. A decade later he's still charming and a refrigeration engineer.

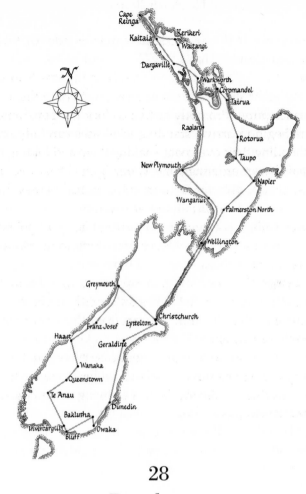

28
Dog home

From the plane window I can see the top of the South Island, the endless ridges of the Marlborough back country, green fading to brown, then building to distant snow. They are huge. I've not set foot in them. I've merely grazed the edges of this country.

Travel is partial. Whatever route you take means a hundred

you don't take. In the course of this trip I've spoken to perhaps a thousand people. That's 99.975 per cent of the population unmet.

As the plane descends into Christchurch, I can make out a river that I've fished, a cricket ground I've played on, the house of a friend who kept a dozen peacocks and two standard poodles. One afternoon the poodles killed all the peacocks. I've got sixteen years of entanglement here.

Friends have brought my dog to the airport. She's lying on the grass outside the terminal. I call her. She comes to me, her body squirming, her hooked tail swinging. I pat the chunky hollow of her chest, run the silk of her ears between my fingers, and I tell her, as I always do, that I'll never leave her again.

I'm lying of course. A few months from now I'll be away fishing, thigh-deep in the Tekapo River in the heart of the Mackenzie, where the heat bounces from the stones, the tussock waves like hair and the snowy mountains glisten.

In the Introduction I posed a question. When my dog dies, should I stay or should I go? Well, while I've been away a friend has rung, an English friend now living in Melbourne. He says he's found just the dog for me, a black lab. Can he send it across? I think I shall say yes. It will be good to have a young dog around again. And it may perk up my old dog in her years of decline.